Praise for *What It Used*

"This is a dear, sturdy, disarming memoir that proves, at the very least, that even dead eighteen years, the masterful Ray Carver knows how to keep the love of a good woman."
— Joy Williams, author of
The Quick and the Dead and *Honored Guest*

"Maryann Burk Carver obviously is a person of immense intelligence and discipline."
— Jonathan Yardley, *The Washington Post Book World*

"Good writers write what they know, but great writers show us what they know to be true. Raymond and Maryann Burk Carver dared to be great in America and, in the end, both paid a terrible price . . . it will break your heart because, like all great stories, it is true."
— Diane Smith, author of
Letters from Yellowstone and *Pictures from an Expedition*

"A testimony of a marriage as well as a portrait of an artist before becoming 'The Author.' It is the story of hunger for education, the necessity of art, in the lives of the working poor. . . . For folks who live paycheck to paycheck, for readers whose books are all stamped 'Property of the Public Library,' this story is only too familiar."
— Sandra Cisneros, author of
The House on Mango Street and *Caramelo*

"A heartbreaking, but bravely told, love story."
— *Seattle Post-Intelligencer*

"Much more than a memoir of interest to admirers of his stories and poems . . . *What It Used to Be Like* is emblematic of its time and place, of our American loss of innocence . . . a love story sure to endure for the ages."
— Douglas Unger, author of *Leaving the Land*
and *Looking for War and Other Stories*

"Maryann Burk Carver writes with clarity and honesty. Ray, one of America's great writers, would have loved this book."
— Adrian Mitchell, author of
All Shook Up and *The Shadow Knows*

WHAT IT USED TO BE LIKE

*A Portrait of My Marriage to
Raymond Carver*

Maryann Burk Carver

St. Martin's Griffin

New York

www.stmartins.com

Photo on page ii of Ray and Maryann, bride and groom, June 7, 1957. From the collection of Maryann Burk Carver. Photo on page v of Raymond Carver with his children, Vance and Christi. Sacramento, 1966. Photo by Violet Lavonda Archer, courtesy of Don Archer.

Library of Congress Cataloging-in-Publication Data

Carver, Maryann.
    What it used to be like : a portrait of my marriage to Raymond Carver / Maryann Burk Carver.
        p. cm.
  ISBN-13: 978-0-312-33259-4
  ISBN-10: 0-312-33259-9
    1. Carver, Raymond—Marriage. 2. Carver, Maryann—Marriage. 3. Authors, American—20th century—Biography. 4. Authors' spouses—United States—Biography. 5. Married people—United States—Biography. I. Title.

PS3553.A7894 Z595 2005
813'.54 B—dc22   2004066285

First St. Martin's Griffin Edition: July 2007

10 9 8 7 6 5 4 3 2 1

For our dear children,
Christine LaRae and Vance Lindsay Carver,
and in loving, vivid memory of
Raymond Carver—the Abba, the Daddy, of our house

Contents

Acknowledgments

When I was a philosophy student at Humboldt State College (now known as Humboldt State University), I wrote a paper on Tolstoy's essay "What Is Art?" I was taken aback when Count Leo pointed out how many people and how much expense are involved in an opera or a stage play. I never imagined then that I would find myself in a position like this to thank so many people for their tireless, devoted efforts on this book. I am indeed so humbled and honored to list some of these people now. And to those of you behind the scenes or neglected here, I thank you as well from the bottom of my heart.

There were people who helped me type my manuscript—1,250 pages; still other people cut down the final version to what you see here. Jeanne MacGregor was the first lady to type, and Theresa MacDonald was the last. In between, there were Jacqueline Dalton and Rene Casebeer, my niece, who also prepared my family photographs for inclusion in the book. Sandy Bonnickson did a lot of typing and organizing, too, as did Kathy Taylor, who took the manuscript, in pieces, to Bellingham author and editor Sara Stamey for preliminary editing. In 2001, dear Kathy also sent the first book off to my agent, Lori Perkins, who had received a section of it as early as 1995. As Lori put it, she kept me in her Rolodex thereafter, determined that I could tell my story myself, instead of other people telling it for me, but by their lights.

Eleven years later, Lori deserves my absolute heartfelt gratitude for her indefatigable, loyal, and loving efforts on my behalf. And, I might add, it is a good thing other people and other projects are making her a living, as she has not made five cents an hour for the time she has spent on me and my work! Another person like that is my first editor, John Stryder, the mastermind who cut those 1,250 pages down to trade-book size, while being minimally invasive and respectful of me, my voice, my story. John is another person whose labor for love, not money—his gift to literary history—made this book possible. Sine qua non.

I owe a huge debt of gratitude as well to editor Diane Higgins, who, when at St. Martin's, demonstrated heart-warming enthusiasm for the book, having been a devoted fan of Ray's and his writing for years. Our hands-on work together on the ending for the book made it much better. Thank you, Diane. And now to Nichole Argyres at St. Martin's, my final editor there, I owe my gratitude for her strict adherence to schedule and procedure; at the same time she lends an edgy, artistic overlay to my work. To George Witte, Vicki Lame, Jennifer Carrow, Emily MacEntree, and all the others at St. Martin's who have worked on and for this book . . . thank you, too!

Part professional adviser, author, but family member first and always, my brother-in-law, Douglas Unger, I thank for years of involvement and support for my book.

And thanks to Merry Reymond. I connected with her agent, Lori Perkins, and that has made all the difference. How kind and generous, Merry! Thank you.

To my friend David Danee, who graciously allowed me to use his Lummi Island, Washington, Eagle's Nest Retreat as a place where I could write, and where I completed the manuscript, I extend my heartfelt gratitude.

Finally, fullness-of-the-heart gratitude to my wonderful, dear family and friends who were readers, characters, and supporters . . . my sisters, Jerry and Amy, gone now—unbelievable—but readers and supporters, both of them. I love and miss you so much! My mom, who loved and supported me loyally and completely no matter what, I thank, love, and miss you beyond imagining. And my dad, that wonderful character and extreme example of strength and humor in my life, I thank you and Aunt May, too. A major joy of this book is having all of you live within it.

I thank my children for surviving and thriving—for the joy and pride they have been in my life. And to their dad, Raymond Carver, who was, as the song goes, "the best thing that ever happened to me." Thank you for sitting me down in your study in Cupertino and telling me to write our story.

The book was abridged and edited by John Stryder.

1950s

Me at fifteen. Union Gap area, Washington, 1955.

1

SPUDNUTS AND ROSES

As the summer of 1955 began I was almost fifteen. I lived in Union Gap—a little town to the south of Yakima, Washington—and in June I was hired to waitress at a shop that sold spudnuts. It was my first real job.

I was so wound up the first morning that I bought a pack of cigarettes on the way in. I hadn't smoked in months, not since March when I left public school to attend a private one. I went into the bathroom of the local Texaco station and made myself sweetly dizzy as I lit and inhaled a Pall Mall fresh out of the new red package. Then I chewed some Juicy Fruit to get rid of the smell on my breath. Then I ditched the gum. At Saint Paul's School for Girls we learned that ladies do not chew gum in public.

The staff at the Spudnut Shop was just the owner, Mr. Ness, and Ella, another waitress. In her early forties, she was a tall, still-pretty Southern belle who loved to feed her sweet tooth with glazed spudnuts. (Spudnuts, by the way, are like doughnuts, except made from potato flour and more delicious.)

Old Mr. Ness had supposedly bought the business for his son. But he so loved tyrannizing everybody—lording it at the sink full of dirty dishes, getting in the way of customers' orders, and supervising our every move—that he hadn't gotten around to turning over the managerial reins. I soon learned that only when he'd left for the day could Ella and I relax.

When the coast was clear, straight into the jukebox went some of my hard-earned tips, five plays for a quarter. First I'd get Al Hirt from New Orleans going with his trumpet. Customers would turn their heads and smile. Then I'd play Nat "King" Cole's "A Blossom Fell" or Al Hibbler's beautiful "Unchained Melody." And oh! "Cherry Pink and Apple Blossom White" from Latin mambo king Pérez "Prez" Prado.

One bright, sunny day the bell on the shop door rang out. A tall, dark curly-haired young man walked in. I happily went over to wait on the good-looking guy. Suddenly I had a strange feeling. As he looked at me, I thought with calm, powerful certainty, I am going to marry this boy.

He didn't seem aware of anything unusual. We smiled at each other. I found out he liked spudnuts and was addicted to Pepsi Cola. He ordered. I served him his order. We smiled some more.

The next day he was back. I had been hoping he would be, sensing as teenage girls can that he might be attracted to me. He came in and sat at a table. Ella saw him and looked as if she was going over to wait on him. So I hurried to get his order and practically bowled her aside in my haste.

"Hold it!" Ella said sharply in her Southern drawl. I stopped short, surprised—she'd always spoken charmingly to me. "I'll wait on him, Maryann." She explained: "That's my son, Raymond. I need to talk to him."

Oh.

What a difference a day makes. Yesterday the boy was a handsome stranger from out of nowhere, like a knight-errant. Because, you see, he was *destined* to be my champion and marry me. Today, as any idiot could tell, he was simply stopping by to see his mother. Cancel the wedding plans. Hold the honeymoon. My other immediate thought—What was wrong with me?

I stood still a long minute. But I trusted my intuition and chose not to let my total embarrassment paralyze me. I just *knew* fate was at work here. Then it struck me—damn, I've already met my future mother-in-law. I looked over at Ella, who was chatting with her son and (little did she know) my future husband.

I learned that Ray Carver came into the Spudnut regularly for lunch, snacks, and endless Pepsis. He had a summer job in a grocery store down the street. He was two years older than I. And he had the nicest manners, the best of any boy I'd ever met.

Ray didn't call his mother "the old lady" or his father "the old man" the way a lot of teens flippantly did out of earshot. He referred to them as "Mom" and "Dad" or "my folks." I thought he was proud of his family, respectful, as I was of mine. He still went on family picnics and outings. I felt that he was a confident, mature person who wasn't ashamed of his background or upbringing.

One day while we were talking at the Spudnut, I asked him whom he loved the most in all the world. Without hesitating he said, "My dad. I love my dad the most." He was proud to be named after his father, I think simply because he loved him so much.

Though Ray was sometimes called Junior, his given and middle names were reversed: he was Raymond Clevie and his dad was Clevie Raymond. The reversal was apparently a birth certificate foul-up and not his parents' intention. Both father and son were called Raymond at home and the right one would always answer when Ella or James, Ray's brother, called, although anyone else couldn't hear the difference. What Ray came to hate was being called Junior by his extended family. His stubborn resistance eventually forced everyone to drop the habit. He was never Junior after that.

My summer days were settling into regular routines. After work I'd still be dancing in my head to exotic jukebox rhythms as I headed over to the grocery store to check for the latest *True Story* or *Modern Romance*. I could buy what I wanted now that I was old enough to have a job—but felt youthfully guilty about some of my choices. (So I hid the "trash" from my mother.) At the same time I was also devouring books on the Saint Paul's summer reading list for students, from Norah Lofts's *Bless This House* to classics like Joseph Conrad's *Nigger of the Narcissus*. I felt entitled to read whatever I craved.

Waitressing at eighty-five cents an hour—close to minimum wage in 1955—I could finally buy the Jantzen sweaters and Pendleton skirts and jackets I wanted for school. I made a list of coordinated outfits, the "civilian clothes" I could wear when we students shed the uniforms that our Episcopalian boarding school required. Number one on my fall list: a white Jantzen skirt and sweater, red belt, red shoes, red purse, and round red earrings with centered clusters of rhinestones. I just loved clothes.

And I loved going to my job. Or at least I did until the morning when Mr. Ness made one too many petty jabs at Ella. She was in the middle of dishwashing. Ella whirled on him, fire blazing in her eyes: "I believe I've washed more dishes in my life than you have! I'm tired of trying to work with you breathing down my neck all the time!" She told the dumbfounded old man that he was welcome to the damn dishes, ripped off her apron, and sailed out the door. Gone.

I was stunned, but thoroughly awestruck. My mother, who was a teacher, did everything according to Hoyle, especially when she changed jobs. I admired Ella's spunk. Then it sank in—I'd have to handle the shop all on my own that afternoon. A further panicky rush of thoughts engulfed me. I was convinced that Ray would never come back. Why should he? His mom wasn't here. He could get his Pepsis other places. I'd never see him again.

The next day I watched the entire eight hours of my shift for Ray. He didn't stop by. My heart sank. The following day it was the same, and I reproached myself for having made something out of nothing. The mutual attraction I was so sure of was a figment of my girlish romantic imagination. Day three after Ella quit, I gave up. Live and learn. Get over it. More fish in the ocean. Sure.

Then Ray came into the Spudnut. I couldn't believe how overjoyed I was. But I acted cool, or tried to. I strolled out from behind the counter. There was another customer I had to wait on. Ray stood in my path, not a lot of open space to maneuver between the tables.

Without any special recognition I went to cross behind him. I don't know why, but I impulsively stepped closer. Close enough to touch and faintly graze my breasts on his back. He stiffened and leaned into me, pinning me for an instant, though it felt as if I were frozen and on display for a short eternity.

I had shocked myself down to my toenails!

My face burning, I broke away and all but ran to the back room, where I tried to compose myself. He's just another guy, I told myself. What am I to him? Just some kid, a nobody waitress in a white uniform. Be cool. Be *cool,* I told myself. . . . Oh Lord, I'd left the other customer sitting there! I had to go back!

Or risk losing my job. What a fiasco. But I needed to keep my job. Resolute (barely), armed with my order pad and a smile, I went back out to face whatever fate had in store for me. Spudnuts, anyone?

DESPITE MY SELF-CONSCIOUS meltdown, Ray kept coming in to see me. I could tell he really liked me, but I started to wonder if the summer would end before he'd ever ask me out. I shocked myself once again by asking him, out of the blue, if he'd like to do something—us, together, somewhere, not the Spudnut?

Well, the next day he was going fishing with his uncle Fred. They'd be gone for a week. "That's why I haven't asked you out," Ray clarified. "I wasn't sure when." He looked at me more intently than usual.

Nine days later he was back.

But he'd been thinking about me out in the wilds and had come up with a plan. We could go to the drive-in. The one where teens from several Washington counties converged every night. Okay?

Okay.

He drove up to my house in his dad's gray sedan, a '50 Chevrolet. I was ready. I dashed out wearing my black cotton skirt splashed with vivid swaths of pastels and a sleeveless rose-colored blouse. I was laughing to myself as I realized Ray had never seen me out of my waitress uniform. But now, now he sure saw me.

In a blur we were on our way. At the drive-in we sat close together in the car. I was so nervous that my hands were wet with perspiration. The double feature that night had *Blackboard Jungle* first up. There was a girl in it who looked and danced (I decided later) a lot like me. I was so excited to hear the movie's hot new song—"Rock Around the Clock"—by somebody named Bill Haley and the Comets. Customers had told me about this new music that was called rock and roll.

As the movie ran, Ray moved closer and put his arm around my shoulders. I felt both awkward and thrilled. Who needed to read romance magazines? This was the real thing.

At intermission I excused myself and went to the girls' room in the snack bar. As I threaded my way back between the parked cars in the dark, I got the usual crude remarks from faceless guys: "Hey, girl, over here!" "Shake it, but don't *break* it!" By the time I was back, the second feature had already begun.

Ray opened the door for me. He had begun to get worried and apologized for not escorting me to the snack bar. I felt a rush of gratitude and, unexpectedly, felt so very comfortable to be with him. After the experience of what to my mind was a creepy public exposure, I was touched by his kind concern. (My magazines hinted at the perils lurking at the drive-in.) As I flashed again on all those half-open car doors and the leering comments, I thought, It feels good to be home.

When Ray later dropped me off at home, he kissed me good night. I made a mental note to myself—oh my God, tonight Ray kissed me for the first time. Another sign we were destined for each other. I was amazed that my dreams and reality were magically becoming one.

After work the next day, Ray picked me up in the car. We drove up South First Street in the sweltering heat, past Layman's Market with the huge containers out front of cantaloupes and watermelons. Next came a motley jumble of small restaurants and seedy taverns until Union Gap was left behind us. Then we drove north as far as the Triple-X Drive-In restaurant on the outskirts of Yakima (the big city of forty thousand or so).

We stopped, ordered food. When it came, Ray said, "Here's your root beer, honey." He said "honey" just like my brother-in-law, Les Bonsen, did to his wife, Jerry. She was my older sister. The word hung in the air. It felt like a commitment.

For years afterward, whenever we were doing some ordinary task like washing the dishes or the like and Ray happened to say "honey," I would remember how thrilled I was on that hot afternoon in Yakima when he said it the first time. I'd remember the sweet expression on his face.

From then on we had to see each other every day. When Ray came into the Spudnut, it was hard for me to take my eyes off him and do my work. We would happily smile away at each other for no reason at all, and talk at my breaks or when there weren't any customers. Ray also liked to smoke. I asked him how long he'd been doing it. "A couple of years now." I could tell by the expression on his face that he wasn't showing off. He was pretty well hooked.

I knew smoking hurt my lungs. The pain had stopped when I was at Saint Paul's, where it wasn't permitted. But cigarette in hand and drinking a Pepsi, Ray was as handsome and sophisticated as a guy in a TV ad, the sort who wore those heavy-framed dark glasses while cool jazz played.

IN JULY, Ray took me on long drives north of Yakima over the dry rolling hills toward Ellensburg. Or we'd drive to the west on Tieton Drive. That's where the great orchards were, those miles and miles of apple, cherry, apricot, peach, and plum trees that had made Yakima the self-declared "fruit bowl of the nation."

One afternoon out on Tieton, we talked animatedly about how much fun it would be to travel someday. We could go places that fascinated us. Imagine—to the Middle East where civilization began and modern politics made it a powder keg. Or to Europe to see art in some of the world's most amazing museums. Like the Louvre! Or even to Russia to walk where Napoleon desperately tried to win against the czar's troops and the Russian winter.

We knew about foreign places only from reading. Ray loved books as much as I did. That really surprised me. We both read several hours a day, always a book out of the library in progress. Few other teens we knew liked to read at all. Spend precious free time buried in some book?

Kids who did got called bookworms. But our shared passion meant that Ray and I couldn't have cared less what anybody thought of us.

When he was younger, Ray had read all of Edgar Rice Burroughs several times over. ("You Tarzan, me Jane," I had to tease.) His voice rose with enthusiasm as he told me about Burroughs. Ray clearly revered these books. And Buck Rogers. Ray had read everything in the series. Now he was busy with science fiction and fat historical novels by popular authors like Thomas B. Costain. (I let him know that I'd just finished reading Costain's *The Silver Chalice*.)

We discovered we were both enthralled with history. Again this was a wonder. No one we knew in public school could stand history, much less respond to it as we did. Ray was captivated by stories of Alexander the Great and knew all about his military campaigns. I had studied ancient history a year earlier, and before I knew it I was telling him about the Fertile Crescent and Hammurabi's code of law. That tumbled into a discussion of the Spanish Armada and the invasion of England. "In 1588 Queen Elizabeth I was triumphant over Philip II of Spain because she was so intelligent. No one expected a woman to have brains. Well, she showed them!"

"Of course having the British navy at her disposal didn't hurt either," Ray retorted. I laughed.

Then I asked him abruptly, "Ray, what would you like to do when you're older? You would be a fantastic history teacher." I could see him in front of a class of adoring students.

He nodded, unexpectedly serious. "I'm going to be a writer, Maryann. A writer like Ernest Hemingway. In fact, I'm going to be such a great writer, I'll be able to flip the bone to the world." He raised his hand, middle finger skyward.

My heart was pounding. This was the most exciting thing I had ever heard in my life. Conviction ringing in my voice, I said, "Ray, I'll help you!" Our eyes locked. It was a pact.

Trusting me more, Ray began to reveal other things about himself. But he was not easily forthcoming. Quite the contrary—he had private issues that took a long time before I knew much about them. I had no idea yet that from childhood on he'd had a serious weight problem. The year before we met, Ray finally made himself diet. Unlike the plans imposed on him by his mother or the family doctor, this worked. To stay trim Ray leaned on other habits, especially smoking, which took the place of food.

His fat-boy childhood had affected his personality and values. Always he sympathized with the underdog and the afflicted. However, for him it was important never to be called fat again. As for a wife—however smart, talented, or accomplished—she would also have to be a real trophy. When I eventually realized this need of Ray's, I was a little taken aback. My mother had always told me that physical beauty was skin deep. Good character counted for much more (and besides it was something you had control over).

Already I sensed that Ray wanted me to be a real showcase lady—and so I would be. He was always making sure I ate enough. At Mooney's Drive-In everybody wolfed down huge, trademark burgers; when we went there Ray urged me to eat. (I felt self-conscious, not hungry.) He wanted me to look "just right," slender but not too thin, because he didn't want his friends to think I was unsexy skinny. He was proud when somebody said I looked like Ava Gardner or Audrey Hepburn, those slim beauties and consummate movie stars of the day.

On the other hand there was more to me than my looks. Ray knew it and never belittled my abilities. This was just the way we were together, fifties attitudes about women notwithstanding. He really listened when I explained to him what Saint Paul's meant to me. "I go to Saint Paul's instead of public school 'cause it's college preparatory. The girls there like to read and study."

Truly I thought the twelve girls in my class were all first rate, stimulating and challenging. After what I'd faced in public school my new classmates had come as a great relief. These were the sort of girlfriends I wanted to have.

Unlike in my public school, I wasn't made to feel unfeminine or ashamed because I openly loved to learn. I may have been an A and B student at Saint Paul's, but I had classmates I considered totally bril-

liant. (There were four National Merit Scholarship winners.) Most came
from very wealthy families with every educational advantage. As I saw it
I was vying with the best, and that made it far more difficult to get really
high grades.

Only with my older sister, Jerry's, help had it been possible for me to
go to Saint Paul's. I was completely grateful. I wanted to become a
lawyer; I had ever since I was eight. So I worked very hard at my studies,
as I would have to qualify for a college scholarship.

After my fervid explanations I waited for Ray to say something. "Oh,
that's why you go there," he finally said. "My mother told me you went
to some school in Walla Walla. But she thought it must be a reform
school." He laughed. "I didn't want to ask." When he saw my hurt look,
he quickly added, "That's the only reason Mom's ever heard for going
away to school."

"No, silly," I finally said, with what I hoped was patience for his mis-
informed opinion. "It's like a reform school, sure, but the opposite of
what your mom was thinking. Saint Paul's is a *finishing* school." And I
certainly meant for Ray Carver to realize yet again what a special girl he
had.

ONE SATURDAY night Ray drove us to the top of a hill, a plateau east
of Yakima in the upscale development of Terrace Heights. You could
park there high above the lights of the city. The brilliant silver-and-
white stars hung elegantly in a concave black sky, and this night they
looked unusually far, far above us. The wide-open view made it the most
magical place in the world.

We talked. We talked and talked. And in the warm darkness we
started kissing each other, laughing, and kissing again. In the midst of
which Ray broke out in a serious sweat. His forehead was wet, his neck,
even his clothes seemed suddenly damp. It was his turn to be bewildered
and embarrassed. I was amused. I was happy beyond measure and
newly, delightfully confident. Loving Ray, I was overjoyed to be alive.

We got out of the car, leaned back on its body, and looked at the stars.
The warm breeze curled around us while songs played from the car ra-

dio. "Stranger in Paradise." "Mr. Sandman." There wasn't one we didn't like. It was as if the universe were beaming songs straight from the stars to us.

"Something's Gotta Give," Sammy Davis Jr.'s current hit, came on and leaped into our minds:

When an irresistible force
Such as you.
Meets an old immovable object like me . . .

I shivered with excitement and a faint undercurrent of fear. I was too young. I wasn't even fifteen, really, not until August. Oh, what could I give? If things went any further with Ray . . . just not now, please God, *not now.* I felt slightly chilled, the night no longer endless and inviting. The stars had gone remote and pitiless. I should go home—with a clear conscience. Somehow we held the line again.

IN AUGUST my girlfriend Pat came down from Billings, Montana, to visit for two weeks, after which we'd go back to Saint Paul's together. I was very excited and looked forward to her good female company. I didn't want summer to end, but I was lonely for my school girlfriends, as I'd mostly dropped out of the local circles. Besides, I sensibly decided, a distraction from Ray was a good idea. My romance magazines seconded the notion. And I'm sure my mother agreed.

Pat was *the* wild girl at school. Smart as a whip, she was a short little thing with a voluptuous body who liked to perch herself up on three-inch heels whenever she could. She had an attractive face, but unlike most of the girls I knew, was surprisingly adult looking. One of her favorite lines was, "I'm wise to the rise in your Levi's." No one doubted it. And she had witty stories of her adventures. Like the time in Montana she ran away with a rodeo star who looked just like James Dean.

Ray had a freewheeling friend, Dick, who was eager to meet her. I thought he'd make a good date. Pat's drink of choice was beer—not the Pepsis that Ray and I usually drank—and Dick liked beer, too.

After Pat arrived in Union Gap, I thought we'd have lots of time for talk and girl stuff. But then she met Dick. Before I knew it we were a foursome. During the two weeks of her visit, Pat and Dick and Ray and I went on long drives, saw movies at the drive-in, and partied on the hot afternoons when we "locals" weren't working.

The place for daytime action was Ashbaugh Park out on the Yakima River. The pavilion had cement flooring and a roof supported by poles, as well as barbecue pits, picnic tables, and a jukebox and dance floor. Under Pat's influence I wore colorful halters and cutoff shorts like hers. That had everyone at Ashbaugh looking us up and down. On my own I'd never have dared to wear such sexy outfits.

After the sun set *the* place to be was Yakima Avenue. The long street ran straight through the center of town. Every teenager's car in the valley had to be seen cruising Yakima, especially on a Friday or Saturday night. Your social rep was on the line.

Couples would "announce" that they were now going steady by drivin' the ave'. They'd sit so close together that the girl was practically in the guy's lap. Somehow he had to steer while they made out. It wasn't what the town fathers had in mind to promote good, clean fun in Yakima.

When cars came to a stop, girls and guys jumped out, shouting jokes and insults. They switched passengers, back and forth, piling in and slamming the doors. Then some guy would shout, "Drive it or park it, asshole!" and that would provoke a chase and maybe a fight. Other cars would rush to catch the action, at least until the cops came and broke everything up. Yet before long the cruising got going again.

That summer of '55 had turned into an endless party. Or so it seemed. I was part of it—despite my good intentions—caught up in the excitement. What's more, Pat and Dick were getting on like a house on fire. The third evening we all went out together our friends had the car's front seat while Ray and I were in back. When we parked they started to make out heavily. Then they whispered something to each other. The next thing I knew, they jumped out, grabbed a blanket from the trunk, and went off into the night, arms laced about each other. Oh my God . . .

Ray and I were still holding the line. But every night was an agonizing experience. We'd reach a critical point, break off, light cigarettes, comb our hair, try to collect ourselves. Meanwhile our friends, who barely knew each other, were thoroughly enjoying their freedom, the night, and each other. They weren't waiting to grow up someday.

The guys started bringing beer on our dates. Ray and I drank together for the first time. Why not? I was fifteen. We didn't have a lot of time left to be together. Pat was having a fabulous time. Saturday night of her first week in town, Ray and Dick came over to my house to take us out again. They had two cases of beer and were in a hilarious mood.

Ray protested when it looked like Dick was claiming more than his fair share. "I need plenty of this for Pat," Dick deadpanned.

"Keep it all," I said. "I don't need beer to be funny or sexy. Unlike some people I know."

"Well, don't mind if I do," Ray said. Dick kept grabbing bottles back. We were all so playful and exhilarated. It was summer euphoria. We were old enough to be out on our own, no longer kids. What more could anyone ask?

We all drove over to Lyle Rousseau's house. His parents were out of town for the weekend. Lyle and his girlfriend, Marlene, were several years older than Ray, so that made them at least six years older than I, a considerable gulf. And they were sophisticates, everybody agreed.

They greeted us at the front door in a cool, blasé manner. What did I know? In our corner of the Pacific Northwest far from the hip circles of the world, they were as close to "young, fair, and debonair" as it got. If Marlene deigned to speak to you, that was special. Every younger girl in town believed it.

They ushered us into the living room where there were bowls of potato chips and peanuts on the coffee table. Marlene went out and returned with a tray and six tall beer glasses filled to the top. "Hi, how're you doin' tonight?" she asked me, but moved on before I got out a reply.

On the hi-fi turntable LPs spun, jazz only—Shorty Rogers, Gerry
Mulligan, Dave Brubeck, Monk. This was the music Ray and his older
friends liked to listen to. Witty, cynical jokes were de rigueur with Lyle
and Marlene, and Pat was instantly a hit with her killer dark humor. "I
thought someone said there was going to be a *party* at this address," she
drawled.

"What do you want, babe?" Dick chimed in. "Whips and jangles, or
you bored with that, too?"

Ray and I were a little uneasy at the direction the jokes were taking.
Everyone was drinking steadily. I drank more beer than I ever had before, even though I didn't particularly like it. Usually I would nurse one
along, or if I opened a second I'd eventually hand it to somebody else to
finish. I cherished the company of my friends—I loved good times—but
only appeared to drink with the crowd. I didn't want to lose control.

After maybe a couple of hours of listening to the cool music and
drinking more beer, Lyle took Marlene's hand and pulled her up from
the couch. He gave us a wink and led her away. Dick reacted. "Hey,
Lyle, where can Pat and I go?" Lyle motioned down the hall. Like that
Ray and I were sitting alone in the living room, deserted.

The record on the hi-fi ended. After a few awkward, silent moments,
Ray asked if I wanted to go for a walk. Holding hands, we went out to
the backyard. We sat down under a big oak tree, just us—the way it'd
been before Pat and Dick. Ray had two beers with him. We sipped and
talked softly. Finishing his, he turned and kissed me.

Soon we were kissing wildly. I realized that the beer helped me to feel
freer than I'd ever felt. More important, there was the joy of my passion
for Ray. Before I fully realized what was happening, I was stretched out
on the grass under the leafy oak. In the air was the scent of the garden's
big-blossomed late-summer roses.

I heard Ray say, "Oh, please, honey, I love you. Please don't tell me
no this time. I love you so much. I want you so much." He kissed me
tenderly. He was unbelievably dear to me.

"I love you, too," I said, closing my eyes. I felt suddenly as if something in my head had made a complete circle, a realization of what life

was about. I remember thinking, What the hell. I reached up and kissed Ray with all the love I had.

He must have sensed the change. He hugged me as hard as he could until I almost couldn't breathe. It was so sweet, as sweet as the scent of the summer roses.

IN THE MORNING I felt shaky and panicky, constantly on the verge of tears. I hadn't meant for "it" to happen. I didn't feel sure of anything. Mostly I wanted to crawl into a cave and hide. But I went to work my Sunday shift anyway.

All those nights up on Terrace Heights or out by the rushing river we'd gone to the edge and then stopped. I'd go home with a good conscience and yet the secret excitement of being in love. It all came back to me in a rush of lost innocence. I planned to shine. I wanted to fly—now he will expect this to happen again.

Just when my thoughts were blackest, Ray called me at the Spudnut. On the phone my nervousness intensified. But his voice was so gentle and concerned—and soft as always. He was sweet and sincere, asking me how I was doing, if I felt okay. The genuine affection in his voice finally eased my terrible discomfort.

But I did a strange thing. I talked as if I didn't remember what had happened, as if the drinking had left me with a memory lapse. Ray was obviously bewildered. I felt slightly guilty because I could tell he didn't know what to do or say next. He sounded a little ashamed as he hinted at what had taken place at Lyle's house.

In the short week left to us before I went back to school, Ray thoughtfully planned familiar outings. We went to a movie downtown, not the drive-in. And we had a nice dinner at his favorite restaurant, the Golden Wheel. Though it was a Chinese place, I knew it made a hole in his budget. But what comforted me the most was that when Ray took me home he simply kissed me gently good night.

Before I knew it, it was two days to go. Our last Sunday Ray picked me up after work, deliberately shaking Pat and Dick so we could be alone.

He drove west from Yakima out into the country through apple orchards heavy with ripening fruit. We didn't say much as we sped by,
contentedly looking at the ordered rows of trees basking in the late summer sunshine. A song came on the car radio. The Four Aces, number
one on the hit parade, "Yes, true love's a many-splendored thing. . . ."
Our song.

Ray pulled the car into an orchard and stopped. He rushed into telling me what had happened at Lyle's. I felt he was being honest and direct, apologizing if he'd taken advantage of me. I had to admit that I'd
been conscious during everything and awkwardly explained that I was
too shy to talk about it on the phone the next day.

"I'm not sure what to do next," I confessed.

Kissing me on the cheek, Ray said, "That's entirely up to you."

I turned to him and said, "I love you."

DURING OUR LAST day together Ray often earnestly declared his love
for me. Eventually it became a small, special shared joke. When he'd
say, "I love you," I'd say, "Do you *really?*" Then we'd both laugh and
he'd say very gravely, "Yes, I really do."

Summer was over. Good-bye, Union Gap.

Pat and I headed back to Saint Paul's. Dick and Ray saw us off from
Yakima on a Greyhound bus. I was very glad to have Pat along cracking
her wry jokes on the long bus ride out to Walla Walla. But I also wanted
to get back to school.

Saint Paul's meant a first-class education for me, a treasure for life.
Yes, I dreaded the thirteen-hour days ahead. It meant study, study,
study— a quiz every day in every subject. I could handle it. I still had a
sense of destiny, a life full of promise. I'd learn about English literature,
Latin, geometry, physics, religious thinking, speech, and drama—well,
let me at it!

THE MAIL at Saint Paul's was laid out alphabetically on an oak table in
the drawing room. After lunch students would circle the table looking

for their names. Unfailingly there was an envelope for me in Ray's dear, near-illegible handwriting.

"That which we call a rose by any other name would smell as sweet." I thought of Romeo and Juliet and longed for Ray. And who wouldn't put her trust in such a sweet person and such a promising world?

2

LOVE LETTERS

I wrote to Ray early in the morning when I woke myself before the school bell, or else late at night. For two years—my junior and senior years at Saint Paul's—we conducted a written courtship with great passion. Back in Yakima, Ray often wrote his letters to me during class, usually Spanish. (He didn't care much for high school.) We wrote back and forth about history and literature and the events in our daily lives that interested us.

We could only see each other freely during school holidays and *the* weekend, the one each semester when students were permitted to go home. That meant mostly waiting for Thanksgiving and Christmas and spring vacation around Easter. I felt our separation keenly. In September, as the fall inched slowly ahead and the days until my next vacation seemed infinite, I believed that my lone hope of keeping Ray's interest was through my letters.

So I wrote constantly about everything and anything. Naturally I wrote about whatever I was studying: Grendel, Beowulf, the great hall, flagons of mead, Caesar marching on Gaul, Rome burning. Ray was *interested*.

I wrote about going with my girlfriends over to Roedel's, a candy and ice cream shop a few blocks from school. It was right out of an *Archie* comic, a hopping place where boy met girl and the jukebox banged out the latest hits. We listened to the Crew Cuts sing, "Sh-boom, Sh-boom . . ." Life could be a dream when sipping on an ice cream soda—and maybe flirting a little.

I told Ray about Saint Paul's students marching en masse to Whitman College to see *Oedipus Rex* or *Death of a Salesman*. Or being shepherded to a cello recital or some other musical offering of the community concert series.

I wrote about the Friday nights when chaperoned students were escorted to the movies. We saw first-run features like *Giant*, with James Dean, Rock Hudson, and Elizabeth Taylor. Later in class we discussed the movies we'd seen as reflections of our society. (Think of *Giant*'s antiracism—imagine, Mexican Americans might be equals!)

And I wrote about Saturdays when Pat and I were unrestricted and could go as far as downtown Walla Walla. We'd shop at the big stores and do lunch—a treat after eating at school all week, although Fong, the Chinese cook, was great.

And I had to mention the Saturday-night social dances.

Ray seemed particularly keen on knowing more about that. I explained that I had to attend when my name was called. Mrs. Fulton, a local dentist's widow and our housemother, ran things. She paired us with dancing partners, young men rounded up from Whitman College or boys corralled from Walla Walla High School. One dance I was partnered with a wealthy doctor's collegiate son, another a cute high school boy.

Well! Ray didn't like it. He kept track of "the situation" by calling me long distance. (His dad never complained about paying.) He knew he could come to Saint Paul's only to attend formal events. At the proms Ray would wear his elegant gray suit and bring me white carnations to wear on my wrist or dress. I was so proud of him. I felt like Cinderella, I joked. Happy beyond words, I'd check off my dance card, never wanting the evening to end.

In his letters to me Ray wrote about going over to Lindy's Diner with Dick. It was a hamburger joint in Yakima that had his favorite pinball machine. Everybody loved the charged atmosphere; it was like going to a party. Ray sported a DA haircut (the punk style of the day) and wore a black vinyl jacket. He would play pinball with all his energy, shoving sideways, back and forth, doing whatever it took to make the silver balls drop home. (When I'd gone with him to Lindy's it turned *me* on to watch.)

He'd likely enclose his latest work for the Palmer Institute of Authorship. This was a Los Angeles–based correspondence course, advertised in popular pulp magazines, that his dad bought for him. I was amazed at how well Ray wrote! He was great. I could visualize whatever Ray described, whether it was a plump, perspiring woman baking bread or a pastoral scene in a meadow, with a creek full of fish and insects buzzing on the water.

His assignments came back annotated with the instructor's high praise and occasional suggestions. Disinterested in his schoolwork, for Plamer Ray faithfully put forth his best efforts. It made no difference whether the assignment was a character sketch, descriptive piece, or point-of-view exercise. He was challenged and worked hard. If more than a day or two went by and he hadn't gotten to his "Palmer," he felt guilty and uneasy. He'd neglect everything else and cut out partying until he caught up.

I think Ray learned the basics of how to write from this course, however formulaic and rote the lessons. And he had all that practice writing letters. But the ambition to write that he announced to me so emphatically had formed much earlier.

During his childhood Ray "slept in" with his dad on Sunday nights to hear his dad's stories. (Another night his brother, James, got his turn.) The stories were about the South. Ray's dad had grown up in Arkansas. He had tales of his father's cousin being an outlaw in the Frank and Jesse James gang. When Ray's dad was a little boy, the family story went, this outlaw cousin had brought the notorious brothers to the Carvers' homestead. Ray's dad said he'd been allowed to handle their guns!

This one night a week was all it took. At some point Ray began to make up stories of his own to tell his dad. When he learned cursive lettering in the third grade, he decided *writing* stories was what he'd do when he grew up. Now he was sending wonderful first efforts to me.

We were such young kids, with so many hopes. I knew I could count on Ray. He championed me, encouraged my studies, and had so much respect and love. Even our separation had a positive aspect. It let us develop our individual identities, instead of spending every waking moment as a high school couple going steady. But we missed each other terribly, and we could only write about our loneliness and wait.

AT CHRISTMAS, Ray had something to say to me. When he asked me to be his wife, I broke into tears. I was so happy I couldn't say anything. I nodded my head yes, then sank against him. He held me tight to his chest.

We were engaged, but it had to stay a secret. I was only fifteen. Ray was seventeen. We weren't even out of high school. Both of us had many expectations to meet and intensely held personal dreams to pursue. We may have been adolescents, but somehow we were going to make it all work out.

IN THE SPRING I was writing Ray about walks I took with a friend. We strolled through the Walla Walla neighborhoods on the way to play tennis at Whitman College. The sunshine was so light and thin it felt fragile and precious, like the clusters of early daffodils I admired in people's yards. Having shed our uniforms for shorts and white tennis shoes, we ambled along, carefree, idly swinging our rackets.

And had he heard this new Elvis Presley record? We couldn't hear it enough. At least ten times a night "Heartbreak Hotel" spun on the phonograph. Our interest in other singers paled. Elvis and that song were "the most," my friend Sally Wilson declared. (It was his first number one hit.) From then on Elvis was always our man, always the King.

Ray had lots to write, too. His group of buddies—Dick and various other friends—bought beer every weekend and went on nighttime "odysseys." They'd go over to a house to drink and play music, drag the avenue in their cars, and then get something to eat at the Lariat Drive-In near the high school. Ray always told me who got drunk—not him, usually.

I was glad to hear it. But not everything about Ray was so easy for me to accept. He had his quirks. I'd already run into a mildly disturbing one the summer we met.

Ray told me he liked to dance. He implied that he was a very good dancer, that he knew how to do the mambo, the tango, the samba, and other popular ballroom styles. I was very excited as I loved to dance, although I was a little intimidated by his expertise. Even though I was a good dancer, I didn't know the Latin steps well. How could I keep up with Ray on the dance floor?

A place called Playland, out at Selah north of Yakima, was where the big bands performed. When we finally went there, I discovered Ray couldn't do *any* of the Latin dances. It was all a lie. At best he slow-danced—which I enjoyed—but he didn't jitterbug or do any of the fast numbers.

I had believed Ray—otherwise so honest and aboveboard—about his dancing prowess. When I teased him about telling a bald-faced lie, he just shrugged it off. He wasn't embarrassed or contrite. *C'est la vie,* was his attitude. He'd been trying to win me over. He laughed. What did I expect?

It occurred to me many years later that being an adept liar went well with being a good fiction writer. Ray was always an extraordinary storyteller, able to embellish prosaic occurrences with humor and imbue them with a mythic air. But it was hard for him, seemingly, to accept where poetic license ended in real life. If pressed, he did know where the truth lay, but he made it his deliberate choice to decide in which situations the "stricter" standard applied.

Ray's lack of dancing ability didn't stop him from encouraging me. Over the years I danced and danced. (I still do, every day.) At home and for Ray alone, I performed. I did go-go. I did ballet I'd studied as a child. I closed out the evenings with my own private imitation of stripper Gypsy Rose Lee. Bright eyed, Ray would sit in his chair, fascinated, watching me. It always turned him on, he said, because the dance was always different.

Dancing made me happy. At Saint Paul's the big formal dance of my junior year was the occasion of my greatest social triumph. What a time we had. Ray and several of his friends came and stayed over in Walla Walla. They put up with all the strict school rules, though we ridiculed and evaded them wherever we could.

His friends enjoyed being paired up with mine. The night before we informally partied to Elvis, and then on Saturday we danced the night away. Ray and I were the envy of the whole school.

IN JUNE 1956 Ray was to graduate from Yakima High School. (Renamed the A. C. Davis High School in 1957 in case you go looking for it.) Right after graduation day his family was moving to California. I was crushed. He had to go with them, our totally secret engagement notwithstanding.

I had so looked forward to spending the summer together. Instead, when I got home from Saint Paul's we had a measly week. Ray and I tried to make the most of it. After a long afternoon parked up on Terrace Heights, we barely made it to his graduation ceremony. The next thing I knew he was gone. Ray, James, and his mom headed off to someplace called Chester. His dad had left town earlier.

I had met Ray's father the previous summer. I'd been shocked by his good looks—at forty-one he was as handsome as a movie star. And sweet! My God, he was sweet. He always pampered Ella and his two boys every way he could. He had taken his sons fishing from when they were little kids. (All three were great and avid fishermen.) He bought Ray a ton of books, Ray's favorite toys when he was child. And C. R. (as most of his friends called him) doted on his pretty wife.

Of course I had met Ella Beatrice Carver waitressing at the Spudnut Shop. She had that temperamental Southern belle personality. But she always amused me, and—strictly to myself—I thought of her as Scarlett O'Hara. Usually she was very charming and very forthright. You knew where she was coming from.

Ray's dad would beam when Ella came back from the beauty shop, looking wonderful. In the living room she'd stand in front of her oval mirror patting and reshaping her hair, fuming about the beauty operator who couldn't do it right. She'd rail on about her hair in her soft Southern accent, which she never lost, though she was always surprised when anyone remarked on it. She liked getting everyone's attention with her feminine "views," the only female in a house of adoring males.

"Dear, your hair looks beautiful," C. R. would say.

"No, my hair looks just awful. It makes me mad to spend all after-noon at that cussed beauty shop and come home looking like this. But thank you for the money for it, dear. Thank you for the box of choco-lates here, too."

The Carvers called each other "dear" no matter what the state of their moods. His wife may not have liked it when C. R. drank beer on a Friday night—because even a little bit "showed" on him—but he was always the loving bulwark of his family and a steady breadwinner. He had worked at the Cascade sawmill in Yakima for ten years.

C. R. was a saw filer. His brother, Fred, ten years older, was a head filer, and C. R. worked under him. As a head filer, Fred Carver made considerably more money. He was responsible for the care and mainte-nance of the huge log-cutting saws, the heart of a sawmill's machinery.

Everyone in the family had a fixed belief that Fred, his wife, Billie, and their daughter, Linda, were the "haves" and that C. R., Ella, and the two boys were the "have-nots." (My understanding was that Fred's daughter had been "brought up like a little princess.") This family peck-ing order was respected, resented, and endured all the years of their closely mingled lives.

Earlier in '56, Fred had gotten into a quarrel with the mill and was fired. He found work in California. C. R. could have stayed on, but out of loyalty he decided to follow his brother. Things looked promising at first. Ray's dad and uncle were employed in the Collins Pine sawmill, and there was a job for Ray, too. It was a chance to make some good money, better than anything he'd find in Yakima. He could buy a car, and in the fall, if he wanted to, he could go to the community college at Susanville, near Chester.

Ray's family had seen some lean times, but they had pulled through and prospered modestly. No one could have imagined that the relatively comfortable, established life they left behind in Yakima was never to be theirs again.

UP UNTIL THE summer I met Ray, my younger sister, Amy, and I had spent summer holidays with our dad on his great farm in western Washington. My folks had divorced when I was five. (My mother, Alice Ritchey, married three times. So she was Mrs. Burk, then Mrs. Higinbotham, and finally Mrs. Reed.) Now we stayed put with Mom because we wanted summer jobs in town.

Amy was only a year and eight months younger than I. So my mom had two teenagers on her hands. She tried to be a disciplinarian but was so sweet she really didn't have the heart for it. She was a teacher who inspired her students, rather than acting like a schoolhouse jailer. I'm afraid Amy and I, full of teenage liveliness, gave her a few more gray hairs.

That sweltering summer of '56 my mom had rented a little house in Selah, north of Yakima on the other side of the river. It was behind the Playland dance hall. Glumly I had resigned myself to a long, lonely three months. I had two jobs—a hard one in a restaurant where I made good tips and an easier gig at the Playland snack bar during the big dances. (Our friends the Paradis owned Playland dance hall and park.)

Ray and I continued writing each other every day. Like me, he was often exhausted from work. His job as an entry-level laborer at the sawmill hurt his mind as much as his body. In a bid to be more independent he moved into his own apartment, but after three weeks he was back with his family. He was lonely and too tired to cook decent food, so a place of his own seemed pointless.

In July, Ray let me know he was getting the first week of August off. Then came the electrifying invitation. If my mother permitted it, he'd drive up and bring me back to Chester. I could stay with his family for four or five weeks and take the bus home.

Mom was worried about my coming home by myself on the bus. The next two weeks I begged her relentlessly until she finally agreed. I started counting the days, hours, minutes until Ray would arrive at our house. When the old familiar gray Chevy finally pulled into the yard, I was beside myself with joy.

I ran out and greeted him in a red-and-white T-shirt and a pair of white shorts. The outfit had been selected for days. Smiling from ear to ear and laughing silently, he took me in his arms. Hello, my secret fiancée.

We took off as soon as we could.

After a long drive, Ray and I got to Chester late at night. His dad opened the front door, glad to see us. But C. R.'s handsome face looked gaunt and sad, and for a moment I hardly recognized him. He had lost an enormous amount of weight and was holding the waistband of his pants gathered in one hand.

What had happened? The story was that the previous spring he'd got a piece of lead in his hand at work and left it untreated. Blood poisoning set in. He couldn't eat and developed chronic, painful diarrhea. Stomach cramps made him uncomfortable in any position.

At night he lay in bed with pillows under his belly, moaning and writhing from side to side. Adding to the pain was the apprehension his illness stirred, as deadly as his deteriorating physical condition. "Carver fear" had set in.

The family believed it was the pall of bad luck in a pitiless world, crippling and baffling. And yet C. R. still somehow went to work every day during my summer visit. (Eventually he gave in to his pain and left his job at Collins Pine. He would struggle for years with failing health, unable to hold any job for long. The shame and depression that followed became an illness unto itself, one that had a dire impact on everybody he loved.)

The elation that Ray and I felt was too heady to contain, even with the simmering crisis in his family. We saw only a month of fun ahead of us. Better not to dwell on what couldn't be helped; better instead to cheer everyone up with our excitement, giddiness, and pure joy.

I HAD MY birthday at the Carvers'. August 7. Ray and I and James (who'd turn thirteen in August) spent the day fishing. We worked a stream winding its crooked way into Lake Almanor through a swampy chartreuse and dark green meadow.

James hooked a big German brown trout that put up a vigorous fight. Ray and I laughed boisterously, crying out encouragingly each time James *almost* had his fish. "That's it, James, you had him. You'll get him yet!" Then he'd lose control and the fish flailed away downstream, line reeling out, all of us giving merry chase. Finally James mastered his catch and brought him in. We were all in awe of that big fighter fish. And we were also muddy up to the knees from tramping up and down the little creek bed.

After our fishing we went to visit Ella at the Copper Kettle, a Chester restaurant where she was working. In high spirits, we ordered ice cream cones. Then we headed back to the house and told Ray's dad our fish tale.

He nodded. "Mary, this fish was a scrapper. He was sent for your birthday. I'll cook him for you." He nodded again. "Sixteen is a wonderful age for a girl." (My name often got affectionately abridged to Mary.)

"I agree," I said.

Although he felt very sick and had worked all day at the mill, C. R. insisted on preparing a special dinner. The three Carver men loved to watch me eat fish they'd caught. It was standard fare they'd been eating all their lives, but to me it was ambrosia.

Ray's dad deboned my serving of trout and in a ritual flourish served it to me. That made Ray and James laugh with pleasure—the master of the house applauded by his sons. But later I broke into tears when C. R. proudly carried in the homemade birthday cake that Ella had baked. Sixteen candles blazed with fire and light.

"You're the daughter we always wanted," Ray's folks told me.

They treated me like one. It was positively embarrassing to go shopping with Ella. All I'd have to do was mention I liked something, and she'd insist on buying it for me. Ray's dad stood by me, always with utmost loyalty and love, which I appreciated endlessly. He'd tell my mother one time, "For my money, Raymond could have searched the whole world over and taken twenty years to do it, and he wouldn't have found as fine a girl as Mary."

RAY AT EIGHTEEN, as I saw him, was as handsome as any young man at that age can be. I hold him in my mind's eye as he was then, right there—perfect, beautiful—with that dark curly hair slicked back and those wise, deep blue eyes—his best black striped shirt on and (for pants) black peggers. A young, cool West Coast Adonis.

All the local Chester girls looked long and hard at him. Like that blonde, cute as Sandra Dee, who worked at the soda fountain. I made sure that his focus stayed on me. As the August moon waxed, I was as happy with Ray as I ever could be. His dad saw how turned on we were by each other. I think he was concerned but felt powerless to say anything. He did try subtly not to leave us alone in the house, but we laughed and drove off in the car. Neither my mom nor his dad could stop us, though I'm sure they might have liked to. Besides, we knew we were engaged, even if they didn't.

It's said you don't know a man until you live with him. Those weeks at the Carvers, I was very excited to be practically living with Ray and learning many things about him. I saw how spoiled he was! And came to realize he always had been. Ray was an only child for five years until James came along. His mother thought him "so beautiful" and "so smart," she was supposedly afraid to have another child.

When Ray was young Ella dressed him in expensive little Eton suits with matching caps. She'd kept them, and one day she got them out and showed them to me. I was very impressed with her excellent taste. She had a picture of Ray as a toddler with long, golden Shirley Temple curls down past his shoulders. He was eighteen months old when his dad took him out and got him a haircut.

I saw that Ella still doted on her older son. She would come to the doorway of the room he shared with his brother and ask Ray what he wanted for breakfast. Ray would ask what she had, and she'd run off a list of everything she could make for him. He would pause, consider, and select whatever he wanted.

I found myself recalling an incident from last summer. Ray and I were out drinking beer with Pat and Dick down by the railroad tracks. A police car pulled up. The cop was out to arrest us. Ray pleaded, don't tell his folks: "Oh please, officer. My parents think the sun rises and sets on me." That must have impressed the cop because we avoided serious trouble. It became a stock joke of Dick's to mimic the scene in a high childish voice: "Oh puh-leez, officer . . ." We'd burst out laughing, but Ray never found it funny, and now I wondered if he more or less believed his declaration.

But he wasn't more self-focused than others in his family. Take the night when only two pieces of homemade cherry pie were left—and all five of us coincidentally converged on it. Ray, James, and Ella put hands on the pie tin and earnestly argued back and forth over who was going to get a piece. No one gave a thought as to whether C. R. or I might like some. While they skirmished, we exchanged a smile of amusement. Had it been my house, everyone would have insisted that someone else have the last piece. A guest absolutely would have been offered first.

For all the closeness between Ray and his mother (and perhaps because of it), they had vicious arguments. They would "get into it" as

Ella called it. Ray's mother tried inordinately hard to please her son, but when she fell short of his expectations, he'd let her know.

"Mom, I told you to go by the drugstore and get that roll of film I left there to be developed. Why didn't you do it?"

"Honey, I couldn't afford to get your film out. By the time I got my groceries, I didn't have enough money left. I'm sorry."

"Well, I'm not surprised," Ray avowed. "My entire life has been one of continual want."

That was typically the point when she burst into heartbroken tears, painful for me to hear. But being a woman with spunk, Ella rebounded, doggedly determined "not to take his shit." She argued back that Ray got the best they could possibly give him and he knew it, damn it. (Go get him, Scarlett, I thought, laughing to myself.) Eventually they'd both run out of gas, and harmony would be restored.

Ray was a sweet, compassionate man like his dad and he was, at times, stubborn—*determined*—like his mother. He'd need both these qualities to become a great writer, though I wasn't yet old enough to grasp what that would mean. But I did sense that Ray had parents who had given him all they could to boost him up the road to a better life.

RAY'S DAD REPEATEDLY offered to send him to Susanville's junior college. He could quit his job, live at home for free. C. R. knew Ray was bright and wanted to write and hated mill work. But Ray declined; he liked the things his paycheck could buy. He also had me.

Our relationship was separating him from his family. His parents knew I was becoming a fixture in his life. Though they wholeheartedly welcomed me, they must have felt they were losing their oldest son. I was partly the reason Ray wasn't interested in college in California—he wanted to return to Washington.

"Love finds a way," we'd said with tears in our eyes back in June. Reunited in August, it seemed truer than ever. I remember our driving to the Chester Pharmacy and stopping out front in the sunshine. We were going to get sundaes or milk shakes at the soda fountain. As he parked the car something suddenly struck me, and all sixteen-year-old solemn I said to Ray, "I want you to know there will always be a *very* special place in my heart for you."

He looked stricken. No, silly, we aren't breaking up! I was trying to put into words how much I loved him. I meant, I'll love you forever. As long as I'm aware of anything. And beyond that wherever God takes me. That's how long I'll love you.

That he understood.

Chester wasn't much of a town, but it did have a little movie theater. Our other favorite haunt was the library. It was cool, clean, and well lighted.

I had a summer reading list from Saint Paul's to deal with. On the seniors' list: *Anna Karenina, Madame Bovary, Crime and Punishment, Fathers and Sons,* and "The Lady with a Lap Dog," along with five other Chekhov stories. We borrowed the Tolstoy, Flaubert, Dostoyevsky, Turgenev, and Chekhov volumes I needed. Ray had never really gotten into any of these writers before. He became very curious after he read the jacket blurbs and sampled some pages.

I tackled *Madame Bovary* first, reading passages aloud. The story was so sad, but even in translation the style was the marvel. For Ray it was a small revelation. And we both loved "The Lady with a Lap Dog," impressed that Chekhov not only wrote short stories but also had been a practicing doctor. I found out that, yes, this was the same writer who wrote plays; I had seen a production of *The Cherry Orchard* while at school.

We didn't have time to read everything on the list but managed to get through the Tolstoy and Dostoyevsky. There were other appealing diversions at hand. For instance, it was just a three-hour drive from Chester to Nevada. We wanted to see Reno.

OUTSIDE THE CITY we came upon a huge sign: WELCOME TO RENO/THE BIGGEST LITTLE CITY IN THE WORLD. For no real reason, it had us laughing uproariously. Maybe it was our heady anticipation.

We spent money saved from Ray's paychecks on movies, clothes, and wonderful food. The real challenge was to sneak into clubs and gamble—wasn't that what everybody was there for? Ray loved to play blackjack and roulette, as well as the slots. We'd have a great time until some club official got the notion we were minors. Then we'd be forced to leave. We did manage to hang on to the little souvenir bottles of vodka, whiskey, and Scotch we bought all over town.

By the time we left Reno, we knew we'd be back. In the car the heat was so intense we stripped off our clothes until we were down to our underwear. Then we made drinks from our little bottles in paper cups. We sped along the dry, hot, country road, getting very high and happy, exuberantly aware that our whole lives lay ahead of us.

Back from our quick trip, we went driving some evenings on the winding road through the big mysterious evergreens that bordered Lake Almanor. Sometimes we stopped for a swim. Occasionally another couple came with us, Sam and Jay. Ray worked with Sam at the mill. They were not from around Chester.

Sam was handsome but pockmarked and had that experienced look. He'd been in prison for car theft. He drank a lot and often stuck by himself in the little trailer he shared with Jay. As for her, she had been an exotic dancer in Sacramento hard joints. Just meeting them, I knew they were out of my league.

On my own I wouldn't have hung out with them. I don't think they would have invited me, either, though Sam stole glances at my body and breasts when he could. Jay and Sam seemed old and jaded. Their vulgar language and boozing were racier than anything I was used to. It was Ray who enjoyed the pair of them, all of them drinking whiskey and water out of tall glasses embossed with badly faded hunting scenes.

As I rationalized it my hope was that Ray was looking for background material. You had to be able to write characters of all sorts, I supposed, like the bad ones I'd read about. (I know Ray would never have put it that way.) But obviously he found Sam's tales of prison life fascinating. He was interested in Jay's life, too. How did a lady of the evening survive in the city? He enjoyed getting Jay going, letting her describe proudly her "success." For me it was a lesson on how the poor dregs of society cavorted.

I was to find out that Sam's "lessons" included taking Ray to his first whorehouse. They went over to Susanville, the little town thirty miles away, where Sam bought Ray an "around the world." (If you don't know, don't ask.) It was ancient history by the time I found out a few years later—but when I did I was jealous and upset anyway. I felt acutely a lack of loyalty and fidelity. I was Ray's first lady, and I couldn't imagine him wanting anyone else, ever.

(My natural reaction upset Ray. He lamely tried to convince me that the experience had meant nothing to him. That's why he finally mentioned it the way you do some old amusing story that comes back to mind. Yet in his heart of hearts, I don't think Ray had real regrets. He was only concerned to soothe my hurt feelings.)

My distaste for Sam and Jay at the time didn't seem to register much with Ray. It never turned into an open argument, but I made it clear I wasn't changing my mind about them. When Ray groused, I laughed. What was the battle of the sexes if not a convoluted, confusing phenomenon? That's what I told him. None of my reactions were intentional—I just responded. And I said, "Besides, you know I still want to be a lawyer. I can't help myself."

Washington girls in the fifties who didn't immediately marry after high school and start having babies usually ended up being nurses or teachers. I didn't plan to be trapped in either of those professions. Or wind up a housewife. After law school and a successful practice as an attorney, I imagined going into state politics or, better, national. Verbal jousting with Ray Carver was just the beginning.

LIKE THAT, AUGUST was gone. I took the bus home uneventfully. Soon after, I was back at Saint Paul's to begin my senior year. Ray stayed in Chester, working at the mill and living with his family.

My big consolation was that my sister Amy had also enrolled at Saint Paul's. She was a freshman. We had always been so close, and we'd loved being at school together.

I went home to Yakima for *the* weekend six weeks into the fall semester. Ray was in town. He met me at the Greyhound Bus Depot on

Yakima Avenue. He had come back, found a job at a pharmacy, and was already moved in with his aunt Von and uncle Bill.

Violet Lavonda Carver—the four-years-older sister of Ray's father—was known as "Aunt Von" in the family. She was married to Bill Archer, and they had lived in Yakima for years. In many ways she was like a second mother to Ray.

We had a weekend reunion that was tender and wistful. Love had found a way. Too soon I was back on the bus to Walla Walla.

AT CHRISTMAS RAY and I again went to visit his family in Chester.

We were deliberately vague about our travel times—that let us squeeze out a day on the road by ourselves. With much excitement we set off speeding down the highway to California. Everyplace we stopped had holiday decorations. Snow had fallen in the redwoods. There were Christmas trees with bubble lights, jukeboxes with Bing Crosby singing "White Christmas"—a wonderful, magical season. We sang Christmas carols in the car, laughing because Ray knew so few of the words and I knew them all.

Now we had "our" day. We rented a little cabin in the trees in Bend, Oregon. It was the first time for us to be together all night. We were so excited to have real privacy. Ray took over the place, turning the covers back on the bed, smoking a cigarette in the big chair in the living room, feeling he was "master of the house" before we went out to dinner.

But poor me! I felt a terrible cold coming on. Ray bought some medicine at a drugstore and doctored me. At dinnertime he put on his white silk patterned shirt with the mandarin collar (I was just crazy about it), and I dressed in my red sweater and red shoes. Forget the sniffles. We were going out to a nice restaurant with all the time in the world to eat and talk.

Music played while we ate, the likes of "God Rest Ye Merry Gentlemen" and "Here We Come A-Wassailing." Ray pretended to be learning them on the fly as he fumblingly sang along. I found his performance hilarious. When I tried to join in, I found laryngitis had seriously kicked in. I could only duet in a croaking voice. What a pair we made.

After dinner both of us were eager to get back to our little house. Giggling and laughing, we took our first shower together, soaping and washing each other. Ray was very solicitous, carefully wrapping me in a big towel so my cold wouldn't get worse. I felt very witty and funny, cracking a whispered stream of one-liners until Ray was helpless with laughter. He responded with his own jokes until we were both laughing hysterically under a tangled pile of blankets on the bed.

Back on the highway the next day, the car radio belted out more Christmas carols. Again I teased Ray for not knowing them. "Where have you been all your life?" I said, laughing. "Where?!"

"That's just *it*," Ray said.

"Just what?" I asked quietly, sensing his more serious mood.

"Where have I been all my life? I've been thinking about that a lot lately. I grew up in Yakima. My family moved there when I was two. Except for living near another sawmill in Northern California for a few months, I've never been anywhere.

"My folks used to take me on train trips to Seattle when I was younger, because they could see how much I loved to go somewhere different. To see the water, the zoo, go to a restaurant different from any I'd ever been to before.

"That was the same time I went to see *King Solomon's Mines* three times. That movie completely captured my imagination. I wanted to share it with my dad. Just like when I was small and we went to movies together. My dad understood why I loved *King Solomon's Mines*."

Ray laughed quietly. I was thinking, What did an old movie have to do with us? Or Haggard's story, for that matter—though Ray liked that sort of book. He was getting to what was really on his mind.

"Two friends—Berghoff and Vashon—are going to go to South America. To Brazil. I've read that at the mouth of the Amazon it's possible to reach down and pick up handfuls of diamonds. Imagine! I got maps. I know just where the diamonds are found. I need something to do while you're away at school. Maryann, the guys and I agreed that before one of us went off to college or got permanently trapped in a job, we ought to go down to South America. We ought to have an adventure we'll never forget."

My stomach felt queasy. Dread descended at the thought of Ray being gone. I'd worry if he was safe. But I loved him, so the decent thing to do was to encourage him with genuine enthusiasm. To inhibit him with my fears would be unfair, I reasoned in a flash.

I told Ray I would miss him horribly. Then I put a great deal of animation into asking encouraging questions about the logistics of the trip. How long would they be gone? How much money would it cost? How much did they have now?

Some answers came swiftly. They were going to leave in January; they expected to be gone a couple of years. "The only problem is," Ray said haltingly, "I surely am going to miss you."

I smiled. "By the time you get back I should be studying prelaw at the University of Washington. I'll get a scholarship. I'll be in Seattle." It all spilled out of me like it was the most ordinary thing to be talking about as we sped down the road to Chester.

One more thing: "Waiting for you, Ray. I'll wait for you," I said.

3

TO CHURCH WE WENT

The Christmas trip to Chester had been shadowed by Ray's imminent departure. As 1957 began nothing seemed to have changed his mind. He called me at Saint Paul's the last week of January. He had quit his job at the pharmacy and really was heading off to the Amazon. His two friends, Vashon and Berghoff, were set to go with him.

"We'll write just the way we do now," I said softly.

"Yes," Ray said. "I've lined up general delivery towns all the way. When I arrive at a town, the first thing I'll do is check for mail from you."

Since his announcement at Christmas, I'd developed a lofty sense of self-sacrifice. His was a necessary quest, the initiation into the wider world of a young man who was destined to be a great writer.

"I love you," Ray said.

"I love you, too."

It would be forever before we would see each other again.

I RECEIVED A postcard from Arizona and then a letter from Mexico.

Philosophically I told myself that Ray's letters were always going to come from exotic places. But they'd contain exciting news. I would be sharing his adventure—the quest—from afar. My life demanded this sacrifice. Hadn't Ray repeatedly said that he considered us both to be very special people? We were destined to live very unusual, out-of-the-ordinary lives.

The third piece of mail I received from Ray was postmarked Chester, California. I stared at the envelope and could not imagine what had happened. But I was surprised and relieved at the letter's news, even as I felt for Ray's disappointment.

Ray and Vashon had gotten into a violent argument somewhere south of Guaymas, Mexico, a Pacific port town about 150 miles from the border. A fight started over a monstrosity of a fish that Ray caught from a little pond of water and brought back to camp. Vashon threw a fit. It was an obvious excuse for venting the hostility and frustration that everyone was feeling.

The situation had become the classic "two's company, three's a crowd." Ray and Berghoff got along well, as did Berghoff and Vashon—but all three of them? No. They just assumed there wouldn't be any personality clashes on the trip. Plus they'd all been sick from eating tainted bologna. Food poisoning hadn't helped anyone's disposition.

The upshot was that Ray gave Vashon and Berghoff almost all his money because they planned to keep going. He kept only enough for bus fare back to California. His dad laughingly told me later how Ray ate two breakfasts, one right after the other, when he picked him up in Red Bluff, 70 miles west of Chester. Three days with hardly any food had left Ray mighty hungry.

I knew Ray felt stymied and hurt. He had always been well liked by everyone. His father's friends liked him. To confess the folly of his aborted trip to his parents and me was not easy. But I loved what he wrote next: "God, I'll be glad to see you, honey." That thought had kept him from being devastated by the trip's collapse. Ray added, "We'll see the world together. We, for sure, do get along," with "ha ha" in parentheses. His joking, as we often did in our letters, truly reassured me that all was well.

I was ecstatic. There was more: "After June, when you graduate, you'll be free. We'll both be free." I couldn't think of a thing I'd rather do than travel with Ray, having exotic adventures. I was thrilled by his enthusiasm and affection. Then I let my whole being glow with the realization and joy that Ray was back.

Ray recharged at his folks' and then returned to his old job in Yakima, driving a pharmacy delivery truck. Al Kurbitz, the pharmacist, owned three drugstores. He took a personal interest in Ray, liking his intelligence and maturity. But as a good businessman, he questioned the practicality of Ray's ambitions, as Al personally had never met a writer.

Mr. Kurbitz offered to pay all of Ray's college expenses if he would become a pharmacist, come back to town, and take over one of the drugstores. "You could always write on the side, evenings and weekends, but be sure of a good living." Ray was very flattered by the offer, but declined appreciatively. He certainly knew that the hard sciences of the pharmacist's curriculum weren't his forte. For the moment Ray was content to have landed back in Yakima, where he had other things to occupy his mind.

Saint Paul's spring vacation came at last. I went home to the apple and cherry orchards in bloom, a profusion of pink-and-white blossoms. And I came home to Ray. He was eager for my June graduation so we wouldn't ever be unwillingly separated again. Until then we had to be satisfied with the next nine days together.

The first evening in town we had a wonderful dinner at my sister Jerry's house. (Although called Jerry, her given name was Bonna.) She was twelve years older, had been married to Les for years, and had two boys. Altogether there were five fabulous Burk girls: Jerry, me, Amy, and Valla and Annette, our two much younger half sisters from my dad's second marriage.

Dinner was great, but Ray and I left as soon as it was polite, saying we were heading over to Aunt Von and Uncle Bill's place for coffee and dessert.

Instead we started driving out into the country.

There were acres and acres of orchard blossoms, the moon lighting the way and so brilliant that our headlights were irrelevant. Ray finally spotted a driveway leading to the heart of one of the orchards. He pulled in with an audible sigh of relief and excitement, stopped the car. We turned to each other.

"Hello there," he said.

"Hello there yourself," I said. We began to kiss each other.

"Honey, I've missed you so much."

We were lying awkwardly on the seat, the moonlight streaming in through the windshield making Ray look silver.

"Do I have to put something on?" he asked.

I quickly counted the days. Fifteen since the beginning of my last period. "No, I don't think so. It's been fifteen days."

"Oh, good," he said. "I just want to feel you."

MY GOD, I THOUGHT, I've got six more weeks until I graduate. I've got to pull this off. *Dear God, I have got to make it through.*

As this resolve set in my mind, I was overcome with an attack of nausea and made for my wastebasket. Later I furtively emptied and cleaned it. I didn't want any of the other girls to see I'd been sick.

Earlier I'd been half naked when my good friend Diana popped into my room without knocking. She took one look at me and said in her typically spontaneous way, "Maryann, are you pregnant? Your nipples are as brown as nuts."

I didn't know what brown nipples signified. "No," I said, "I'm not pregnant. I've lost five pounds since spring vacation."

"Oh, well . . . those breasts of yours . . ."

"Don't say a word to anyone, Diana. For God's sake, you know how everyone loves how you blurt out things. Don't blurt this out."

"I won't," she said very seriously. And she swallowed hard.

I knew then.

I had tried to convince myself otherwise. I had a history of missing one or two periods a year during the three years I'd been having "those days." This was just a missed month, I reasoned. Young girls are sometimes irregular—I'd read that lots of times. And aren't you supposed to get fatter? I was skinnier than ever. But I hadn't been able to account for my swollen, sensitive breasts, except to think that my period would start any minute.

With a last burst of optimism, I went into my clothes closet to be sure of privacy and looked at myself. For the first time I really saw what Diana had seen. Two very dark brown nipples. Not like normal pastel pink ones.

Oh God.

A week later my period still hadn't begun. My breasts hurt under the white Ship 'n Shore school uniform blouse. Before, I had always been relieved when my period started after Ray and I had been together, even when logically there was nothing to worry about. I had been scared, then relieved, so many times that I couldn't believe it really wasn't going to come.

A couple of days later, unable to keep my secret all to myself any longer, I snuck downtown at the three o'clock school day break. I used a pay phone to call Ray at work, person to person. I didn't expect him to be there, as he'd probably be out making deliveries, but I left a message: Call me tonight during dinner.

I was summoned into the little telephone room that evening. On the phone Ray sounded out of breath over the long-distance connection. "What's the matter, honey? You've never called me at work during the day. What's the matter?"

Losing my courage, and afraid that someone might be monitoring the line, I couldn't say more. "Oh, I was just lonesome for you today." At least that much I said truthfully. "Ray, could you possibly come down this Sunday and see me? If you can, then I think I can make it through until the end here."

"Sure, honey. Isn't this funny? The thought hit me this morning, I wanted to see you so badly. I was thinking of whose car I could borrow that would make it down there. I'll work on it. I'll ask my friends and come up with something."

"Go see Jerry." My voice had a trace of desperation. I tried to stay composed and think. "If she knows this far in advance, they won't plan anything. Her car is brand-new but she'll let you borrow it."

"Yeah, maybe I'll ask Dick to come along, and he can visit Pat while I visit you."

"Oh, don't do that!" I blurted out. "I mean, I don't feel like making small talk with them and laughing and joking. I just want to see you."

"Is there anything the matter, Maryann? You don't sound quite like yourself."

"No, I just miss you," I said, tears starting in my eyes.

"I'll see you on Sunday. I'll be there by one-thirty. Just after you've gone to church and had your Sunday dinner, little Saint Paul's girl."

"I love you, Ray. I love you so much."

"I love you, too, Maryann. I love you so very much."

We hung up. As I started back to the dining room, tears were in my eyes again. I had to step back into the telephone room and bring myself under control. He loves me. He truly loves me. And I truly love him. Everything is going to be all right. We've just got to make a plan, both of us, and do what we have to.

RAY ARRIVED AS promised on a fair Sunday in May. I was waiting for him in the sitting room, my coat already on. "Do you want to go for a walk?" he asked. Whenever he'd visited Saint Paul's we had kept to the school grounds, our rendezvous as platonic as a fifties school picnic. But today I wanted to leave campus. I felt I was maintaining a monumental charade.

As we started casually out of the building, we ran into Miss Zorb, the headmistress. She had warmed to Ray—unbelievably—as she never did to any of the pimply boys who came to the school dances. It was totally unheard of for Miss Zorb to approve of a boyfriend. I thought of what she'd said to me privately after first meeting Ray. "That young man— there is something about him. I have the feeling he is definitely not run of the mill."

Saying almost nothing, I listened to her chat with Ray about how his writing was coming. "Write about what you know, from your own experiences. Write about the Pacific Northwest. It is an enchanted territory. You could be the one to do it—put it onto the map."

After the unnerving encounter with Miss Zorb, Ray didn't want to seem furtive or overeager to leave the school grounds. "Let's take a walk around. The birch trees must be in bloom by now."

"Fine," I said—not really. Today I didn't want to preen; I often had, walking arm-in-arm with Ray in front of girls playing badminton or students taking solitary strolls. I shrank from seeing anyone I knew. Miraculously no one was down in the meadow with the lovely circle of tall white birch trees. Ray and I walked there in private, holding hands.

After a few minutes of pleasantries and local gossip, I had run out of anything more to say. Except what I had to say. "I think I might be pregnant."

Ray turned to me and hugged me hard. "Don't you worry, little thing," he said. "Don't you worry."

"My period is two and a half weeks late. My nipples are a strange dark brown color. But I'm losing weight—perhaps it's all nerves or *youth.*" I tried to laugh as if I had the goofiest notions.

Ray had his own answer. "What we'll do is get married. As soon as you graduate. Then, if you are pregnant, that will be covered. If you're not pregnant, that's okay, too. In either case we'll be married."

He had it all figured out like lightning. "I'll start right on it, planning the wedding. I'll bring Jerry in. I'll work with her. I'll go out and see your mother. My mother, too. Don't you worry, honey, we'll have everything ready for you. You just concentrate on your studies. Have the fun of graduation with the other girls. When you come home, we'll be together and can plan anything we want."

I started to weep, overwhelmed with gratitude. "Love finds a way!" I said, laughing and crying.

AFTER THAT SUNDAY with Ray, I was on a high and confident of my decisions. Of course I could make it. I'd study and keep my grades up— whether I went to the university next year or not. Every day would be well spent, no matter the future.

I was fortified by my family's values and emphasis on education for women. My mother, my mother's sister, and my Grandma Ritchey were all teachers. Two of my dad's three sisters were teachers, and the third, my aunt Anna, was a nurse. They had worked to put themselves through school at a time when most men didn't even finish eighth grade. Saint Paul's college preparatory courses were only a first step for me. I was not abandoning the dream of higher education, even if I had to put it on hold for a while.

It was no wonder that I was privately distressed by Ray's hatred of school. His education of choice was reading the books he loved or being out in nature. He had no desire to go to college. I had written letter after letter to him explaining how bored and frustrated I was at public school, but how different Saint Paul's had been. College would be different for him. Everyone said so. Ray couldn't possibly know what he might be missing.

Right before I got pregnant, I concluded that Ray didn't have a practical strategy for moving his life forward. I had written how we could move to Seattle and go to the University of Washington together. We could travel summers, work at national parks—we'd see beautiful places while we earned school money. Maybe we could get jobs on steamships, see Europe or the Far East. Maybe we might take some time off from school, save our money, embark on an open-ended trip around the world! Whatever we decided, after June we'd be free to become exceptional people with exceptional lives.

Now travel had to wait, too. My immediate future was the reality of marriage and motherhood, barring a surprise reprieve. I barely grasped the import of these irrevocable changes. I was caught up in the rush of events, convinced as only a sixteen-year-old can be that I was doing exactly the best thing.

Ray and I let the word get out to our relatives and friends of our "impetuous" decision to wed. This happy news had one unforeseen reaction. When I told my sister Amy, she cried brokenheartedly. Why? Why? she wanted to know.

I knew Amy liked Ray, but I realized that she felt she was going to be abandoned. Our parents divorced when she was three. Amy had three more years of high school. To her it seemed as if I were bailing out of the family, too.

Mom had just dropped her own little bombshell. She was getting a divorce from her second husband. She already had a steady new boyfriend, but her situation was anything but stable.

My heart twisting, I tried to comfort Amy. I told her nothing would change. We'd still be sisters and spend just as much time together. But I was graduating. Ray and I had been going out together for two years. I wanted to live with Ray, not just date him. Please try to understand.

I went ahead and sent out my graduation announcements. I was going to make it.

The day before, my mother took the bus to Walla Walla. She came early to spend some time with Amy and me. We were elated to see her. We went downtown to a nice restaurant for dinner, and the three of us reveled in being together. All of us were caught up in the rush of feelings that the end of a school year brings.

As a teacher, Mom lived by the academic calendar. How exciting but bittersweet graduation time could be, and she had been through so many. While we ate, Mom talked brightly about my big day. Amy interrupted her. "Well, that's not the biggest thing. Maryann is getting married!" My mother's face tightened, and she said tersely, "Let's not talk about that now."

I wondered if she knew something more. Not about the wedding, as that cat was officially out of the bag, but about my pregnancy. Was it possible? Neither Ray nor I had told her. Meanwhile, he was right in the middle of the wedding arrangements.

After he bought our rings he had made trips to Jerry's home and my mother's to show them the bands. The flowers, the timing of my father's arrival, the honeymoon preparations—he was going to have everything ready by the time I got back to Yakima.

I couldn't believe how fast everything was happening. One last night

at Saint Paul's. Then it was graduation day. Never-to-be-forgotten graduation day.

Jerry and Les came to the commencement ceremony with their two
boys, Lynn and Lanny. When it was over and every student had her new
diploma, they were the ones who drove us all home. Thank God, they
were not loath to speak about my wedding. I found that they were supportive, jolly, and festive. I was so glad to see them and hear what was
being planned.

Ray was waiting for me at Jerry's house. We were both thrilled and
excited beyond belief. This final homecoming from Saint Paul's sur-
passed all our past reunions. The days of separation and waiting were
over. We couldn't stop hugging each other.

THE BUSTLE OF preparations picked up right where my graduation
left off. My commencement was June 4. Ray and Jerry had chosen the
seventh for the wedding. The ceremony would take place at Jerry's
house, a long, low ranch on the outskirts of Yakima.

Aunt Von threw a bridal shower for us at her house. The roses and
peonies were blooming outside, and the dining and living rooms were
full of beautifully wrapped gifts, many of them homemade, fancy work
by the women.

The afternoon gave way to a fragrant, moonlit evening. The men
stood outside in rolled-up shirtsleeves, leaning against cars, laughing
and talking, while the women congregated in the homey living and dining rooms. Children were everywhere, in and out. Everybody in the
Carvers' extended family was there. I met people from Yakima I had no
idea Ray was related to.

Ray's paternal great-aunts, Ollie and Lena, came. So did their children and grandchildren—the Hunts, the Carvers, and the Greens. Uncle Bill's family, the Archers, of course were there. They were fixtures at
these family gatherings. Most of the neighbors dropped by as they were
much like family, too. I realized these were all people who had come to
Washington from Arkansas and had stayed in touch—even twenty-five
years after leaving the South.

. . .

THE DAY BEFORE the wedding I went out to do some last-minute errands. I bought more clothes for the honeymoon: Ray and I were going to Seattle for a week. Without any conscious intention, I found myself wandering by the office of Jerry's gynecologist, Dr. Waters. Suddenly, I felt I had to *know*. I felt Ray should know. Was I really, truly pregnant?

Dr. Waters was a handsome man who looked like Gregory Peck. He gave me an examination immediately. "From all my experience, I'd say you are pregnant. But I could give you a test that would determine for sure."

Not necessary, Doctor. I almost ran out of his office, tears flying from my eyes. All I wanted to do was to see Ray. I couldn't wait to share the news with him. I wanted him to comfort me. I wanted to see his reaction. It had hit me—we were going to have a baby!

I was suddenly filled with the most incredible sense of joy. I was going to be Mrs. Carver. Get that—Mrs. Raymond Carver! And we were going to have a baby! We would be a family.

I ran the last six blocks to Ray's house. I was out of breath, crying again, but ecstatic when I got there.

"We're going to have a baby," I was finally able to say.

Ray hugged me, as happy as could be.

LATER THAT DAY we went to an appointment with the Episcopal minister who was going to marry us. When we were seated in his office, the Reverend Baxter intoned that married couples faced three standard problem areas: sex, finances, and religion. I popped right out, "Oh, we don't have any disagreements about sex or finances. But I'm very concerned because Raymond doesn't believe in God."

Ray's face reddened. He ambivalently glossed over his lack of faith. To my amazement, Rev. Baxter, perhaps sympathizing with a fellow male put on the spot by a talkative female, now skirted the very issues he had raised. He acted as if he had done his duty by simply *mentioning* the areas of potential discord. It was not necessary to press on and discuss

with a young, starry-eyed couple whether they had any practical conception of what they were getting themselves into.

Turning to more congenial matters, the minister told us that although
he was willing to perform the ceremony at Jerry's house, we were more
than welcome to use the church. Gripped by instant snobbery and the
tempting offer, I now decided that taking our vows at my sister's was
akin to a near-pagan ritual. How could that simple, profane setting com-
pare to vows at a church altar in front of majestic stained-glass windows?

I imagined it easily: guests filling the choir stalls. Others encircling us
as we stood before the minister, and more guests in the main pews of the
lovely church. I thought of people like Miss Zorb and our dear Saint
Paul's housemother, Mrs. Fulton. They were both driving up to attend.
Wouldn't they take one look around the church and totally approve of
such a sacred setting?

With that I forgot about all the preparations my sister had made and
embraced the minister's suggestion. Ray and I would be married in
church. Jerry might be a little hurt and disappointed—I felt bad about
that—but a church ceremony was a sign of respect for God and the
sanctity of marriage. It was what I wanted.

Not surprisingly, when I told Jerry of the change in plans, she broke
into tears of anger and disappointment. Didn't I see the efforts she had
gone to, neglecting her own family?! But she soon put aside her hurt
feelings and gamely conceded that it was my wedding. I should do what
my heart desired.

Although it was a bit of a scramble to get the ceremony plans back on
track, that task was soon accomplished. Tomorrow was the day; a last
night of freedom as singles remained for Ray and me. We both made the
most of it.

Ray went off to his bachelor party. My celebration was with Jerry and
Amy. My two sisters were ready to make my last night as a maiden
something memorable.

We drove out to the officer's club at the Army firing center where
Jerry's husband worked a civilian job. Dressed to the nines in colorful

linen sheath dresses (out of Jerry's closet) and clad in our high-heeled sandals, we sat at the bar and drank all we wanted. Then we danced with three soldiers we met. When everyone grew tired of the songs on the jukebox—like Connie Francis's "Little White Lies"—the six of us left the club and went to get something to eat. We hit our favorite place, the Donut Shoppe, an all-night breakfast joint in downtown Yakima.

My suave, handsome soldier escort was young and healthy, with brown hair and a tan that made his skin golden. He was a lot of fun. Like Ray, he had a ready laugh and the ability to see the humorous side of life. He knew I was getting married the next day and wasn't looking for more than a few innocent kisses to salute my departure into happy matrimony. We were having a lighthearted time on an exciting summer night. A celebration! And how better to spend your last night of being single than with a bronzed, eye-catching young soldier?

Sitting in the Donut Shoppe, the gang ordered ham 'n' eggs, waffles, hash browns, steak, whatever anyone wanted. We ate and talked and laughed. When I next looked up at the clock on the wall, it was almost five in the morning. I wrapped my arms about myself and happily thought, Today is my wedding day. I'd never been so happy in my life.

The bachelorette party finally adjourned. We three Burk sisters floated merrily back to Jerry's house.

That's when someone decided we should call Ray on the phone and sing, in unison, "For He's a Jolly Good Fellow." So we did. At 5:30 a.m.! Ray weakly protested that he'd just gotten to bed. His tone was half amused, half really aggravated—the way men talk to very naughty children.

"Party pooper!" Amy told him on the phone, something I wouldn't have dared to say myself. Notwithstanding our intimacy, Ray and I were respectful and polite to each other. I wasn't about to dispute his right to be riled.

OUR WEDDING DAY was here. It was a Friday. Friends and family gathered from all over. Ray and I would walk down the aisle of Saint Michael's Episcopal Church in downtown Yakima in the late afternoon.

We'd speak our vows from the service of the Episcopal Book of Common Prayer, the Reverend Robert Baxter presiding.

My school friends Pat and Diana had flown in—Pat from Billings and Diana from Portland. They checked in to the Chinook Hotel, Yakima's finest, before coming over to Jerry's to assist the bride. Boy, weren't they excited and flippant, wisecracking away as they helped me with the last-minute details of my trousseau.

My dad had driven in early that morning. His car was loaded down with gifts from the Coast—a fleecy white bedspread from my aunt May and his gift, a silver set. With a happy expression on his face and quick, good energy in his step, Dad spent the day being useful and supportive of his "Deedle," the nickname he gave me before I could walk or talk.

Sometimes when I would amuse him as a kid, he'd laugh and call me Oxy Deedle. I had grown so fast—I was my full height at eleven—that I seemed clumsy compared to my more graceful sisters. But I was the one who looked most like him. He adored me the way I was, even if he loved teasing me when I stumbled into an "oxy."

Today I noticed that he didn't call me Deedle but addressed me as Maryann. It caught at my heart. He was preparing himself to give his little girl away.

Dad took my out-of-town girlfriends in tow and gallantly paid for their hotel room. He took them out to lunch and bought them a bottle of liquor for later. Pat and Diana declared to me that the party "officially" began when my dad, Mr. Val Burk, arrived.

I wanted the church to be filled with three times the flowers originally ordered. Dad enthusiastically bought more. We also ducked into Lou Johnson's, an exclusive clothing store, where he bought me four extra honeymoon outfits. Then he picked up the tab at Gordon's, the chicest hairdresser in town.

When we got back to Jerry's, I bathed carefully and dressed in the sitting room. Pat and Diana squirted me with their favorite perfumes and helped me into a white linen sheath of Jerry's. It was her best dress and looked right out of the pages of *Vogue*. Last they adjusted the cloche of white feathers I wore instead of a conventional veil. It was my own idea.

Admiring myself in the mirror of the dimly lit sitting room, I saw a tall, willowy white bird—a dove—swooping out of the sky.

Because I had spent a good part of the afternoon at Gordon's, and what with other last minute emergencies, the bridal party was running very late. An appointment to take pictures at a local photographer's studio had to be canceled. No one could reach Ray, either, so he and Neal Shinpaugh, the best man, showed up right on schedule at Jerry's. (Nonsense that it's bad luck for the groom to see the bride before the ceremony. We were young and blithe and did what made sense to us.)

When I saw them get out of the car, I stepped out onto Jerry's circular driveway and walked to Ray. He was dressed in his new navy blue suit, white shirt, and tie, handsome as could be. It was our first sight of each other that day, and we laughed aloud in joy. What a sight to see us all dressed up to get married!

It was time to go. We piled into Neal's car: Ray with Neal in the front; Pat, Diana, and me in back. We took off for Saint Michael's Episcopal Church, careening along, having the time of our lives. All that ran through my mind was, How totally, totally cool.

SAINT MICHAEL'S WAS stately; it had been modeled on Sir Thomas Gray's church in his poem "Elegy for a Country Churchyard." Climbing ivy covered the huge gray stone walls up to the wooden roof. The church looked solid, enduring, unbreakable. I wanted my marriage to have those qualities and last forever. I would do whatever it took to make it work. I had been so hurt and crushed by my own parents' divorce that I never wanted my children to go through such a traumatic experience. Most of all, I knew I would never love anyone as much as I loved Ray.

I was waiting for my dad in a back room of the church with the minister and my attendants. Out a window I saw Jerry's car arrive, then my dad pulling in behind. I said, "Oh, it is they!" " 'It is they,' " Rev. Baxter repeated. "I hear Saint Paul's grammar in that syntax." He was obviously pleased. I felt cherished and protected, as if I were back in school in the familiar atmosphere of an early-morning prayer service.

In the church were so many of my friends and family, I wondered if all these people would ever be in the same place again. That day we were all so young. I was sixteen; Ray was nineteen. Neal, his best man, was no older. My sister Jerry was the matron of honor at twenty-eight. My immediate family was together, my divorced mom and dad both smiling. Only Ray's father, of all people, was missing. (C. R. knew his failing health might soon cost him his job in Chester. He didn't dare lose a day of work.) But Ella was there in a light spring tweed suit and matching hat, looking dignified and proud for her son.

Our family's "kid contingent"—how adult we felt in comparison— was looking good: Ray's brother, James, and Amy (both fourteen); my cousins Spencer and Irmagene Kulp; and my nephews Lynn, ten, and Lanny, eight, the family mascots. The boys were the youngest guests. They looked like preppy angels with black pants and white sport coats with pink carnations in the lapels.

Aunt Von and Uncle Bill, along with most of the folks from the bridal shower, came. Many of my friends from Saint Paul's were in the pews— I was the first in the class to get married—as well as old friends of mine from public school (Highland High School in Cowiche, a town north of Yakima) and friends of Ray's from Yakima High. And to my delight, Miss Zorb and Mrs. Fulton attended as promised. They had come a hundred miles from Walla Walla to be there.

All these guests filled Saint Michael's choir stalls and the pews of the lower level. Even more would be at the wedding reception out at Playland. (I had limited the invitations to the ceremony as originally it was to be held at Jerry's house, a much smaller space.)

There was hushed anticipation in the church. My dad hurried into the back room. I took his arm. Dad was wearing his brown suit—his only suit. He looked as handsome as any man in the place as we walked into the nave and the processional music began to play. The massive organ pumped out "Here Comes the Bride" through its big brass pipes, and we came up the aisle on the long maroon carpet.

The glowing white candles looked celestial next to the white wicker baskets of tall white flowers. As my feet glided over the thick carpet, I

We're legal! I'm watching Ray sign the marriage papers, with his best man, Neal Shinpaugh, witnessing. Saint Michael's Episcopal Church, Yakima, Washington, June 7, 1957.

glanced at guests in the wooden pews. But when I saw Ray at the altar steps, I could see only him. He was smiling at me, waiting to marry me. Flanked by Dad, I joined him and took his arm.

Rev. Baxter began the wedding service. When Ray had to "repeat after me," he spoke his vows right out, poised and intelligent. But then something happened I never could have imagined or anticipated. I realized that nothing in my life would ever outshine this moment. Try as I might, when the minister told me to repeat "I, Maryann Elsie Burk, promise . . . ," I had no voice. It was gone.

Ray put a reassuring arm around me. But I could not find my voice. Then my dad, in a loud stage whisper, said, "Deedle, do you think there's going to be enough beer at the reception? Maybe I should leave now and get more." "Shh!" I said, incensed. Wait, I could speak! Then what Dad said hit me and it was all I could do not to dissolve into helpless laughter. I winked and smiled at him.

I spoke my vows. The minister gave his final blessing and pronounced us man and wife.

. . .

ON TO PLAYLAND. The Paradis family had offered their dance hall for the reception. My friend Cheri Paradis made it a labor of love to do all the preparations and decorations. But my mother still insisted on a big, white tissue wedding bell, without which, she declared, "all was lost." So we had one. It was hung above the table where the cake was displayed, also a gift from Mom.

A full buffet was prepared by the cooks of a gourmet restaurant the Paradis also owned. Load up your plates—there was roast beef, ham, turkey, several kinds of salads, baked beans, rice and potatoes, and homemade hot rolls. In addition to supplying kegs of beer, Bob Paradis had made up two huge batches of punch, alcoholic and nonalcoholic. Cheri saw to it that the punch bowls stayed full. (The alcoholic punch was vodka-spiked and certainly put people in a cheery mood.)

Ray and I led off the dancing with "The Wedding Song," followed by our "personal" song, "Love Is a Many-Splendored Thing." Then I danced with my dad. The children danced with each other, danced with their older relatives. My friends were sitting with Ray's, and Ray's relatives out of Arkansas were eating and dancing with my mother's Canadian ones. Everyone was mixing and matching, and it seemed to me that it was a great, wonderful, interesting party that should never end.

(My dad even shook hands with Clarence, Mom's new boyfriend. In the past, Dad had gotten testy, even near violent, with any man that my mother got involved with. Not tonight.)

As I went around the room talking with everyone, I occasionally looked over at Ray. He was laughing and talking and smoking with people from the pharmacy where he worked, poised and charming. Yet there was something new about him. He seemed almost visibly stronger and more mature, happy, and relaxed.

I was longing for a cigarette as well, so I sneaked out behind the beer kegs and lit up. Jerry caught me. "You don't have to hide anymore, Maryann," she teased me. "You're a married woman now. You come right out here with the other adults and smoke your cigarette like a lady." But I didn't want to. I was embarrassed, fearing I'd look like a ju-

We cut the wedding cake . . . and I fed the groom a piece.
FROM THE COLLECTION OF MARYANN BURK CARVER

venile delinquent. But Jerry got me thinking. I was now a wife. I was Mrs. Carver. I could stand with a cigarette in the middle of a room, and it was nobody's business but my own.

As the reception party rolled on, Ray and I were having such a good time that we didn't want to leave, even when we were reminded by several older female relatives that we really ought to get along. We were supposed to seem very eager to depart. Once we exited, others who were ready to go could leave. It was grossly impolite to leave before the bride and groom.

"Too bad," Ray and I first replied when asked to be considerate of others. After another round of reminders, I finally said, "Oh, all right."

Ray and I made the rounds. It was almost impossible for me to say good-bye to my dad. All my life I'd never seen enough of him. He had only arrived that morning. It felt too soon to say farewell, but it always did, no matter how long or short our visits. I hugged him hard.

Dutifully we left Playland, the music and the crowd's laughter still going strong. We hopped into Ray's little Chevy coupe. It had been decorated with plenty of cans and a JUST MARRIED sign.

The Reverend Robert Baxter, Episcopal minister, observing his handiwork:
Ray and I joined forever in holy matrimony.
FROM THE COLLECTION OF MARYANN BURK CARVER

Laughing and cuddling, we drove over to the Tops Motel on North First Street. We had a reservation. In our room we happily talked over the day's events, relaxed at last. We were so high, enthusiastic, and romantic. Jerry had given me "something new" to wear. I was delighted with the beautiful, sexy, mint green baby-doll pajamas. I saw Ray was too.

MY NEW HUSBAND was sound asleep. I lay there beside him, exhausted yet sleepless. The events of the day whirled in my head.

My mood had deflated and I thought, My God, what have I done? My youth is over. Poof, I'm an adult! I'm a wife. All the mystery and anticipation of my future life had vanished. Signed, sealed, and delivered, that's how I felt.

I didn't want to disturb Ray, but I couldn't stop my stifled sobs. My tears didn't ease my misery. Crying often came as a relief, but tonight the longer I cried, the more hopeless I felt. Just think, two months ago I was fretting about my grade in physics. What sort of joke was the world playing on me? Finally I couldn't stand feeling so bleak and alone. I had to wake Ray up.

"Ray? Ray?" I shook his shoulder gently.

"Oh, honey," he said groggily. "If you'll just let me sleep five more minutes, I'll do it again."

Now I had to stifle my laughter. Ray's humor was our saving grace. Oh, I'm fine, I thought, I have this tender, wonderful man. I wouldn't trade places with anyone in the whole world. I snuggled up to Ray and finally drifted off to sleep.

4

YOUNG, MARRIED, WITH CHILDREN

The next morning, before we left on our honeymoon, we drove over to Fred and Billie Carver's cottage. That's where Ray's mother was staying. The moment he sat down at the kitchen table, Ray said, "I've never been so hungry in my life!" His mother laughed, and I blushed with embarrassment. Ella cooked us a big breakfast of Ray's favorites: sausage, scrambled eggs, and hash browns.

James was sweet to me that morning. I think he needed to feel that no one had lost anyone. Well, we all needed to feel part of a larger family now. I had never before had such a sense of being so important to others. Having all these folks rallying around me was heady. I was, amazingly, the celebrity of the hour.

I was sure I was looking lithe and attractive in my new yellow toreador pants and a brown striped T-shirt of Ray's. I also had on a big silver pendant cross presented to me during graduation week. And a wedding ring.

After breakfast we paid a visit to some of my family. We went over to Jerry and Les's house. My aunt Amy and uncle Elmer were there, with my cousins Spencer and Irmagene. We were an affectionate family supportive of one another, and we chatted away happily.

At a lull in the conversation, I knew it was time to get up and get going. Taking our empty coffee cups out to the sink, I signaled as much to

Ray. There were some mild protests as nobody wanted to see us leave just yet, but everyone knew we had to hit the road.

They trooped outside with us. Ray got into the little Chevy coupe and I climbed in beside him. We waved good-bye and drove off into our married life.

ALL THE WAY to Seattle I sat close to Ray, laughing and talking. In my head I kept saying "Maryann Carver" over and over. I was trying to get used to it, like new shoes. Ray was still Ray Carver—a name I always thought sounded great. For me to be a Carver, too, instead of a Burk, meant . . . what exactly? I am Maryann Carver. But who's that? I'd have to find out.

Driving into town we were eager to explore the busy streets and waterfront, Woodland Park, and the big stores like Rhodes and Frederick & Nelson's. But first thing, we had to find a hotel. We hadn't made a reservation.

As Ray was parking, I saw a tall, dignified-looking brick building up ahead of us. I was drawn to its height and stateliness. A tasteful red neon sign stood high above the building. It said simply, VANCE.

"Look there, Ray, that must mean the Vance Hotel."

"Yeah, but look over there." Ray pointed the opposite way and laughed. He had spotted a smaller, nondescript building with a small sign: RAY HOTEL. Thinking that this was a more prophetic omen, as well as being an obviously less expensive place, I said, "Oh, we have to stay there. I feel a story coming out of this!"

That settled it. We got out and walked straight to the front desk. Without really looking at the lobby or asking to see a room, we checked right in. The proprietors were Chinese, an inscrutable old couple who barely spoke English. When I mentioned that we had just gotten married, neither cracked a smile or offered congratulations. On the contrary, they looked us over suspiciously. All of a sudden I felt as young as I was, a girl not quite seventeen.

"A first-rate welcoming committee," Ray muttered.

They counted Ray's money carefully and grunted some half-intelligible directions to our room. We were on our own as we went to climb the rickety-looking stairs. Then it hit us how musty and dusty the lobby was.

The room was worse. Walls in shades of pea-soup yellow. Grim. With oppressive air that smelled of strange, stale cooking. "Oh my God, I'm afraid we're in for it now," I said nervously. Why, oh why hadn't we checked in to the Vance? I could see Ray was thinking the same thing, so I quickly tried to be more positive. "I knew this one would be cheaper." Which was true. But what a fleabag.

Anyway, we weren't going to hang around the room. Ray had a plan. "Let's get out of here. Let's go eat at Ivar's Acres of Clams down at the wharf. I've heard about that place all my life but never been there. Let's go look at all the big ships in the harbor."

"Let's!"

Ray laughed and gave me a kiss. "Jesus," he said, "this is going to be some adventure."

The next day we spent walking the entire Seattle wharf and eating seafood until we thought we'd never order it again—until we did the next meal. That night Ray and I made love in our hideous hotel room. We laughed that we'd changed its yellow aura to rose. Then we turned to each other for a kiss.

"Good night, darling."

"Good night, Ray."

In a sudden afterthought I said softly, "Let's always kiss each other good night just like this. Let's never forget to, because if we always kiss each other good night, I know we'll always love each other, and we'll always have sweet dreams."

Ray leaned over and kissed me again.

In the morning we reinspected the grimy bathtub and decided it was still unthinkable to use it. So we sponge-bathed with towels, dressed, and dashed out to have a big breakfast at a workingman's café on the same block as the hotel. Ray loved the look of the place. We weren't disappointed when the food came, either. We got big pancakes—three as wide as the plate—with ham and eggs on the side.

When the waitress learned that we were in Seattle on our honeymoon, she brought us little bowls of applesauce to go with our monster breakfasts. We joked with other diners as if we lived in the neighborhood and had known them for a long time, and drank cup after cup of coffee. Dipping a forkful of pancake into a puddle of maple syrup, I said, "See, Ray, this is why we saved our money, so we could eat like this."

"Yum yum." And then he added as an afterthought, "Yep, this certainly beats working."

I thought of the wealthy girls at school who had proved to me that holiness and poverty need not go hand in hand, as I somehow had gotten the notion. "Noblesse oblige" was the attitude taught at Saint Paul's. Everyone there had great expectations for the future, for herself, and I had been right in the heart of it less than a week ago.

Ray was watching the longshoremen at another table. He felt invigorated to be in the same place with them. "They work and live, live and work. They aren't writers, but I like these people. My people are working people. My dad. My uncle Fred."

"But not Aunt Billie," I teased. "She's an aristocrat."

Ordinarily I think Ray would have laughed, ready to agree about his snobbish aunt by marriage. But he had a serious idea that he was working out, and he brushed off my remark. "I like these people. I can tell their stories, I think. Maybe I'll be able to tell their stories as well as anyone."

Over the past two years I had become more accustomed to the way Ray's inner life surfaced unexpectedly. I had seen a local production of Arthur Miller's *Death of a Salesman* when I was at Saint Paul's, and the pitiable, ordinary Loman family came back to mind. I had felt a strong identification. As I explained to Ray now, "I kept thinking about poor Willy, who didn't just want to be liked. He wanted to be well liked."

"I know," Ray said. "I know that feeling myself."

WE TOURED THE University of Washington campus. Then we spent time in the university district looking at books and listening to records. Fats Domino and Ricky Nelson were both singing "I'm Walkin'" over store speakers. Ray and I were walking all over Seattle, holding hands, mesmerized by the sights and sounds.

Sometimes we just sat together in the park, in the sunshine, and read our books. Every day we watched the Bremerton ferries sail, looking farther out to where the pale blue sky and pale blue waters merged on a horizon of deep blue. Behind us, the distant, snowcapped peaks were covered by an umbrella of white, floating clouds.

The third day in Seattle, we returned to our room in the Ray Hotel after walking and walking, and the first thing I did was take off my sexy white high-heeled sandals. Shyly I unzipped my brown sheath dress, doing with a few days' experience what Ray called "the bride's striptease."

"Don't get undressed for a minute."

I looked over at Ray. He sat on a hardbacked chair, obviously tired. "Why not?"

"I don't feel like making love just yet," he said.

"Oh." I looked at him more closely, noticing how tense he was. "What's the matter, Ray?"

"It's nothing."

"Oh please, honey. You can tell me. If you can't tell me, who can you tell? Besides being your wife, I'm your closest friend. That part hasn't changed. I care about you the way I care about all my friends, deeply, as well as being in love, crazy in love, with you. Friend to friend," I urged more insistently. "Tell me what's wrong!"

"Oh, Maryann, I don't want to be here. I don't want to be doing this. If I didn't love you so much, I'd walk out of this cheap, grimy hotel this minute and start driving. But I can't. I do love you. I love you so much. And none of this is your fault. It's nobody's fault."

"Oh," I said.

"I fear that years from now, maybe, if push really came to shove, and I had to choose between you and my writing . . . Maryann, I'd take my writing."

"Oh, for God's sake, Ray. Things will never . . . they're two different things, me and your writing! It's comparing apples and oranges. Both things you love, but they are never meant to be in competition with each other."

"That's the point. I just hope I never have to choose."

"You won't," I said. "I'll see to it. I'll try so hard. I'll work so hard. I'll make sure that you can have both and . . ." I shut up. I realized I was beginning to ramble. My stomach was knotted and beginning to ache. The baby? I was seized by a wave of sadness. He doesn't really want the baby. My brain was ablaze. Yes, he does. He loves me. I know that for sure. He is just being hit by the enormity of the situation. I sat down on the bed.

But was it my job to preserve Ray's opportunity to be a writer? With nothing left for my own ambitions? I felt truly for the first time how burdened my personal situation was. I won't tell you this, Ray, but I wouldn't mind getting in the car myself, right now, and just start driving. To be sixteen years old. The way I was just a few months ago, with a wide-open future.

I would have to be the one to make it work. I'd have to wait my turn. In the meantime my biggest challenge was to keep others afloat—Ray, the love of my life, and the yet-unborn little baby who had all the potential in the world. I didn't just want Ray, I needed him. I needed him desperately. I couldn't imagine having a baby without his help. With a steely flash of determination, I thought, I *want* this baby. I already love it to pieces. No baby of mine is going to come into this world unwanted. And I wouldn't let it come from a broken home, as I had.

I would walk the tightrope between Ray's writing life and our fami I'd walk it better than anyone ever had. And if that turned out to be only achievement . . . This is what it means to be a woman, I sudd realized; this is really what it means to be a woman, and like it o that's what I am now. I felt jolted with disappointment and dete tion, the oddest mix, but that's what it was.

"I'll make it work out, Ray. I will."

He leaned over from his chair and kissed me hard on the l love you, so very much." He sounded as if he was on the verg

"You are a remarkable girl, Maryann. Come into bed with me. One thing is for sure. I will never as long as I live have enough of you."

Later that night in the dark I stood at a window in our depressing water-stained room and gazed at the tall brick building up the block, with its sign, VANCE. The Vance Hotel. It looked respectable and bright. It looked upstanding. The red neon letters held my eye, and I wondered if any better omen was being signaled.

A WEEK LATER we were back in Yakima. We brought gifts from Seattle, cartons of chowder from Ivar's Acres of Clams for everyone. Luckily we had a place of our own—or would have shortly. Dr. Coglan had offered us the basement apartment beneath his office.

He was Ray's family doctor and had known the Carvers for years. At seventy he was still practicing, with no sign of stopping. He'd delivered James, taken care of both boys' cases of measles, doctored Ella's early menopause, sewed up C. R.'s cut arm, and generally acted as the family's unofficial psychologist.

He was greatly revered in town. Notably Dr. Coglan hadn't gone to medical school until he was thirty-eight and had served as a colonel in World War II. Besides his loyal wife of long standing, there was the "other woman" in the good doctor's life: faithful, virginal, white-haired Miss Olson, his nurse. She always dressed in a starched white uniform, stockings, and hat. Together they ran his thriving practice in Yakima.

Ray and I would have free rent and utilities in exchange for cleaning the office nightly. Dr. Coglan said that the job would take half an hour, although periodic more thorough cleanings were necessary. Ray's dad, who had spoken to the doctor, took the offer for us on the spot, with heartfelt gratitude, knowing full well how precarious our finances were. For six days' work at the drugstore, Ray took home forty-six dollars. Fine for a single fellow, living free with his aunt and uncle. However, supporting himself and a wife was another matter.

The apartment would not be ready for three more weeks. It wasn't a problem, as we could move in with Jerry and Les. (More honeymoon, cha-cha-cha.) Their basement became our temporary home. Like a pair of newly acquired older children, we regularly emerged for the wonderful gourmet meals Jerry served.

WE RESPECTED AND loved Les and Jerry. I had babysat for them when I was younger, when they dressed up and went out dancing.

Jerry had her own money from her night job at the best supper club in town. She enormously enjoyed drinking and having a great time, laughing and talking. She was such a beauty: elegant, blond hair; big, exotic, brown eyes; gorgeous figure set off by those exquisite clothes. For his part, Les was an ace mechanic who had risen to ably overseeing three shops at the firing center located by the military base outside Yakima.

They kept their own scenes out of sight. Apparently Les would reach a boiling point over Jerry's vivacious, extroverted ways. He occasionally blew up and hit her. None of us realized it. They had married during World War II, just as Mom and Dad were giving up and separating. After seventeen years I thought they had to wind up with the most enduring marriage. But it wasn't to be.

We had a grand time, a three-week summer party. Dressed in shorts, we ate watermelon, drank beer, rode horses, and went off on family fishing jaunts. Ray and I would squeeze into the backseat of the car with Les and Jerry's boys, his arm around my shoulders, holding my hand with his other hand. In the evenings we started going over to Dr. Coglan's basement apartment to paint and move in furniture. Finally it was ready.

We moved in.

The first afternoon, shortly before Ray was due home, I left the Rome in my head of busy streets and ambiguous morals—I was reading Alberto Moravia—and wondered what to do about dinner. Ray and I had been discussing everything under the sun since we'd met. But one thing had not been discussed. It never came up—I really didn't know how to cook!

When I was home I'd been surrounded by good cooks like Jerry and my mom. My husband would be home soon, and he was always starved after the long workday. I hurried out to the store; I had two dollars and twenty-seven cents in my purse. So I bought a can of Spam, a small can of shortening, four little potatoes, and a can of peas.

Back at the apartment I used several new pans we'd been given as wedding gifts and fried the potatoes, fried the Spam, and heated up the peas. The bizarre, old-fashioned gas stove, I discovered, either gave no flame at all or just blazed, burning everything. I heard Ray come in.

Time to eat. I turned off the stove, relieved to have that ordeal over with—I was wringing wet with perspiration. Ray came to the table. He was delighted to find his supper ready, as it should be.

When I dished up our plates, I could see that the food was under-cooked. Everything was cold and swimming in grease. Ray and I took a couple of bites. My face was downcast, my eyes focused on my plate. I felt tears coming to my eyes.

"This is terrible," I finally muttered.

"Oh, everything's really good, honey."

"No it isn't," I said shakily. "You know, we've talked about everything in the world, but not about whether I could cook."

"That's all right, sweetheart," Ray said. "There are other things you can do."

He came over and began kissing my neck, my wet eyelids, and then my mouth. After a "joust" in the bedroom, we laughed at my first dinner in our new apartment, threw our clothes back on, and went out for hamburgers.

The next day I walked downtown and bought a *Better Homes and Gardens Cookbook*. I studied it with the same concentration I used to apply to physics and Latin. I also asked Aunt Amy to type me up some of our family recipes, basic ones for couples on a tight budget—meat loaf, goulash, ribs, and the like. I deliberately evoked images of my mother cooking a chicken or roast, amazed at how much I had observed without realizing it. Soon I was turning out tasty casseroles, pork chop dinners, and homemade chocolate and lemon pies.

(Years later Ray still raved about my cooking, a sweet, kind habit I always appreciated, doubtless originally inspired by that first fried Spam dinner.)

. . .

CLEANING DR. COGLAN'S office made us groan profusely. Our deal for free rent and utilities was biting us back. Sometimes we got it done early in the evening, but other nights we'd let it go until one or two in the morning. We just dreaded it. Sometimes Ray cleaned by himself or I did—to give one of us a break. But usually we wanted to be together, even when cleaning toilets.

We joked about the bloody bandages emptied from the office wastebaskets.

We used the examining tables, including the stirrups, to play doctor and patient.

I helped myself to Miss Olson's stationery and used the typewriter. Several times I became distracted and left my typing in the machine. I'd usually remember it after Miss Olson was already in the office. Initially I was horrified and stricken with guilt. But Ray would find my oversight hilarious, so I soon did too.

We never intentionally tried to offend the doctor or Miss Olson. But our friends could hardly wait to hear the latest episode of *The Carvers versus the Doctor and Miss Olson.* That inspired us to perpetuate our serial, I'm afraid.

There was the time we borrowed all the ice trays from the office refrigerators for a weekend party. (Ice packs were used to treat the doctor's patients.) On Monday morning, Miss Olson came downstairs to see if we had the missing trays.

As Ray would tell the story: Coming down the stairs, the first thing Miss Olson discovered was Amy in the hallway. Sleeping nude to the waist on a cot. She had stayed over after the party.

The next thing Miss Olson found were the trays. They were out in the kitchen. Ah ha!

On the stove burners.

My mother couldn't find any pots so she was cooking vegetables by making do. They were steaming away in the metal trays!

Then there was the time Ray was sitting at Dr. Coglan's big oak desk, his feet up, sucking a Rolo candy from a pack the doctor had left on the desk. Ray was talking to me over the intercom when the doctor walked into his office. Just as I asked, "Have you cleaned up the doctor's slimy, bloody, stinky gore yet? Roger, over and out." "Over and out, all right," the good doctor muttered as Ray . . . Of course Ray smoothed things over, explaining our plan to rent a big buffer (at our own expense) to polish the floors—one of these weekends.

Some years later I said, "Ray, you ought to write a whole book of stories and call it *The Landlord Stories.*" We had certainly collected more "specimens" of the breed. Ray never wrote that book as he wanted; however, "Put Yourself in My Shoes" and "Chef's House" evolved from the fear, contempt, and occasional appreciation we felt for numerous landlords, beginning with old Dr. Coglan.

Besides evading polishing the floors, we went to a lot of movies, perhaps sensing that we ought to while it was uncomplicated to grab our hats and go. We'd do whatever we felt like on the spur of the moment. We took short drives out to the river where Ray could enjoy the outdoors and signs of wildlife. We visited friends and relatives, and then everybody came to visit us.

Ray's friend Del Mayer brought his elegant fiancée, Vicky, over to our apartment. She was from Seattle. We talked about the previous few months. I told them, "Ray arranged the wedding. He was behind me all the way."

"Behind you?" Ray said, laughing. "I wasn't behind you, Maryann. I was riding my white horse ahead of you, lance held out." Ray looked directly at me. "You are my sweet lady. I am your knight in shining armor."

Vicky's eyes filled with tears. She reached into her expensive handbag for a Kleenex.

"That's what you get when you marry a poet," I said happily.

ON AUGUST 7 I turned seventeen. We celebrated passionately after a get-together, gifts, and cake with my family. It was another milestone. I wasn't sweet sixteen anymore. I was about four months pregnant. Life was perfect, I felt.

. . .

IN THE FALL our lives took a more serious turn. Ray had two weeks of vacation in September, so we went down to Chester in the old Chevy. On the trip I was reading *Grapes of Wrath* for the first time. My thoughts were full of Rose of Sharon and her pregnancy.

Ella and James were back living with Ray's dad. The three of them seesawed between Yakima and Northern California. They could stay in Fred and Billie's cottage up our way, or go back where C. R. might find work in a mill.

The little cottage was behind Fred and Billie's big house, which they'd been renting out since moving from Yakima. They let their family stay in the cottage rent-free because C. R. was ill. In time it became clear to me that never had Ray's family paid more dearly for a roof over their heads. They were no longer independent and self-sufficient, as they always had been. Now they were beholden to Fred and Billie, and there wasn't a waking moment when they weren't keenly aware of it. They talked about it often.

I saw them virtually tiptoe from one room to the next, the little hovel's uneven flooring a symbol of the imbalance into which their lives had been thrown. It was particularly tough on James, but his parents needed him with them. He was also very good looking and bright. But his dad's illness limited his educational opportunities until he was older and could pay his own way.

Over the next several years the Carvers made the trek repeatedly. They were a pitiful joke to some in the extended family who couldn't understand why they didn't stay put. Ray was troubled by the way they were living and their reduced circumstances.

Driving the road to Chester that time—still three hours away—Ray was simply exhausted. He couldn't go another mile. I had never gotten my driver's license, nor had there been much chance for practicing since the days of summer visits to my dad's farm. But I took the wheel. And I drove.

Ray slept, his head on my lap. When we reached the mountains outside Susanville, I wasn't sure I could navigate the tremendous heights and curves the road took. I shook Ray to see if he could drive again, but he was dead to the world and kept right on sleeping. With an increasing sense of exhilaration, I managed to drive on and brought us to Chester, my little family safe and sound. From then on I felt I could drive any-thing, anywhere—and from then on I often did. (Of course I promptly went and got my driver's license.)

AFTER THE VACATION trip to Chester, we definitely entered a new phase. Ray and I began to speak often of the baby. On the way back I had felt life move inside me. I broke into excited tears.

While I began to stay home more and read my books, Ray liked to go out fishing or hunting. He would come home flushed and happy from his day in the wilds, and if luck was with him, there would be fleecy geese he'd shot. He would take them over to my mother to pluck and prepare. But soon he'd be back at our apartment.

Almost ceremoniously Ray would strip off his boots and long under-wear, shower, and then sit down to an enormous plate of food and lots of coffee. Afterward, sometimes, he would spend several hours writing po-ems. Sunday night was his best writing time, especially after a day in the goose bluffs overlooking the mighty Columbia River.

That was the fall Ray began college. He took two classes at Yakima Valley Junior College. One was a history course taught by an exchange professor from Germany. She subtly made World War II and Ger-many's horrific role in that conflagration come alive for Ray. Through-out his life he read books about the war and its major participants. The professor, when pressed, recalled how people in her home village could smell burning flesh from the nearby concentration camp but still refused to speak of it. When they met neighbors in backyards or out shopping, they didn't look one another in the eye.

As for me—well, my mother enrolled me at the local "business col-lege" and paid my tuition. I had no interest in studying filing, typing, and business machines, but my mother thought otherwise. Rather than sit around my apartment, she declared, I would be "on a roll" somewhere, interacting with other students, and gaining marketable skills.

I really wanted to be at college. Like Ray. I wanted to study literature and philosophy. His response when I found the resolve to bring it up: "What do you plan to do, Maryann, take the baby to school in a suitcase?" Jerry had offered to take care of the baby if I went. But that one remark inhibited me totally. I didn't want Ray to think I wasn't going to be a conscientious mother.

I tried to content myself mixing with the divorced women and young girls who made up the business college's student body. They had no interest in going to a regular university. They wanted to learn to type and to get a job. Compared to my brilliant classmates at Saint Paul's who were now at schools like Berkeley, Stanford, Wellesley, and Vassar, I felt out of place in this crowd.

When I got bigger, obviously pregnant, I was able to convince my mother that I'd be a lot more comfortable waiting for the baby at home. Better to be at my apartment reading and baking cookies or a pie for Ray. I'd had enough of business college.

RAY WENT HUNTING on Sunday, December 1. I felt strange; not well. Apathetically I lay on the couch in our apartment for most of the day. The baby wasn't due for another six weeks. When Ray returned I was delighted to see him, glad to watch him remove his damp clothes, woolen underwear, and socks. I could hardly wait to go to bed as he ate his dinner and read for a while. I felt like being held, my pregnant body against his long, lean one. In that position I always fell instantly asleep.

I awoke an hour later. The bed was wet, the queasy feeling I had all day had intensified. I shook Ray, who was exhausted and sound asleep. "Ray, something's happening. The bed is soaked. I didn't wet the bed. Did you?"

"No. I haven't wet the bed in years. My shorts are dry."

"Uh-oh, my nightgown is wet. I guess I'm going to have the baby. But it's so early . . . I don't know."

Ray's eyes popped open, and he sat straight up in bed. "My God. Are
you sure?"

"I don't know for sure! Maybe you better call Dr. Waters. Maybe you
better call Jerry."

"Are you having pains, contractions?" Ray asked. "You're supposed
to have contractions when you have a baby."

"I know. I'm not having pains, though. But I haven't felt well all day.
I've felt very queasy and odd."

Ray got up and brought me a dry nightgown. I waited in bed, listening to him first phone Jerry and then Dr. Waters. When he came back I
knew from the look on his face that I was to get up and get dressed.
Time to go.

There was snow on the ground. The caked, crystalline surfaces glis-
tened in the distance, and if you stepped on a fresh section, it cracked in
pieces. We warmed up our old car sitting out front of Dr. Coglan's office. With hot water and a scraper, Ray worked to clear the windshield. I
sat in the car. It was two o'clock in the morning.

A patrol car pulled in. Out popped a policeman. He was authoritative
and accusing, with a loud, mean voice: "What do you kids think you're
doing out after curfew? You know better!" He walked to the side of the
car, looked inside at me. He assumed we were underage.

Dramatically I opened my coat and watched the expression on his
face change as he got a good look. "I'm taking her to the hospital," Ray
quickly added. "She's in labor. She's going to have our baby."

"Oh, pardon me," the cop stammered. "Would you like an escort?"

"No, thanks," Ray said firmly. "There's not that great a rush."

We roared off toward Memorial Hospital, giggling, happy to be one
up on the police. I huddled up close to Ray.

At the hospital I was put in an area with a woman who was having her
fourth child. She was hollering and yelling as loudly as she could. "Not
a very auspicious beginning," Ray said skeptically.

"Don't worry. You won't catch me doing that." I reminded Ray of all
the books I had taken out of the library on natural childbirth. Dr. Wa-

ters said I was too young for that sort of approach. But I read everything anyway.

Just then the woman let out a bloodcurdling scream. We both shivered.

"You should go home and get some sleep, Ray. Dr. Waters will be along when he feels he should be. I guess the nurses will call him."

He barely had a chance to say, "No, I'll be right here," before they kicked him out to the waiting room and left me with the veteran childbearer.

DR. WATERS ARRIVED early the next afternoon. I was lying on a hospital gurney parked by a brick wall. He sat down on a chair next to me and took my hand. This is strange, I thought. He's never held my hand before or touched me, except in the most impersonal professional manner. Strange—he has looked and felt inside me, I was thinking, as he began speaking softly and earnestly. "Maryann, try not to be too disappointed if the baby doesn't make it. It's too early, and you're small. The baby is too small. We'll do the best we can, but I want to warn—"

I turned away to the brick wall, unable even to cry.

When Mom and Jerry came in to see me, I couldn't say a word. I didn't tell them what Dr. Waters had said. I looked at the wall and pretended to be caught up in my contractions. Jerry was sympathetic. She said, from the heart, "Oh, baby sister, I wish I were lying on that gurney instead of you." Like others in my father's family, the Burks, her feelings ran deep. My mom, on the other hand, subscribed to the stiff-upper-lip school and pretended in an upbeat manner that all was well. That was her "positive" style of dealing with heavy situations, as her father had done.

At the hospital gift shop, Jerry had bought a beautiful, yellow hand-crocheted sweater set for the baby. The bonnet and sweater were trimmed in white, appropriate for either a boy or girl. When I took the gift in my hands, I *knew* the baby would make it. Why else would I be given this by my sister for a baby who was going to die?

After they left I was alone when suddenly my back was seized by the

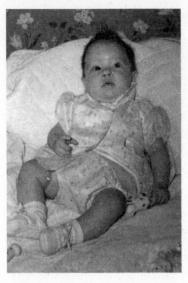

Our baby girl, Christine LaRae Carver,
at four months. April 1958.
FROM THE COLLECTION OF
MARYANN BURK CARVER

most powerful surge of strength I
had ever experienced. It had nothing to do with my volition. My back
rose completely off the gurney, as
though I were going to levitate to
the ceiling. At the same time something was breaking loose inside.

This is how it feels to have a baby!
The universe takes over. Nothing I
had read even began to capture the
sensation. It's like trying to describe the taste of cherry pie to someone
who's never tasted a cherry.

My contractions were starting. And what was I thinking? Weren't Indian women known to gallop their horses to a meadow beside great
boulders to give birth? Behind mammoth rocks an Indian woman would
squat for a minute or two, then come back bearing a healthy son, a brave
for the tribe. She'd wrap the child in a colorful woven blanket, mount
her horse, and ride off with the baby. The experience of childbirth was
no more than a short part of an Indian woman's summer afternoon.

Here in Yakima, in December, the nurses phoned Dr. Waters, and he
trudged back through the snow to the hospital in the late afternoon. I
looked ready. I was taken into the delivery room. Dr. Waters arrived,
took charge, while the nurses acted as if they'd somehow held me back
until he got there. He ordered a saddle block immediately. It would ef-
fectively paralyze me, taking me out of pain. I reminded him that I
didn't want anything, but he said softly, "No, Maryann. You are too
young. I don't want to put you through that. See up there, that round
mirror? Just watch and see. Just watch."

So I did. I watched the little, round, dark, wet head emerge. I saw
Ray's hair, dark, curly. Finally the head was out, then the rest of the

baby's body slipped out in a quick series of bumps and snags. "Oh, it's big enough," I heard Dr. Waters say gently. Then, "It's a girl!"

I HAD BEEN almost certain that the baby would be a boy. But here she was. I hadn't even admitted to myself that I passionately wanted a girl. "Thank you, God!" I cried. I watched in the round thick mirror as Dr. Waters placed the baby across my chest. I wasn't crying anymore. I was laughing. This is the happiest day of my life, I thought. Without question, this is the happiest day of my life.

Ray and Jerry were waiting when I was wheeled back to my ward room. We talked a little. Everyone was excited and happy. Jerry teased me about how unfair it was that I had a girl first time out. She had wanted a girl and gotten boys both times. She loved them, of course, but no bones about it, she'd wanted a girl.

Right then a nurse brought the baby in. I could see Dr. Waters out in the hall, smiling, basking in the spiritual reward of his profession. I took the baby in my arms. Ray moved in closer to see her. I heard him make a soft little crooning noise. I looked up and was amazed and enormously touched. Ray was crying.

"Say, are we a happy group?!" Jerry exclaimed. "Look, this is earlier than we'd planned, so we haven't said much. But we expect you to bring the baby home to our place and all of you to stay there while we get this little doll off to a good start."

I agreed with Jerry.

Then I turned to Ray. "She looks to me like a Christy. You know how you love to listen to June Christy? I'd like to name the baby Christine, so we can call her Christi." (I'd spell it with an *i* to make it stand out.)

"Sounds good to me." Ray smiled.

And so it would be: Christine LaRae Carver, born December 2, less than a week after Thanksgiving. (As I learned some years later, Christine means "female follower of Christ." I had unknowingly honored my belief that he would send her safely into the world.)

After Ray visited us in the maternity ward on the third floor, he went up to the fifth—the psychiatric ward—to visit his dad.

C. R. had made it back to Yakima from California, amazingly thin from the lead poisoning in his finger. He felt bad, unable to work anymore. His doctor suggested an observation stay in Memorial Hospital. At the hospital his doctor and a psychiatrist soon recommended shock treatments for acute depression.

That day Ray found his dad sitting out in the hallway in a flannel bathrobe, dejectedly smoking one of his innumerable Camels. Ray told him, "Dad, you became a grandfather today. We had a little girl."

"Oh, hello, son." His dad looked up, worn and downhearted. "I feel like a grandfather today."

AUNT VON AND Uncle Bill came to the hospital and were loving and enthusiastic about the baby. Bob and Loretta Archer stopped by, too. Jerry came several times a day. My mother came, with an exquisite little green bunting for the baby.

Conspicuously absent was Ella, Ray's mother. The last time I had seen her was at the Carver Thanksgiving table. Admittedly she was under a lot of stress, but she had cried in front of everybody and said she was too young to be a grandmother. It hurt me that she hadn't rushed over to see her granddaughter. I realized she was dealing with C. R.'s hospitalization, but by the last day of my stay in the maternity ward, I was more emotional about her snub. For goodness' sake, I was only two floors down!

I was so excited I didn't sleep the entire night after Christi was born. I hardly slept for the three days I was in the hospital. I was just too high. Now I knew what old ladies meant when they spoke about being "blessed with grace." When Ray came to get us and I carried the baby out to the car, there we were—a family of three. As we drove off, I looked around, at the snow on the ground, the tall buildings of Yakima, the light of day, a few Christmas decorations in the windows. I realized that in a few years it would seem as if Christi had always been with us.

I decided to remember it all. I knew that Ray and I, teenage parents of this little girl, would never forget this moment as long as we lived.

Christi was our love child, a crazy-in-love child, and what child could be more welcome than that?

I was happy to go to Jerry's. She put us in their own big bedroom. Jerry gave the baby baths while I watched. She supervised the baby's nursing and laundry. She cooked beautiful dinners so I would eat properly. Les helped do the laundry, dishes, and extra housework our presence inevitably created, without complaint. My nephews, too, liked Christi, and an atmosphere of love and excitement surrounded us all.

Our first week passed in a blissful blur. But then I noticed that Ray was spending more time down at the apartment. He still had to clean the office, and I assumed he was also getting in some reading and writing. He was always back to sleep with me, always at Jerry's table for dinner. Things were settling down to normal.

NOT EXACTLY. One night in bed Ray asked me what I'd think if he went off to Spain for two or three years. After which he'd come back to me and the baby. Or, if he found a good little village—warm from perennial sunshine, where the prices were cheap, the fish plentiful, the music romantic and welcoming—then Christi and I would come over to join him.

"I don't think you should be thinking about Spain right now, Ray." A little sarcastically I added, "Ernie's already done it. He chased the bulls down the street in Pamplona. I think you should wait and go another time."

Christi was nursing while we talked. I was sitting up in bed, wearing Jerry's white satin nightgown that matched the satin sheets. One moment you feel like Lauren Bacall wrapped in satin and golden light, and the next your husband is announcing he's heading off to Spain.

"I'm so sorry, Ray," I finally said. "Sure you want to travel. I want to travel, too. Spain does sound bright and colorful." Then I put my finger on what I thought was bothering him. "Are you getting tired of being here? At Jerry and Les's? Would it help if we all went home now?"

"I just wondered what you'd think about the idea. I've been thinking about Spain a lot lately."

"Ray, it's the dead of winter. It's almost Christmas. She's only two weeks old. Last week she had yellow jaundice, and Jerry and I had to take her to the doctor. I want to be a good wife. I want to be supportive. But please don't go away now." I began to cry. The baby got the hiccups.

"Just skip it," Ray said. There was silence except for Christi's little soft toylike explosions of air. "I think we should go back to the apartment tomorrow. We need to get our lives back. I don't want to sleep in Les Bonsen's bed anymore."

"You've got it. Christi and I will be packed tomorrow."

Back at the basement apartment Ray was happy again. We were in our own bed. He could read and write after work when he wanted to. We cleaned the office together as we used to, or I did it when the baby was asleep. I was in love with her, and I was in love with seeing Ray on the bed with that little pajamaed infant lying beside him, her head on his arm. She looked like Ray, with her dark hair, round face, and blue eyes—but those fair eyes, I thought, were almond-shaped like mine.

That night I told Ray how much his mother's attitude was paining me. It was upsetting my care of Christi. Looking disgusted, as in his younger days when Ella hadn't done something she'd agreed to, Ray promised to speak to his mother.

ONE AFTERNOON RAY'S dad walked into the apartment unannounced. He was newly out of the hospital. I was nursing the baby when he came in.

"You look just like Mary with the baby Jesus," C. R. said simply.

He was so openly sincere that my initial embarrassment evaporated. I smiled and welcomed him to come see his new granddaughter.

"Some people . . ." He was unable to say more, but it was obvious he was referring to Ella and her attitude.

"I know."

"Always there have been some hard things . . . ," and he didn't continue.

The next day Ray's parents came together. They brought Christi a beautiful, frilly pink dress. It was instantly the prettiest item in her wardrobe. I felt much better—the breach between us would mend. I realized I cared for Ella as much as ever. But I also knew now that I'd never unthinkingly trust her again.

CHRISTI'S FIRST CHRISTMAS came and went. Amy was home from Saint Paul's and met her new niece. The year was over before we knew it. The winter languished, the baby grew, and our sense of being a family gathered solidity and strength.

In March I went back to Dr. Waters for my three-month checkup. I dressed Christi up in her frilliest pink organdy dress. Waiting in the examination room in a paper gown, I nursed Christi.

Dr. Waters came in. He began a pelvic exam, noting with pride to his assistant that I didn't even look as if I'd had a baby. But as he probed further and more seriously, he couldn't believe what he found. But facts were facts. So he told me: My uterus was soft again; I appeared to be with child.

I couldn't believe it. I didn't *want* to believe it! I thought it was impossible for a nursing mother to get pregnant. Yes, Ray and I had been "relaxing" again. I thought of those late winter Sundays, baby dozing in the crib nearby. But weren't we following my natural rhythm for some protection? Now this.

Dr. Waters looked concerned. "You'll have to stop breast-feeding immediately, Maryann. Your body can't support more than the new baby you're carrying and yourself." Great. Christi had to be weaned.

When I had my clothes back on, I gathered up Christi and wandered out of the doctor's office into the bright sunlight. Practically stumbling over my own feet, I hailed the first Yellow Cab I saw and went to the drugstore where Ray was working. He was glad to see me, all smiles. He took Christi and showed her off to his boss and fellow workers.

Then he got a good look at my face. "What's the matter, honey?"

"Can you take us home? I'm not feeling well."

"Sure, Maryann. Al will let me. The car's right outside."

On the way home I told Ray the news. I could hardly speak coherently in my agitation and shock. "I'm just overwhelmed," I said. "God, I don't even know what to feed Christi. I'm supposed to stop nursing, and she just loves it." I felt so sorry for her, to be pushed aside, so little and so young.

"Let's not talk about it now. Or fantasize about two kids playing with little toys and so on," Ray said rather sharply. "Let's just go on as we are. Then we'll be able to cope." He dropped us off at the apartment. "You're an angel, Maryann. Get some rest now. We'll talk about all this later. I've got to get back to work."

That evening after dinner Ray and I sat on the couch in the living room. We had already cleaned the doctor's office, and Christi was asleep.

"You know, Maryann, I was thinking. There are several foreign countries where a person can go—Japan, Sweden—where operations are legal to terminate pregnancies. Of course it would take some organizing and financing to—"

"Never mind, Ray, I wouldn't think of it. Even if I could go upstairs tomorrow and have Dr. Coglan do it!"

"Do you think it's entirely up to you, Maryann?"

"This baby is another potential Christi—or someone equally interesting. I couldn't destroy a baby, if for no other reason than it was created by you and me."

Ray didn't say anything. He looked dark and forbidding.

I had already begun to love the little one growing inside me. Eventually Ray would love this person too. It was all destined to happen, I was convinced of that. I didn't know why it was happening to us just now, but I did know I would always protect this baby's life. That was not negotiable.

IN JUNE I got a job in a warehouse packing cherries. I wanted to make enough money to buy Ray a typewriter for Father's Day. Jerry pitched in with baby-sitting for Christi.

It was strange, tedious work to stack rows of little cherries just so—row after row to create a perfect layer, then start all over again. There was no

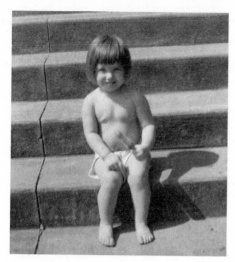

Our daughter, Christi. "As cute as a little girl gets," we said. 1958.

PHOTO BY MARYANN BURK CARVER

loitering on this job. Everyone was timed. If you didn't make the quota you were out, and another willing cherry packer got the work.

The Underwood typewriter I wanted was on layaway. Finally I had enough cash to purchase it. On Father's Day, Christi and I presented Daddy with his first typewriter. She looked beautiful, almost seven months old, in a little blue silk-and-lace dress.

Ray was happy—gloriously, thoughtfully happy. He couldn't stop smiling, and kept stroking his new machine over and over again. Like a good musician with a new rosewood guitar.

5

A TOWN CALLED PARADISE

Some three months after Ray got his typewriter he came out of his study on a fall day with his breath practically crystallizing. Our Paradise house was so cold. It had been our home for only a few months.

But he was jubilant. Ecstatic. He had a story. It was unlike the science fiction piece—a "little green monster" tale—which he wrote first after the move. That one faded out at the end without a real resolution. The new story, called "The Aficionados," interested me enormously. Its premise harked back to civilizations ruled by high priestesses but was more subtle than a pulp adventure tale. Set in a vaguely prehistoric Mexican or South American city, this priestess cuts the heart out of a willing male victim.

In Ray's world fiction and fiction writing were taking on a heightened reality. Our bedtime stories, even as told around the dinner table, were more consciously shaped. We both saw everyday events in a new light, looking for the unusual, the interesting, the offbeat vibration in our reality. These metamorphosed into the anecdotes we told our friends and relatives. (In due course we became known for our ready repertoire of bizarre and amusing stories.)

Sometimes I think we lived on the edge almost intentionally, as if we saw these personal situations as necessary grist for the mill. One of them might contain the raw material for Ray to write into a story or poem. We didn't know when, or even whether, he would use any specific situation. So all of life had to be lived, we thought, like an ongoing saga, an unfolding history sweeping us into the kind of consciousness an artist needed for stimulation and vision. Our reality was often tough enough, but we could endure it. We sometimes embraced it. But, if there was the potential for a good story or poem to emerge from our experiences, then that was the reward for the choices we made.

WHAT TOOK US to Paradise, California? Fate. Destiny. My sister Amy. She had been restless her junior year of high school. The summer of '59, she wanted to move to the San Francisco Bay Area, specifically, to San Mateo. That was where Judy lived, her last Saint Paul's roommate. More important, she wanted to meet Judy's ex-boyfriend, Dick.

Dick's father was an executive of the American Can Company, and the family was well off. Dick himself worked part-time at American Can and drove a good car. He was attending San Mateo Junior College—to find himself and his future.

Dick was confident and arrogant, a real asshole who liked to give girls a bad time. Amy sensed an interesting challenge, I suppose. In any case he was the unwitting reason that she and our entire family eventually moved to California. After much cajoling, Mom took Amy on a reconnoitering trip to the Bay Area, and fate intervened.

On the long drive they were passing through Northern California, south of Red Bluff and north of Chico. They saw a for-sale sign on a house and decided to take a look. It was in Paradise, 840 Roe Road. Astonishingly my mom bought it. My mom figured the house would be a good fixer-upper for Clarence, her now-steady boyfriend, to work on over the years.

But how had she managed to buy a house? She had withdrawn her Washington State Teachers' Retirement Fund account, that's how. My mom meant to move to San Mateo, rent an apartment for herself and Amy, and find a teaching job. That surprising plan, now in full bloom, looked either like a retreat to—or an advance on—the golden state of California, depending on whom you asked. Maybe it was both. And

Mom had found the surefire way to get us to follow along, with the granddaughter she loved: She offered us the house rent-free. (No more cleaning Dr. Coglan's office.) Also, as she candidly pointed out to Ray, it was only ten miles from the state college in Chico.

True to form, my mother never did anything decisive she didn't later regret with loud lamentations. She displayed her typical great gusto over the move but later deplored losing her Washington pension. As I saw it, she really didn't need the scant retirement income later half as much as she needed a change of scenery, and luck.

OUR FIRST WEDDING anniversary was the only one in Yakima. What a year it had been. A graduation, a wedding, a honeymoon, a baby girl, and another baby to come. Incredible.

Ray and I celebrated privately and at a big party with lots of others of our crowd: Marian and Jewell Hill, Shelby and Helen Skillings, people we'd known forever. "Happily married for one whole year!" we kept repeating.

We danced. We kissed each other. We watched Christi asleep in her crib.

Before we left town, I turned eighteen. My dad came from Blaine to celebrate. Pregnant, I went all over town with him, shopping for birthday presents. We bought beautiful Oriental print cotton pajamas, baby-doll style, in blue and white, shot through with fine lines of gold. Next, a bathrobe and black velvet slippers, gold trimmed, that went with the pj's. I was ready to look like a princess from the *Arabian Nights* as I awaited the new baby.

My dad invited the whole family to my birthday party out at Sportsman Park on the outskirts of Yakima. Jerry was pregnant and about to give birth to a third boy. (Loren came nine years after Lanny, her second son.) Les claimed that Jerry had gone baby crazy all over again from baby-sitting Christi.

It was a wonderful birthday party. I basked in my dad's affection, the caring attention of Ray and all the family. Dad also bought a big square sheet cake. It was decorated with white frosting and blue letters: HAPPY

BIRTHDAY MARYANN. When we got back to our soon-to-be-vacated apartment, I sat out on the lawn with Christi. My dad tossed a hundred-dollar bill in my lap, overcome with emotion, then got in his trusty '47 Plymouth coupe and took off for his home on the Washington Coast.

In August's high summer, the traveling party (Ray and I, Christi, Mom, and Amy) got ready to cram ourselves into the Chevy for the move to California. Our plans were set.

Mom had an apartment and a teaching job lined up in San Mateo.

Amy could be boy crazy until she went back to high school in the fall.

Ray would enroll at Chico State College for the fall semester—who says a wife can't influence her husband?!

I'd be pregnant and—what else?—counting.

BEFORE OUR DEPARTURE date, I was stricken with a sudden illness. Ray and I and the baby had been over at his parents' cottage when I felt odd and realized I was burning up with fever. I started feeling numbness in my hands and arms, then it spread everywhere. In less than an hour, I went from numb to a kind of paralysis. I began quietly to panic. My God, I thought, what will this do to the unborn baby?

I asked Ray to call Dr. Waters. He had us go immediately to Saint Elizabeth's, the nearby Catholic hospital. Meeting us there, he put me in the care of Dr. Uber, an internist. (I knew who he was, as he belonged to the same mountain-climbing club as my mother.) Dr. Uber ordered spinal fluid taken, from which he hoped to diagnose my condition. In muffled tones I heard him say something to Ray about polio.

The next thing I knew I was in a room with very high ceilings. I had never even been in a Roman Catholic church, so the rosary read over the PA system, the crucifix on the wall, and the giant statue of the Virgin Mary out in the hallway were strange and unsettling. Alone, I found myself crying.

Besides the paralysis, I'd never been so nauseated. I couldn't even keep down the 7-UP or soda crackers the nurses gave me. I was lost in a sea of overwhelming sickness.

The next day Dr. Uber examined me again. I remember him asking

me about smoking. I told him truthfully that I smoked about ten cigarettes a day. Ray and Amy came to visit me before he was finished. They
had a pair of large, round red earrings for me. I held them in my hand,
smiling, unable to try them on.

Then, in another day, the illness receded as mysteriously as it had
come. The nausea came under control first, and then gradually I was
able to move. I still felt very weak and strange, as if I'd been living in a
cave—the light of day almost overwhelmed me at first.

Dr. Uber prescribed some shots and medication. I was to rest a week
at home before traveling, and I should lie down in the car all the way.
What I probably had was an infection that mimics the symptoms of polio. (No wonder Dr. Waters was so quick to send me to a specialist.)
There was no permanent damage. I knew I was truly blessed when I
walked out of the hospital three days after admission.

As I walked by the Virgin Mary statue, I stopped for a moment. I
stroked her robes. Over the long hours of my paralysis, she had become
my comfort, my refuge in that mausoleum of illness. She had been my
light and comfort, and I loved her.

Time to go. I found Amy in the "bed" made for me in the backseat of
the car. She was sick with a cold, so I sat up front with Ray, holding
Christi. After I came home from the hospital, she wouldn't let me out of
her sight. There was nothing to be done but to take care of my family,
doctor's orders for rest to the contrary.

We picked up my mom. Paradise, here we come.

On the road to California we spent more of my mother's retirement
money on motels, hamburgers, and milk shakes. That lump sum seemed
to burn a hole in her pocket, and she went so far as to splurge on a few
new dresses for herself to wear at her new teaching job. Ahead of us was
"the smorgasbord called California," as Ray later dubbed it in a poem.
We had all left behind the stable roots of our hometown for the promise
of something better.

HOW PARADISE GOT its name was pretty self-evident from the first
time we drove there. Down in the valley was Chico, and up nestled in

the clouds was, naturally, Paradise, at the end of ten miles of road straight up.

The little village was awash in flowers and fruit trees. The shops were well established, as were most of the people. Many were retirees on fixed incomes—a good thing, as we discovered early on, since there were no jobs in Paradise. Ray and I would have to commute to Chico if we wanted work. The house Mom bought had not been vacated yet, so we booked into a motel and had more take-out food, our caravan party shortly to end when Mom and Amy continued on to San Mateo.

The new house was at the end of Roe Road, a dusty little country lane. There were big trees for shade and enough space to separate us from the street's other little nondescript houses. The carpentry was crudely finished—a fixer-upper indeed.

Ray and I weren't inclined to do the fixing ourselves. Clarence, Mom's boyfriend, was to stay with us when he came down from Washington, and after he fixed things up, he would eventually share it with my mother. Even if he had had the time, however, Ray was not drawn to carpentry, or to tackling the endless maintenance on this pig-in-a-poke house my mother had bought on a whim. I was willing to keep the house tidy, mopping the floors daily. Christi, who wasn't walking yet, needed to be able to get down and crawl freely. To me that devotion to cleaning was commitment enough.

In Chico, Ray found work at a drugstore. He took as many hours as they'd give him, sandwiched around his full-time school schedule. Since we had only one car, and Ray had to drive to work, that meant I was isolated with Christi from very early in the morning until late at night. I was in a strange place without a car and knowing no one. As a result Christi and I became even closer. I talked to her all day, read her stories, and took her out for long walks. During those long, lonely days of waiting, waiting for my new baby, waiting for Christi to talk, waiting for Ray, I often felt incredulous that I made it through the long hours without seeing a single other soul.

I felt I had been transported to another planet where they grew kumquat trees and dust, and all the people had disappeared. I wondered when I would have a close girlfriend again. When I finally heard the car drive in at night, my heart would begin to pound, and I half questioned if it had been beating at all.

SO THERE WE were in September, mired in sunny, chilly California. (It's not all L.A.'s balmy temps, as uninformed newcomers discover.) And Ray was writing. As cold as the spare bedroom—now Ray's study—was, he never seemed to mind. I offered him an electric heater repeatedly, but he wouldn't use it. Wearing a sweater and maybe gloves, Ray would read, study, and write, revise and edit, and then contentedly type up his longhand on the Underwood.

That first semester of "real" college, I watched Ray come into his full intellectual powers for the first time. His mother had always felt he was gifted since he was a small boy and carried a book everywhere. From the time he was eight, Ella had sat him down in the kitchen and asked his advice about every puzzling situation she faced. Ray would listen, think for a minute, and give her a logical response. Now his professors at Chico State noticed his special talent and the extraordinary person he was.

In English 1A, for example, he startled the teacher during a routine grammar exercise. Given the choice of "quick" or "quickly" to complete the sentence "Get the medicine——!" Ray alone picked "quick." He argued that's what real people would say in an emergency, and if he wrote a short story about a sick baby, he'd have someone shout, "Get the medicine quick!" The teacher saw what Ray meant—and knew he knew the "right" answer—but she backed the grammatically strict position. And gave a lengthy lecture on adverbs. Then the class got into a lively discussion about poetic license and the exciting, flexible tool language can be in the hands of a writer.

In his 1B class, a speech course, Dr. Glenn was so impressed with Ray that he kindly worked with him after class. When Ray was called on to give a formal speech, his shyness and soft voice made him practically inaudible. Dr. Glenn couldn't bear to give Ray a poor grade, so they rehearsed repeatedly until Ray could get up in class and give the required speeches. It was still psychological torture for Ray—public speaking always would be—but he couldn't let Dr. Glenn down.

Financially Ray and I were more strapped than ever. Yes, we didn't pay rent, but we paid utilities. And we needed gas for Ray to go to school and work, and a small amount sent monthly on what we owed the obstetrician. In our budget we had seven dollars a week left for food—three went for Christi's baby food.

This was all before federal college loans or grants for students. The GI Bill was a major source of college aid, but was available only to military veterans. There was no one we could, or would, turn to for help. "We are living on love," we said. Ray and I ate cold cereal and Campbell's soup all week. Sometimes we had a loaf of bread and could make toast. On Saturday night we'd splurge and have meat loaf, a small can of peas, and mashed potatoes, and on the table, candles brought from Yakima.

We claimed we didn't care about food. During the week we often ate on the fly while reading a book or attending to Christi. Besides, we weren't going to be sellouts to the crass American system! For us *The Man in the Gray Flannel Suit*, Sloan Wilson's universally acclaimed novel, defined American culture. Like John Gardner, whom we were to meet the following year, who drove the plainest black car on campus, we, too, would be unpretentious and nonmaterialistic.

Amy noticed that we had changed since the move to California. She and Mom visited weekends when they could. They knew Ray had to work in Chico and that I was spending a lot of time alone. One time Amy said to us, "You two have gotten so serious. You used to just laugh and have fun all the time. Nothing seemed to change after you were married. Now you guys seem so serious and responsible. You seem . . . very married."

Well, what could I say?

Ray answered, "We *are* serious. We *are* married. And with one kid here and another soon to be here—yep, you have it, we are seriously responsible. We have to be."

Yep. It showed. I was losing weight instead of gaining. My doctor was concerned and wondered what was happening. I was too proud to tell him that we couldn't afford groceries.

JERRY SENT ME a letter with thirty dollars enclosed. Bless her. I'll never forget the fun Ray and I had picking bright, fresh food at the grocery store and lugging it home. I ate. I had peanut butter sandwiches on toasted brown bread, crunchy red apples, and celery. We even bought a small roast beef and had a wonderful dinner, with leftovers for sandwiches.

I gained seven pounds. I knew in my bones that this good food was going to make all the difference for the baby. That weekend I was ill with a terrible cold; my mother and Amy came up to help. On Saturday afternoon we made the trip down to Chico to see my family doctor so Mom could hear exactly how I was and what should be done. The doctor prescribed a histamine medication for my congestion and ordered me off my feet and into bed. I was not to pick up Christi, who weighed twenty-five pounds. I was cramping as well. Unless I was very careful, I'd be thrown into premature labor.

It was October, and I had two more months of pregnancy ahead of me.

Mom was so agitated she could hardly drive our car. Amy and I laughed hysterically as she jerked the car through the gearshifts. Back home, I got into bed. Ray worked until 10:00 P.M. Then I realized I was having the same pains I had before Christi was born. I timed the contractions by the Big Ben alarm clock next to the bed. I was going into labor. At least I hoped the medicine would soon let me breathe normally, if I rested awhile longer.

I watched Christi stand up in her nearby crib, smiling at me. She looked so cute and dear. I felt sad that she would have to share me with another baby when she was still such a baby herself. I wanted to suspend the moment, just Christi and me in the room. Above all I didn't want to go to the hospital until Ray got back.

The minutes ticked away. Finally Ray was home. I told everyone I was having pains. He and Amy would take me to the hospital, leaving my mom with Christi.

We twisted our way down the mountain road from Paradise to Enloe Hospital in Chico. It was on the Esplanade, a long street lined with tall trees. As the contractions swept over me with greater intensity in the hospital, nothing seemed safe and familiar except Ray's comforting presence.

Now we learned that my new obstetrician, whom I'd only seen a couple of times, was out of town. All of a sudden the pain was different, too. When I was examined by a nurse, she determined that the baby had changed position. Unless something changed again, I was going to have a breech birth.

As we waited, before they took me to the delivery room, Ray carried me into the bathroom several times. He rubbed my lower back during contractions, and said kind, encouraging things, hugging me and trying to make me smile.

On the delivery table I labored to no avail. I had a handsome new doctor (on call for my labor) who worked and worked, trying to shift the baby with his hands into a headfirst position. Pain. I was blind with pain. I remember receiving shots, and I remember crying periodically. What kept me going was my new doctor's singing. All night long he sang the current smash, "Volare." "Volare, oh oh, E cantare, oh oh oh oh Nel blu, dipinto di blu. . . ."

Saturday turned into Sunday. Finally at five o'clock in the morning, the baby turned and came out. I broke into copious tears of relief. The singing doctor said softly, "He's a beautiful little boy."

The next morning bright sunshine streamed in through the Venetian blinds. Ray strode into my room, smiling from ear to ear. I had never been so tired and weak in my life, but I was smiling as if my face would break.

"Well," I said proudly, trying to sit up, "we had a boy."

I had taken one look at the newborn and had known he should be called Vance. To my delight Ray agreed. Vance Lindsay Carver, born

October 19, 1958—not "junior," of course. I had expected another girl, but here he was, two months premature like his sister.

Ray reached for me and hugged me. He finally broke away with a laugh. "I guess I better go and call all the folks." Had any couple ever been as close? I wondered as I settled back to rest.

I LEFT THE hospital with my baby son wrapped in a blue blanket with satin binding. My handsome husband was there to drive us home.

We stopped to pick up food and treats like banana nut bread and hot chocolate, courtesy of the congratulatory money relatives had already sent. I indulged in $2.50 of material for a navy blue skirt, though I couldn't really sew. It was on sale, and I was so happy to be relatively slender again that I had to celebrate. (I never made the skirt, but I toted the material everywhere we moved for years. It made me happy to see it, to remember how high Ray and I were, taking Vance home.)

We quickly settled into a new routine.

There was a crib on either side of our bed. If one baby awoke and stirred, the other usually did. Ray would go to Christi's crib, and I'd go to Vance's. Often the four of us cuddled in bed against the winter cold. Christi would drink the bottle her daddy warmed for her, and I would nurse Vance.

Flanked by the cribs with our pretty sleeping babies, we had parties for two, daringly beginning when Vance was only nine days old. There was no way we could be together and wait the six weeks the doctor recommended. The wonder of a nursing-size 44 bust and a nonpregnant wife were too much for Ray to resist. In the evening after dinner, as each of us grabbed a baby to diaper, we'd wink and chuckle. In bed we drank hot chocolate with marshmallows afterward.

An electric heater kept that one room warm at night. Otherwise the house was cold. Very cold.

When Vance was two weeks old, I bundled him up, took Christi, and went with my mom by Greyhound to her apartment in San Mateo. It was a good idea. I could take it easy—just turn up the thermostat if it was cold—and eat and build myself up. It was great to be really toasty and warm.

Besides, Mom and Amy were eager to have me come with the babies to spend some time with them. Mom was especially excited. After teaching elementary school all day, she'd come home and cook a big delicious supper, totally reenergized just because we were there. I ate cookies and drank milk between meals.

One day I was in the middle of a good book—James Gould Cozzens's *By Love Possessed*—when I realized that Vance wasn't behaving normally. His nose was clogged, and he couldn't breathe. He wasn't satisfied when he nursed. After a long restless night, my breasts were sore and red.

The next day, after Mom went off to teach and Amy headed to school, I felt panicky. What do I do in this strange place? My mother didn't even have a car. What should I do? I believed nursing infants were pretty much immune to colds and the like. By ten that night, he was worse, more stuffed up than ever; and just never off my breast. Okay, what to do? Call a taxi!

At Sequoia Hospital over in Redwood City, the emergency-room doctor diagnosed pneumonia. One more hour in Mom's hot apartment, the doctor said, and the baby would have been dead. The next day a pediatrician had more news: Vance had a heart murmur.

In that strange hospital the baby was fighting for his life. He was placed in a crib in a room no warmer than sixty-eight degrees. To be with him I had a cot and was freezing all the time. Once a day I went to the cafeteria and grabbed coffee, sandwiches, and fruit to keep going. (Christi stayed with my mother and Amy, my saviors.)

Ray was absolutely wonderful during this time. He soothed and comforted me by phone as I kept him up-to-date on the baby's condition. I had been inconsolable when I learned of the heart murmur; Ray wrote me a beautiful, poetic letter in response. He created images of our boy who couldn't play football and sports but would instead learn to love poetry and good literature, serious music and philosophy. Nothing important would be lost. He'd simply have a different destiny.

Slowly Vance got better. He was going to make it. He'd live.

We could be discharged—as soon as the hospital had a down payment on the bill. Welcome back to the real world. We had no medical insurance and could no more afford to pay than when our children were born. We still had those bills.

Ray had to sell his shotguns. They were his pride and joy, guns used for years hunting ducks and geese. I realized what a sacrifice it was, but he never complained. He was in his forties before he was able to buy another gun. (He would also buy a rifle for the writer Richard Ford, a special friend of his. What better gift, Ray thought, than something he himself had waited twenty odd years for?)

From the proceeds, beside the hospital payment, Ray bought groceries. He took a whole day off and did laundry, mopped all the floors. He had the house spotlessly clean, a roaring fire going in the fireplace, when Christi, Vance, and I arrived home.

(Happily for Vance, in three or four months the doctor could no longer hear a heart murmur. He could be physically active after all. I was beginning to wonder if our life was always going to swing rapidly from the highs to the lows to the highs. Probably. If we could pay for it all.)

SATURDAY NIGHT WAS our weekly special dinner. One time Ray added a small bottle of Thunderbird wine. He bought it for $1.38, as he put it, right off the top of his paycheck. Ray wasn't even old enough to buy liquor. We knew no stores that would sell to minors, had no relatives or friends willing to buy for us. So Ray felt blessed that he had found a grocery store checker willing to sell him the wine. (He was buying baby food, too, which likely made him seem mature enough.)

The "T-bird," however, had aced out the hamburger for the meat loaf. We didn't care. We'd eaten meat loaf the weekend before, and we'd have it next weekend. With a fire blazing, the babies fed and asleep, we were free to spread out on the couch and enjoy our glasses of wine. This was more like it. Amy was right. We had gotten inordinately serious since coming to California.

How good to laugh and relax. I stretched out, and for no other reason than the joy of life, broke into giggles and laughter.

Vance Carver with his eighteen-year-old mom, me. Fall 1958.
USED WITH PERMISSION OF THE
ESTATE OF AMY BURK UNGER

"I say, what's so funny?" Ray asked.

"I don't know. You, the Thunderbird, just everything is cracking me up."

"I'll give you something to laugh about." He was laughing resoundingly as he pounced on me. I eluded him and beat it out the door, Ray in pursuit, the way we used to chase each other in Dr. Coglan's basement apartment.

In the cold darkness I doubled back behind a woodpile. Ray couldn't see me, and almost jumped out of his skin when I ambushed him. I couldn't control myself any longer. I was laughing so hard, I fell on the ground. Ray fell on top of me. We laughed so hard we were in tears.

The next day we sat on the couch with newfound wisdom. Thunderbird was cheap and went down like lemonade. But, my God, the hangover! Our heads were pounding. From our separate ends of the couch, we commiserated. Our missed meal of meat loaf was looming large.

"The only thing I can imagine would be a huge pot of mashed potatoes, with lots of butter and pepper." That might make my headache go away.

We gradually recovered a little and didn't regret our night of fun. Ray said he would do it again. Then he went out to buy some potatoes.

IN NOVEMBER I went to work. I hated to do it. Vance was a month old, and Christi wouldn't be one until December. I didn't want to leave them in someone else's care, but I hated even more seeing us all starve. It felt very strange to be walking the streets of Chico looking for work, my breasts full of milk. I walked from one store or restaurant to the next, asking if they needed someone.

Jobs were hard to come by. There were few businesses in sleepy little Chico, and many college students to fill the menial ranks. I know I was supposed to feel very lucky when the owner of a pleasant, clean little restaurant seemed interested in me. He took my name and phone number.

That night he called. I could start work right away at Mr. Chips Coffee Shop. It was, in fact, Mr. Chips himself on the phone. His wife also worked in the shop, even though both had college degrees in English.

I found a nice young baby-sitter. She had a two-year-old, which made me feel better about leaving my children with her. I had to get everybody up by five so I could breast-feed Vance, cook Christi her favorite boiled egg with toast, dress them, take them to the baby-sitter's, and then get to work in Chico by seven.

It was strange working hard for eight hours, stressed out by everybody from customers to the boss's wife, and then facing all the work at home. It made for a long, long day. On our joint day off Ray and I worked ourselves silly, doing massive loads of laundry, changing the sheets, mopping the floors, always one more thing to do.

That's why our "parties for two" at night were so important to us. Finally we could laugh and be ourselves. We could refocus on our wonderful goals. We could be passionately in love.

The money I earned did help. We survived. And it was clear that my wages made the difference. We had starved as long as we could. (I was so thin that, undressed, I practically looked concave.) The babies needed shots and examinations. The car needed a long-overdue oil change and tune-up. We needed to pay old bills.

I did what I had to do. Several times a day I went into the women's bathroom at the coffee shop and squeezed the milk out of my breasts into the sink. The pressure relieved, I could continue waiting on patrons.

I put my tips, mostly dimes, in a jar up in a kitchen cupboard.

. . .

CHRISTMAS WAS COMING. Jerry and Les announced that they would pack up their new baby and two older boys and come on down to California to visit. We were thrilled to think of the family party we could have. Jerry and Les always had the money to celebrate, and they were going to make it happen for us, too.

Everyone came to Paradise for Christmas Eve. Mom and Amy, Jerry and Les, and us—and a house full of five children. Thanks to the unexpected event of the week, there was plenty of food for dinner. Whatever else we needed was provided by my relatives.

What had happened? We cracked everyone up with the explanation. Ray slyly set the scene: "I've seen some of you wondering why we have all the cans of food with no labels. We don't know whether we're going to encounter pumpkin pie filling, olives, or green beans. Well, one day last week, Maryann was in the living room in her slip, ironing and drinking a beer. Suddenly thirty-five Boy and Girl Scouts arrived at the door with their teacher and principal."

It was true. They had come in a big yellow school bus. I stuck my head out the door and improvised. Wait a moment, I said, till I get some clothes on, and I'll invite you in to see my babies. Why were they here? Maybe it was some sort of weird California welcome wagon thing. Then one of the little boys explained loudly—we were a poor family. The class had collected a Christmas basket of food for the needy. We were it. (Goodness knows which neighbor had provided our name!)

I was extremely embarrassed, but I didn't want to hurt the children's feelings. They were "doing good." Quickly hiding the beer—the first we'd had, a real splurge—I threw on some clothes and made them all welcome. They filed through, looking this way and that, taking in what a poor family's house looked like, what a poor mother looked like, what poor babies looked like. Of course they were enthralled with the cute little babies.

Ray was chuckling. "Maryann let a couple hold Vance and Christi, and then she quickly mixed up packages of Kool-Aid left over from the summer. Every child got a few sips of Kool-Aid at the poor family's house and went off to have a happy Christmas, having shared with those less fortunate."

Bob Cratchit move over. Merry Christmas, one and all!

We had barely finished our expansive, no-label dinner when it was straight from the high to the low. Christi tried to take a bite out of a red Christmas tree ball. She was bleeding and cut on the lips and tongue. Fearing she'd swallowed glass, we rushed her to the hospital emergency room. Fortunately the cuts were superficial. She'd be all right.

I wasn't so sure about my mother. "Grandma Alice" was crying in near-hysterics. I wasn't far behind her, but I tamped down my agitation so I could comfort her.

Later that night, after dinner and gifts, Ray and I, Les, Jerry, and Amy headed off to Reno. My mom, newly restored to her customary bravery, was staying behind at the Paradise house (it was hers, after all) with the three babies, Christi, Vance, and Loren, and the two boys, Lynn and Lanny. We all piled into the Bonsens' car. Freedom!

In Reno we changed clothes and dolled ourselves up to the max in a service station bathroom. Then we hit Harold's Club. Unlike those in our party who never got enough of slot machines, blackjack, or roulette, I wandered into the lounge shows and enjoyed the free entertainment.

A highlight of all my trips to Reno was catching Louis Armstrong. When I saw him, Pops had a band with a well-built black singer. She wore a strapless white formal with a full net skirt, and looked about seventeen. I'd never seen such a wild, unbridled woman in my life. She sang and pranced all over the stage with such energy that I thought she'd bring down the ceiling. All the while Satchmo grinned, even as he played. He clearly loved the girl's wildness as much as we in the audience did.

How we grew to love what became our annual family jaunts to Reno! That Christmas, however, the trip wasn't completely carefree. Strange how some little, irrelevant thing can trigger, sometimes, a straight-from-the-hip response. In this case it was mushrooms. We had ordered steaks topped with them, but Jerry didn't take a bite of steak or anything else; she went at the mushrooms.

"What are you doing gobbling mushrooms as if there's no tomorrow?" I kidded her.

"I'm having chest pains. I want to make sure I've eaten my mushrooms. I like them the best."

Jerry was thirty. At twenty-six she'd had a coronary thrombosis. Her doctor scoffed. She told him she had crawled across the living room floor to get outside for air. The doctor said she was too young—and female— to have a major heart attack. But when he read her EKG, his expression turned grave. Yes, it had been a coronary. If she wanted to live and rear the boys, she would have to speak to Les, avoid housework, stop smoking. She had to quit her job.

"What about if I quit my husband and kept my job?" Jerry countered sardonically.

She did try for a time to follow doctor's orders but nearly went crazy from boredom and loneliness. If this is what her life had come to, she decided, she didn't want it. So she went back to work, resumed smoking, and had another baby, the bouncing boy who was back with our mother in Paradise.

She hurt. She had other attacks. But she always ate her mushrooms *first*. For the Burk sisters that became our way of declaring: Live your life to the fullest.

Jerry, in turn, was concerned about me. How was Ray treating me? We had deftly turned the Christmas charity basket into another of our oh-so-amusing stories, but she was not having any smoke blown in her eyes. I told her I was determined that my marriage would last. I'd seen the pain breakups caused. That's why I was willing to work any cruel job to keep things together, two at once if I had to. Besides, I knew I'd go right out and pick the same type of guy if I were free. I had joked with friends: "I know me. If I weren't with a writer, I'd be with a jazz musician. The same merry-go-round. So what's the point of making a change?"

NEW YEAR'S EVE. We were by ourselves. Everyone else was safely home, and we were reading *Ulysses* out loud, cuddled by the living room fireplace. After Leopold Bloom bought a kidney to eat, we welcomed in 1959. We kissed and toasted with the champagne Jerry had bought us.

And we made a decision. We would be happier living down in Chico, even if we had to pay rent. We'd had it with icy roads and commuting. Also we'd be closer to the pulse of college life. But we wouldn't be living in one of those large white stucco houses, once grand dwellings, that now housed the Greeks—the fraternities and sororities. The frat boys and sorority gals seemed at times to dominate the streets and bars of Chico. We watched from afar with contempt. This was never going to be our experience of fifties college life. We wouldn't have wanted it, even if it were possible.

As winter lingered on, we found an upstairs apartment a few blocks from the college. The landlords, the Scotts, looked as if they had stepped out of van Gogh's *The Potato Eaters*. Fat, bald Mr. Scott. Fat Mrs. Scott. They had fat, doughy-looking boys. We moved in.

Then I realized that Christi, now walking, might in an unguarded moment tumble down the exterior stairs or slip through the railing and fall two stories to the cement below. We bought a little safety gate for safety's sake. Every day I chided myself. What had possessed me to think we could live here with a toddler? I also knew we were stuck. It was impossible to raise money a second time to rent somewhere else.

At the apartment doing laundry was particularly unpleasant. The old wringer washer sometimes lost its rubber hose, sending water cascading and inevitably leaking down to the apartment below. That's where the Scotts lived.

If water seeped through the floorboards, it turned a deep yellow color from old paint. We didn't know it until one day our landlords came running upstairs. Mr. Scott was so angry that his bald spot was red. The wife was right behind him, her fat shaking.

"Do you folks realize you're leaking down pee water from the kids' diapers all over our house? All over our food! All over our beds! All over our TV! All over everything!" Ray and I just stared at them.

It was their damn washer in the first place. Why wouldn't *they* fix the hose? Their ad had offered laundry facilities; it was one reason we took the place. First we were frightened, and later that night we were mad. They had no right to dress us down in front of our children.

This was our introduction to strangers for landlords. As might be expected, it wasn't the last lesson. For the time being, though, we cuddled up, feeling closer and more united than ever, while those tyrants slept below us.

ON MAY 25, Ray turned twenty-one. For his birthday I went to the best men's store in town and bought two wonderful, short-sleeved summer shirts. I can remember them vividly. One was a kind of white linen material, its two vertical stripes (gray and black) matched under a pocket by two little appliquéd balls. The other shirt was also white, but silky, with a subtle off-white pattern. I just knew Ray would love them.

I baked Ray a chocolate cake, his favorite. As I frosted it, I listened to Frankie Avalon singing "Venus." Christi was in her high chair and learned to lick the frosting spoon.

Ray was pleased. After a special dinner of fried chicken and mashed potatoes, like Ella and Aunt Von made, Christi give Daddy his presents. Vance looked on from his high chair. The shirts were a big hit.

Then Ray decided it was time to go out and have his first legal drink. It was fine with me. I still had two years before I could join him for a toast in public. After Ray left I did the dishes and mopped the kitchen floor. With two babies dropping food from high chairs, it was a foregone necessity.

After the kitchen was cleaned up and the babies put to bed, I spent some time looking at them in their cribs. Christi was a plump baby girl of about thirty pounds. She was sucking her bottle languidly, pushing it to the side a little to smile up at me.

"You little doll," I said, picking her up. "You have no idea what we go through to fill that bottle with milk." I hugged her to me. "You are my best friends now. All of you. Your daddy, you, your brother. I'd be lost without you."

Just then Ray came back. "I only had one drink. It wasn't any fun, Maryann. I'd rather drink coffee here with you than have a whiskey and water in a bar by myself."

"Thank you," I said. "Thank you. Would you like another piece of cake with a cup of hot coffee?" That was what I planned to have.

"Don't mind if I do," Ray said.

IN JUNE THERE were openings for operators at the telephone company. I was willing to take the tests and go through the battery of interviews, if for no other reason than I could sit down. At home I was perpetually chasing after Christi or trying to protect Vance from being scratched by his sister. She was still too young to understand why there was another baby—one had been quite enough as she saw it.

I was hired. "Number, please?"

At the phone company I soon realized I was the odd duck among the operators, all women. The night shift was dominated by fat, peroxide-blond Maxine and her equally fat friend, Joyce. At three hundred pounds plus, with breasts as big as buckets, they bragged back and forth about their husbands loving to wallow in their creases and folds.

They saw me reading *Lady Chatterley's Lover* on a break and for the first time deigned to give me the time of day. They wanted to borrow it, as they'd heard it was "a real racy story." When they did they discovered they had to wade through a lot of densely written pages to get to the juicy parts. Neither had the patience, and they returned the book. Then they went back to ignoring me, like a spot on the wall, as I sat right next to them.

IN THE SCOTTS' lousy apartment after a lousy shift at work, I finally admitted to myself that I was lonely. It was hard working a job I wasn't interested in. Hard to be with people I had nothing in common with. It was a far cry from Saint Paul's, studying poetry or analyzing literature. More than anything I wished I could go to college. But it was out of the question with two small babies and a full-time job. As the man of the family, Ray should go first and get a solid education. He was the one with a great talent. He was the one destined to become a great writer.

6

ALONG THE WAY AT
CHICO STATE

Chico State's 1959 fall semester offered Creative Writing 101, taught by John Gardner. Gardner was only five years older than Ray and at the time unpublished. But he was already a great teacher. Ray immediately signed up.

Day one. Professor Gardner came into the classroom, immediately lit up the first of the endless cigarettes he chain-smoked (against the rules), and let everyone know that there was nothing more important in the world than to write quality contemporary fiction. He did it himself. And maybe they could too.

Gardner had a doctorate from the University of Iowa. He was young, still practically a boy wonder, and had last taught at Oberlin. Ray always liked to think that Gardner left Oberlin under some kind of cloud, but perhaps John's antipathy for the administration got reciprocated. Or perhaps he simply got a better offer from Chico. The college was out to lure top-notch talent to enhance its reputation. Generously financed by a progressive state government, the California university system as a whole was entering its boom years.

Along with his ubiquitous cigarettes, Gardner had brought a box of magazines to class. "Little magazines," he called them, devoted to real literature. This, he informed his young students, was where promising writers and poets first published. When one young student said he'd never heard of any of them, Gardner replied that everyone in the class probably hadn't heard much of anything worth knowing.

That was the premise he started with: They needed to be thoroughly educated. Had they read Faulkner? Had they read "The Bear"? If not, they hadn't read Faulkner. Had they read William H. Gass, Flannery O'Connor, Frank O'Connor, Chekhov? How about Jerry Bumpus, Curtis Harnack, Hortense Calisher? Any student without a resounding yes down the entire list—the smart aleck who slighted the little magazines sank in his seat—ought not to make any more smug, ignorant comments. Period.

The class wised up fast after Dr. Gardner established his literary credibility. His students were inspired. John was the first to show them how embryonic their early writing attempts really were. His criticism and positive encouragement spurred his students to redouble their efforts.

The stimulation of Chico State already had Ray reading everything he could get his hands on: Ford Maddox Ford, James Joyce, John Dos Passos, T. S. Eliot, Richard Ellman, Ezra Pound. Now he added all the short-story masters Gardner assigned or casually mentioned in class. When he wasn't reading, for the first time Ray was writing fiction daily.

Before long Gardner started inviting Ray and some of his other students to carefully orchestrated parties at the apartment he shared with his wife, Joan. The members of the little group were so primed with belief in their futures that they were sure they must be the next Fugitives (a circle of influential early-twentieth-century poets and writers formed by John Crowe Ransom and Walter Clyde Curry in 1914). Well, history was repeating itself! This was the extraordinary enthusiasm John Gardner summoned forth.

IN THE SUMMER months between semesters, we had not been idle. After biding our time at the Scotts', we got out as soon as we scraped together enough rent for the next place. They'd seen the last of our money. Good-bye leaky washer and steep stairs. We settled into a dusty apartment complex just down the road. The units were linked by carports, and the landlord was bland and noncommittal—the best thing about the whole place. It looked, to be honest, like the "tourist camps" of my old *True Story* magazines—where poor tragic folks lived.

We no sooner got moved in than school was out. Ray was preparing to go over the mountains to Humboldt County on the coast. He was going to work with his dad that summer in a sawmill. Humboldt was where the work was. Tedious, dirty, hard, sometimes even dangerous work, but work that paid more than anything in Chico.

We were in debt. Although I worked full-time at the telephone company and Ray part-time at the college library, we barely squeaked by. We had a stack of doctors' bills and other past-due obligations that we simply couldn't handle from what we were earning.

Before he left Ray had taken on some extra work in Chico, a temporary job cleaning up some lady's yard. I decided to surprise him one day with a late lunch, brought to him by his charming young wife and kids. I packed a picnic basket full of sandwiches, grapes, and homemade chocolate chip cookies. On the way I stopped and got a cold six-pack of Pepsis.

Ray was delighted to see us. He wiped the sweat off his brow, put down his rake, and took a break. He gave me a nice kiss, and then one to each baby. I spread the picnic out on a red-and-white-checkered tablecloth, complete with matching napkins. I wanted it right out of *Better Homes and Gardens*—thick sandwiches, well-groomed little children playing amicably, and me in my white shorts, matching top, every hair in place, makeup fresh and moist. Oh, yes . . .

"This is great," Ray said. "I was about to die of thirst."

"Have a Pepsi. I have glasses and ice in the basket."

"Just what is the occasion, anyway, honey?" Ray asked.

"Well . . . I'm glad to see you. That's part of what brings me here."

"What?" He was suspicious and slightly alarmed. "Or should I eat my lunch first?"

"Well, my period is about a week late. I had to share it with you, and put fear and anxiety into your life, too."

"Well, in for a penny, in for a pound," Ray said, obviously not amused. "On the other hand, let's try this. I'll pack *my* suitcase and put it under the bed. When you start your period, I'll unpack it again." Otherwise . . .

We laughed. I thought about the prospect of having another baby. Oh my God! The next day my period started. No need to pack just yet, Ray.

RAY LEFT TO join his dad.

With my husband in Humboldt, I was left at the "tourist camp" to take care of the babies and work split shifts at the phone company. I came home in between to tackle housework, like hanging wash on the community clothesline. The kids mingled with several other children in the dusty grass. The whole place was always dusty and dirty from cars stirring up gravel, constantly in and out. The play area left the children looking like dirty little urchins. I had to bathe and dress Christi and Vance again before taking them back to their baby-sitter, Crystal. Then I went back for the afternoon operator shift.

Crystal, their meticulous and efficient German baby-sitter, affectionately cared for my children along with her own two. Her husband fixed Volkswagens at the local dealership. Luckily for me she fed the kids delicious food, often from her garden, and let them play in her pretty fenced yard or in her immaculate house. Without her I don't think I would have been able to cope as long as I did that summer.

FOR A TIME Ella and James stayed in our little apartment, too. Ray and his father were sharing a cabin, provided by the mill at a hefty price. All of us felt displaced and temporary, an emotional state of emergency that left no one comfortable on either side of the mountain. We wanted to be like human beings who know who they are and where they belong at nightfall.

That hot, fly-ridden, lonely summer was becoming increasingly tough. Go to work. Come home and work some more. Ray felt the same way. He was serving a sentence of hard labor for the sheer benefit of our

Always her boys. Ella Carver with sons, Ray and James, on the campus of Chico State College. Chico, California, 1959.
PHOTO BY MARYANN BURK CARVER

creditors. But the debts had to be reduced if he was to resume college in the fall.

I was totally caught on the treadmill. My job required jumping on a switchboard light the moment it lit. You plugged in while simultaneously saying, "Operator." Then you placed the call. I was perpetually counting the minutes until my break. One day followed another, relentless, over one hundred degrees. I don't remember cooking, eating, or enjoying a single meal. I didn't go to one movie or really get to see any of my friends. I had to use all my energy to survive and keep my family going.

A coupon came in the mail offering a package deal at a local photography studio. I knew I should pass it up, as I always had, but I *wanted* a professional picture of my little dolls. This was the only advantage of being alone, I realized. I could take action when I wanted. There was no one to stop me.

I curled Christi's hair and bought her a new dress; and for Vance, a little boy's shorts outfit. I took them to the photographer and was so pleased when he and his assistant raved about how cute the kids were. Getting those pictures taken was my only high point in July.

On top of everything else, I noticed the car needed repairs. The brakes were increasingly spongy, and I habitually pumped them when coming to a stop. I had never dealt with getting a brake job, and didn't know exactly what was involved. Besides, I had absolutely no money. When I got my paycheck and paid everything on my list, I was stone broke.

One afternoon I dropped Christi and Vance off at Crystal's and headed back to work. I drove two blocks, where I had to cross the main intersection as I had a hundred times before. There was a stop sign. As I approached, I dutifully started pumping the brakes. This time, however, the pedal went all the way to the floor. The brakes were completely gone.

I could see another car rapidly approaching. Throwing mine into second gear, I pulled on the emergency brake as fast as I could. The car slowed, and as I sailed into the intersection, I only clipped the rear fender of the car that would have broadsided me.

I called in to a nasty, unsympathetic supervisor whose only concern was whether I would be at work precisely on time. I thought I had reacted well. I dealt with getting the car towed, took a cab to work. But I soon realized how agitated I was. Suddenly I could no longer bear being a stranger in Chico.

When I got home, I phoned Ray, words tumbling out: "You are receiving a call from the hand that rocks the cradle, and I insist you come home right away. Punt your job. Let the bill collectors get five dollars a month in good faith. Everyone we owe is wealthy, while our payments come out of our hides. We need to be together as a family. I can't take it alone anymore. I was almost killed today."

Ray heard, really heard. "Don't you worry, little thing. I agree. Enough is enough."

We gave Ray a hero's welcome on his return from Humboldt. We were so happy to see each other, grateful that we were all right, that I hadn't been hurt or Ray maimed at the mill. And thank God the babies were not with me in the car.

THREE DAYS LATER it was my birthday. I was nineteen. Ray and I went all over Chico celebrating. With his last sawmill paycheck, we went out for dinner. We listened to music. We danced, first in one place and then in another. We ran into some people Ray knew from school and they joined us for a while.

I hadn't had such a good time since Christmas and Reno. Dressed up and feeling pretty for a change, I was full of energy and eagerness. Life was wonderful. I was married to my Prince Charming and our cute little toddlers were sleeping soundly in their cribs at home with Grandmother Ella caring for them. I felt on top of the world.

SHORTLY AFTER my birthday, I begged Ray to move from the dirty little apartment before school started. In the paper I had found a place that sounded wonderful. A brand-new house no one had ever lived in. It had hardwood floors like Crystal's, which always gleamed from her polishing. I wanted floors like her floors, flowers like her flowers, and a yard for our children like Crystal had.

Naturally several people had already called about the house by the time I got hold of the owner on the phone, but I begged the man with the foreign accent not to rent until Ray and I could come see it. I kept saying, "My name is Maryann. Could you take that down? M-a-r-y-a-n-n."

"Yes, I write that down," the gruff old voice said.

"Well, don't rent that house to anyone," I laughed, "unless her name is Maryann. We'll be over this afternoon, when I finish my shift."

"Okay," the voice said. "I wait for Maryann."

I fell in love with the place instantly. In addition to a large living room and two bedrooms, there was a tasteful kitchen with new oak cupboards—still with shavings in them—and a green stove and gleaming refrigerator. There was also a magnificent lawn, front and back, completely enclosed by a white picket fence. The huge backyard had a huge old oak tree, its branches a shady refuge from the inhuman Chico heat. There were even a picnic table and benches, made to order for summertime meals.

"Isn't this tree amazing?"

"You know what William Blake wrote," Ray said. " 'The tree that reaches upwards to heaven has its roots in hell.' "

"That's a good one," I said.

"Well, we're still in debt and having trouble making ends meet. How can we take on ninety-dollars-a-month rent? That's thirty dollars more than we're paying now."

"I know it will take real sacrifice on our parts to afford the rent. We'll have to cut out any extras."

"I don't know. It worries me to take this on, as nice as it is."

"Well, if I had this house I could hold my head up high again."

Ray got tears in his eyes. He squeezed my arm with his fingers. "Okay," he said. "You've got it. We'll go from here."

I was scared about money, too, but I figured we'd manage somehow. We always did. So we took it.

When I told Crystal about my upcoming move, she said, "You know, Wolfgang told me at lunch that they need someone down at the VW shop to detail the cars. The guy they had quit. Maybe Ray could get the job and solve the money worry." When Ray went to see about it, they offered to hire him immediately.

Back at school he'd also resume working at the library for a buck an hour. That was his favorite job. He could help himself to every periodical and all the books he could want.

There was a job at the VW dealer for James, too. Business was booming, and more than one man was needed. Ray was happy to have his brother's company. James was happy to land a job in Chico, a town where virtually no jobs got advertised. And Ella was happy to have both of her boys working—James, now sixteen, could help her out financially.

OUR LATEST LANDLORDS were Portuguese and spoke almost no English. The old man had been a laborer all his life, ever since he came to America to make his fortune. He had expected to pick up gold off the street after the boat brought him to America. He didn't mind working hard, though. As in the old country, his wife stayed home, minding the children and growing tomatoes. She had almost no contact with other people, despite having been in California for many years. The children were long since grown and rarely came to visit.

After the old man retired, he built a new house on a lot across the street. However, when it was completed, he felt it was too perfect for them. What would he do without his old toolshed? What would his wife do without her old flower beds and vegetable garden? Enter the Carvers, the first tenants to occupy the new house.

Personally I had no compunctions about worthiness. I could hardly wait to get into the house. I had thrown caution to the winds.

For no reason I would look inside the new cupboards, my dishes and foodstuffs carefully stacked. Or I'd wax and polish the shiny hardwood floors, even though they were already spotlessly clean. I'd sing, "New house, new house." I'd look out into the yard and see ten-month-old Vance standing in his playpen and Christi playing with her toys, and feel happy.

We had only been in the new house a few days when we realized how shabby our old furniture looked. And didn't we need a couch and a chair, not to mention a coffee table and end tables? Of course, since we had just paid the rent, there wasn't a dime left to buy new furniture. In fact we didn't have a prayer of more furniture next month, the month after, or any time in the foreseeable future.

If that wasn't bad enough, one night I came home from work at 11:00 P.M. and found that Ray had hung a blanket, normally on our bed, over the living room picture window. It made my lovely house look as if tasteless people lived there, or else that something terribly clandestine was going on.

Inside I found Ray unpacking books and manuscripts, drinking a beer, and listening to a new Tom Lehrer record. Funny, but slightly off-color.

"What's with the blanket?" I asked. "It looks like hell."

"Well, when I was in the kitchen earlier, I saw the landlord standing out by his shed. Looking through a pair of binoculars. So I didn't want the Portuguese to watch."

"Oh," I said. It sank in. My beautiful new home wasn't underground, like Dr. Coglan's apartment. Or heatless in Paradise. Or up a death trap flight of stairs, like at the Scotts'. Or smack in the middle of a dusty tourist camp. What it was, was my foreign landlord with binoculars, right across the street, watching every move we made in his perfect house. Perfect . . .

The next day Vance awoke with a scorching fever and couldn't keep any food down. I was scared. I asked Ray to come with me to the doctor, after I called in to take off work. I knew we needed the money, but this was too reminiscent of San Mateo. I began to cry.

The doctor was concerned as well. Vance was already seriously dehydrated. We wrestled for days with diarrhea, vomiting, and a white-faced little baby. At last he improved and cuddled comfortably into sleep.

By then the rest of us had his bug. We went through bottles of Kaopectate and gallons of pop and juice before it was all over. What a housewarming. I thought we'd have a real party, like the old days in Yakima. Well, I'd thought a lot of things.

MY OLD PUBLIC school friend Marion Hill and her husband, Jewell, visited us in late August. They were on summer vacation. Since they would have spent the grocery money anyway, they figured they only had to pay for the gas to get down from Yakima and back. I was so pleased they had come.

But as their boys brought in tricycles and other toys from the car, I sensed that the landlord would wonder if another family was moving in with us. That tension hung in the air, and doubtless the Portuguese was manning the binoculars. Ray borrowed more blankets from his mother and covered more of the windows.

On a Thursday evening we decided that the grown-ups needed to go out without kids.

The baby-sitter arrived as Marion and I put the finishing touches to our makeup and outfits. We had on high heels and summer dresses with cinched waists and full skirts. My dress was pink with spaghetti straps. Marion's earrings practically blinded, they were so sparkly and beautiful. After a couple of drinks out of Jewell's big bottle of whiskey, we all felt good as we got in the car. We were hot to go.

As we backed slowly out of our driveway, the Portuguese came out his front door and ran into the middle of the street. He stretched out his arms and waved them around, apparently to stop us from getting away.

"Well, I'll be damned," Jewell said. "Would you get a load of that crazy old son of a bitch."

"Disgusting," Ray said. "Jewell, run over him. Don't slow down."

"No, no," I said. "Look at his face. It's red as a beet! I think he's going to have a stroke or a heart attack."

The Portuguese charged our car, stumbling, kicking up gravel, and grabbing his chest. I really thought he might collapse and land us with a manslaughter charge. So, out the window, I tried to appease him. As he stood there I explained that our company was leaving on Saturday. Not to worry.

"They are not . . . the only ones . . . going on Saturday!" the old man shouted, his neck and face beet red again.

"Hey, listen, you old fuck," Jewell said. "Move out of my way because I'm driving through."

Jewell meant what he said. The old man barely made it out of the way. We looked back as he picked up a handful of rocks and threw them wildly, sputtering like mad.

Well, we had plenty to talk about that evening.

Marion and Jewell and their boys did leave on Saturday. Soon after, we left the "perfect house" that was going to let me hold my head high. We moseyed down the way to another rental a few blocks away.

OUR NEXT HOUSE was as large as the Portuguese's, though shabby by comparison. It was, however, cheaper, and a marvelous setting for our ratty old furniture. In short, a great student pad. We had parties in that house that became famous.

The Green House, we dubbed it. It had a dark green exterior, with shaggy, long, dark green grass, no fence. On the inside there was cracked linoleum here and there, which I tried to cover up with playpens and throw rugs. We did the best we could.

At one of our first soirées, Ray got tired of the party, tired of the people. He wanted to go to bed. Without being caustic or rude, he simply went and got all the guests' coats and deposited them in a pile in the middle of the living room. Everyone took the hint. With polite chatter about how late it had gotten, they grabbed coats and were out the door.

At subsequent parties, when the hour got late, knowing guests would ask Ray if he wanted to go to bed.

"No, no," Ray would say, "I'm having a better time than anyone."

"Just checking with you," they'd say, almost reverently. "We don't want you to get our coats and . . ."

That incident was never forgotten as long as we lived in Chico. People laughed about it. They told other people who hadn't been at the original party. Before you knew it, folklore. Did you hear about the time Ray Carver . . . ?

It was in this friendly green house that Ray wrote his first long, elaborate story, "The Furious Seasons." Because Ray manipulated the tenses, relating past events in the present and present ones in the past tense, it was considered a bit of a tour de force. John Gardner was very pleased with it. He not only read it enthusiastically to the writing class but also had his colleague Lennis Dunlap do a review for the school paper. (They were jointly editing a textbook, *The Forms of Fiction* [Random House, 1962].)

Ray's friends at Chico were also elated. With our house already "the" place to hold parties and gatherings, that story made Ray king of the group. His closest rival was his good friend Ernest J. Finney. Finney was a Hemingway imitator, both in appearance and style, but talented enough to go head-to-head with Ray. He was a little older than Ray, and much louder. When he got on a verbal roll at a party, he'd dominate the whole scene with his voice.

Finney had written a story called "The World Is Flat," an initiation story that was first-rate. His subsequent stories for class he entitled, "The World Is Flat II," "The World Is Flat III," and so on. At our house, arguments—mostly started by Finney himself—broke out as to who was the better writer, Ray or Finney. He would try to draw Ray out in self-defense, though the whole thing was really just drunken macho good fun and bonding between true friends.

IN OUR PART of the world the year 1959 slid into 1960 without much fanfare. Granted, the sixties didn't even start, technically, until the following year, but the larger truth is that *the* sixties—that media-annointed decade for love, sex, and rock and roll—was still several years ahead. There were, however, already stirrings all over the place, even in out-of-the-way Chico, California.

Ray decided to start a campus literary magazine. Certainly he was motivated by what John Gardner had already begun, a national literary magazine called *Mss.* Its first issue featured a W. H. Gass story, "The Pederson Kid." (Gass is also the author of the incredible story "In the Heart of the Heart of the Country.") Nancy Parke, a very bright writing student from Connecticut, went for Ray's idea like gangbusters. She jumped up and down, literally, to be the coeditor. "Pick me, pick me!" He did.

Soon Nancy was calling Ray and talking to him for hours about the magazine. They were both on fire about the project, which was to be called *Selection*. Ray had the idea of writing to one of his heroes, the elderly William Carlos Williams, to ask him for an original poem.

Improbably Williams responded. He sent "Moon Shots," a poem about two old men discussing going to the moon. The signed manuscript was Ray's most prized possession. Well—at least until the day when poor Nancy sneezed wetly all over it.

I was excited about *Selection*, too. But one day I went to the campus to pick Ray up, and there he was strolling along chummily with Nancy, whom I'd never met. Fine, I thought, I'm just going to step right up and meet her. As I hailed them, I noticed big, wet rings of perspiration on her blouse under her arms. To me the blouse was the tip-off—she had other things on her mind that did not include meeting Mrs. Carver. I was jealous and pissed.

Later I confronted Ray. How could he spend all his time with Nancy while I slaved away at the phone company? Ray finally cracked and said, "Maryann, if I did have something going on with someone, I'd probably choose someone more comely!" Ray felt bad about his remark, and when I pictured Nancy's protruding teeth, thick Coke-bottle glasses, and mousy hair, I felt bad for goading him into it. However, as usual, I did have a point when I really blew up.

Once Nancy took up with Ernest J. Finney and we palled around as a foursome, I stopped worrying about her being after Ray. Still, because I wasn't a Chico student, especially a writing student in Gardner's class, I was the odd person out. Except for Ray, who knew better, it seemed that everyone else assumed I liked my job with Ma Bell and had no interest in literary matters. Or aptitude.

There was another thing that this student writing crowd did that enraged and hurt me. These budding "intellectuals" who graced my home for parties had more than once referred to Christi and Vance as little animals. These "friends," behind a thin facade of objectivity and wisdom beyond measure, were sneering at our babies.

One night I'd had enough. I told that evening's assembly of campus wits to take their offensive remarks elsewhere. If anyone said another word about my adorable, smart little children, I could not be held responsible for what I did next.

Yet though there were students I didn't care for, I still longed to join the coeds at Chico. I did enroll in one class—Art History—but it turned into the proverbial straw on the back of my camel. I couldn't do class work and all the domestic chores. It was too hard on the babies to spend extra time at the baby-sitter's three afternoons a week. When I was at home, I was busy with laundry and housework because I'd been away in class. While in class I was worrying about the chores I had to do at home.

As much as I loved the college atmosphere, and as often as I cried every time I left the campus, I dropped the course. Instead I focused on the children and our meals. Immediately our home life improved. Surprise.

I SAW A poster at the college advertising an upcoming concert by Ray Conniff and his orchestra. I was determined to go. I loved his harmonies, his music that made me feel uplifted and carefree.

After a lot of swapping with other operators, I got the evening off. I also did baby-sitting for my friend Dorothy Bernache. Her husband, Joe, was in the writing program, too. In return she'd baby-sit Christi and

Vance. Having finagled that far, I called two bill collectors—better keep the electric company placated—and made extended-payment arrangements. That gave me enough money to buy tickets and get a new outfit.

These were my first new clothes in I-can't-remember-when. What I got was a sky blue, straight tight skirt, with a matching blue-and-white print blouse. With high heels, the outfit was positively smashing. Everything was set. When I had dressed, Ray looked me over. "Voluptuous. You look positively voluptuous. Good enough to eat."

Then, half an hour before we were due to take the babies over to Dorothy's, Ray changed his mind. "Honey, would you be too disappointed if I didn't go to the concert with you? I was just going to please you. But I have a paper I have to write that I feel like working on tonight. I don't mind baby-sitting. You could invite Dorothy to go with you."

" 'Disappointed' isn't the word for it," I said. "I'm not 'disappointed.' I'm crushed. I don't want to go with Dorothy. I want to go with you."

"Maryann, please call Dorothy and see if she wouldn't love to get out of the house tonight. I really want to work on my paper."

"Jesus, what a fine time to tell me! The evening is totally spoiled. I got up at five-thirty to work the day shift. I was so excited to be going out, to have new clothes."

Ray went to call Joe. He was willing to take care of their children, and Dorothy did jump for joy at the prospect of a night out. She and Joe had four children, including a four-week-old baby. They were even poorer than we were. Joe had a small monthly GI Bill check, and like Ray, got minimum wage for working in the college library.

I left to pick up Dorothy. She was twenty-six and had been around the block. She had been in Germany when Joe was in the service, and now with four kids living on practically nothing, she was a bit cynical and tired of the struggle. She could hardly wait for him to graduate in June, get a real job, and, as she delicately put it, "end this bullshit."

"What about his poetry? Joe writes really fine poetry."

"I wouldn't know," Dorothy said. "It makes me yawn. I got together with Joe because he's good-looking, a good lover, before he ever wrote a poem. It wasn't poetry that attracted me."

At the concert I could see from the first number that Dorothy was fidgeting. She had gladly put her hair up and applied her best bright mauve lipstick—and she did keep saying how good it was to be out—but clearly the music wasn't doing much for her. At intermission she asked me, "Why don't we ditch this farce and head on over to the Silver Room?"

"The Silver Room. You know I'm not old enough to go in."

"Don't worry," Dorothy said. "They know me. If you're with me, no one will suspect anything. Let's go."

"Oh, please, Dorothy," I said rather sheepishly. "I really am enjoying the music. I'd like to stay and hear it."

"Well, if we stay, are you game to go to the Silver Room after?" Dorothy was closing a deal like a saleswoman, quid pro quo.

I didn't want to go. I had work in the morning, and the concert wouldn't be over until at least ten-thirty. I was afraid of being asked for ID, and I also wondered vaguely what Ray would say if I went to the most swinging cocktail lounge in Chico. But I wanted to be fair, so I agreed. Jesus.

"Okay, but if I do get served, I don't want to have more than one or two drinks."

"That's no problem," Dorothy said. "I have to get home to nurse the baby."

Dorothy hung in until the end of the concert and then practically *ran* us over to the Silver Room. The bartender served me with a smile, a very big smile, as he looked me up and down. "I don't think I've seen you here before. I would've remembered."

"This is my friend Maryann," Dorothy said, first drink in hand.

We were just finishing our second drinks—I was expecting to go— when Vince and a couple of other guys walked in. They spotted us and headed our way. Vince was—yes—in the writing program. He was the stunner in that group of good-looking guys. Unlike our husbands, he was single, with marvelous hip clothes and black hair carefully styled and slicked back. Welcome the consummate stud-about-town.

"He's a slut," Joe and Ray liked to joke. They liked him. He was a fun, cool guy, the coolest in the class, though his writing didn't begin to measure up to Ray's. Ray was an artist; Vince was a hack in the making.

Dorothy had ordered me two gin fizzes, and I was feeling really good. I looked around as Vince and his buddies pulled up stools. The room was silver, with blue lightbulbs, a cavern of fantasy and music that made it hard to leave. But I had to go. I tried to get Dorothy's attention, but she was planted on her bar stool, always laughing and in heavy conversation with someone.

Vince was now buying us drinks. He was talking to me, politely and respectfully. The first question he'd asked was, Where was Ray? He asked me if I'd like to dance. Of course Vince danced exquisitely. He could slow-dance with the most confident, romantic rhythm, or fast-dance with style and humor. Whatever the tempo, it was a blast to dance with him. We were laughing and having fun, dancing, stopping to order another drink.

Over my shoulder, in the middle of a slow dance, I saw Ray walk in. He was looking mean and grim, wearing his big house slippers and wool car coat. Christ, he looked like Nanook of the North!

"Oh my God. There's Ray."

"Be cool," Vince said, holding me tightly so I couldn't break away. "Keep dancing, so you don't look as if you're doing anything wrong. Which you aren't. This is all among friends."

When the number ended and we returned to the bar, Ray had three drinks stacked up in front of him. Everyone had hastily chipped in. He ignored Vince, though ordinarily he'd have shaken hands, patted his shoulder.

"Who's with the kids?" I asked.

"Nobody," Ray said, as he slugged down his first drink.

"Nobody! How could you have gone off and left the babies alone?"

"How could you sit down here with that barfly Dorothy and get drunk and make a spectacle of yourself?"

"I'm not drunk. I haven't done anything wrong. Let's get out of here right now and go home to the kids."

"Not until I finish my drink. You in any hurry?" Ray slugged down his second drink. He finished a third, and with that, we left, Dorothy tipsily in tow. When we got to her place, Ray got out and opened the passenger door. She slumped down over me, her head under the steering wheel and her legs sticking out of the car. When Ray bounced the door off her legs she didn't feel a thing. I knew there were going to be repercussions from this evening. Somehow we managed to get her out of the car and into her house. We zoomed off for home.

Usually we were considerate and gentle with each other, aware of how sensitive we both were. Not tonight.

"I'm going to leave you, Maryann. I'm going to take Christi and leave you. You can keep Vance."

"What? Don't do that. Please, Ray, don't do that. Don't even think about it. And, besides, over my dead body will you take my little girl."

"She's *my* little girl, and I'm taking her with me."

"No, you're not. Everybody knows little babies need to be with their mothers, especially girls."

"She looks just like me. She *is* like me. She belongs with me."

"Well, then, maybe you ought to support her, too."

"You know, Maryann, you have a razor tongue. Tonight's a perfect example of that. You do things on impulse. And if I hadn't gotten down to the Silver Room, you might've gone off with Vince. All it would've taken is maybe a few more drinks. The only thing a person can say for you is you have a good personality and you throw a good piece of ass."

We pulled into our driveway.

"Oh, Ray, do you really think so?" Smiling my icy little smile now, I continued, "I hardly know what more a woman could need than to have a good personality and be good in bed. Speaking of which, let's go to bed. I'm awfully tired. But I'm not too tired to make *you* happy." We got out of the car and went inside.

I meant what I'd said—about making Ray happy. And I did. Just to make it clear what he could lose.

The next morning Christi climbed out of her crib, as she was now able to do, and crawled into our bedroom. She repeated over and over the first word she had learned: "Eat, eat, eat." I laughed and poked Ray.

"There's your kid. She's all yours. She badly needs you to change her diaper." Phew!

SELECTION CAME OUT and hit the stands locally. It was a major triumph. Everyone loved it, and all over campus people talked about it. Ray sent copies to out-of-town friends and relatives. Besides editing, he wrote all the notes on contributors and staff, including himself. The coeditor, he noted, was twenty-one, married, with two children, and studying fiction at Chico. And "recovered" from the move to the Golden State with his wife's relations.

1960s

With Christi, Vance, and my twenty-first birthday cake.
Eureka, California, 1961.

7

EUREKA

With summer 1960 approaching, we decided to move to Eureka, over the mountains in Humboldt County. It was right on Humboldt Bay, about two hundred miles northwest of Chico and a hundred miles south of the Oregon border. For one thing, I couldn't bear another summer separation. I also found out I could easily transfer to the local phone company branch without missing a paycheck.

I think Ray was feeling a sense of completion at Chico State. He had enjoyed the exceptional privilege of using Gardner's campus office on weekends to write in quiet seclusion, but he had basically gotten what he could from John's tutelage. The creative writing class had been pivotal. The parties and get-togethers with other aspiring writers had been exhilarating. *Selection*'s first issue was out and very well received. So "done that," as my sisters and I liked to say, meaning a good experience we didn't necessarily want to repeat. In two years Ray had learned much. But Chico was getting a little stale; there might be greener grass over the mountain.

Truth is, we both wanted to take a look. Humboldt County also had a four-year college, Humboldt State, with courses in creative writing. Ray could transfer—we checked with a call before packing up. We knew from last summer that Humboldt had better-paying jobs, even if many of them were tough and dirty.

So why not? Well, it would disappoint Mom to have "her babies" move so far away. She was teaching in Willows near Chico and spent every weekend with them. But our "why nots" shortly gave way to "let's go."

In our enthusiasm, we got a few of our Chico friends to move, too— Jon and Sharon Remmerde, and David Pierce. We were disappointed that Ernest Finney and Nancy decided not to. They were happy in Chico, and there was no financial advantage for them. Nancy was pregnant. (She'd put aside writing short stories.) They were living on his GI Bill benefits. But they promised to visit, as did we.

After *Selection* came out, Ray, Nancy, and other students hawked the magazine. In a long Saturday festival at school, they sold off all the remaining copies. That final effort made everyone proud and happy, as well as hungry. The four of us—Finney, Nancy, Ray, and I—slipped out afterward to a good, funky restaurant. It had big picnic tables and a sawdust floor, and we aimed to indulge in the house specialty, barbecued ribs.

Ray kept ordering another round of drinks, dipping into the crumpled little brown paper bag Nancy carried to pay. The paper bag, of course, contained the proceeds from the magazine sales. We all had ribs, baked potatoes, salad, and corn on the cob, which we relished like the poor students we were.

"You're getting in over your head," I told Ray as he ordered a fourth round of drinks, again dipping into the brown bag. But I chose not to create a scene. It wasn't my business or responsibility. It was Nancy and Ray's. The production of *Selection* had been financed with state funds allocated to the English Department. The proceeds were supposed to be handed back in.

Well, Ray had a little outlaw streak in him. Nancy, pregnant and in sort of a daze, was powerless to stop a man hell-bent on celebrating hard work. As the evening wore on, Ray dug deeper and deeper into the little brown bag. Soon there wasn't going to be a nickel left.

Our gang of four came up with a plan. If Nancy was questioned, she'd blame it on Ray—*shock! gasp!*—who had moved away. If Ray was questioned, he'd say he knew nothing about it, in the midst of moving—

shock! gasp!—he'd assumed Nancy was handling things. I lost track of who said what, but it was making perfect sense at the time.

One more reason for us to pack up quietly and slip out of town.

WE HAD BOUGHT another car, an old, cream-colored Ford, used, from PG&E, the power company. We were excited to have a car we thought could make a long trip. (It could, and did.)

There was only one small problem. The power company had removed the car's backseat to haul equipment around. We were well up the highway to Washington before we discovered the consequences. The nice black coating on the backseat area was rubbing off on the children's faces, hands, and clothes! I had to nickname the car "the Black Hole (of Calcutta)."

Surviving that debut, the car was ready and able for our getaway as soon as the spring semester ended. Ray and I packed up and struck out for Humboldt County. The kids were staying with my mother until we found a place.

Eureka, here we come!

The Trinity mountain range has peaks above nine thousand feet. At the top of the highway pass, the motor blew.

We sat by the side of the road in our stalled car, unable to think. Here was our first fresh experience—before we were anywhere near the green grass of Humboldt. We were looking at four or five hundred dollars to fix the car or purchase another. We didn't know anyone with that kind of money. *What to do? What the hell to do?* It was going to take every penny from my paychecks just to rent a place and to live.

Finally I thought of someone who might come to our rescue. A friend of my mother's, Coralee Holt. She was the secretary to the superintendent of schools. She had helped my mom, and I knew she was interested in us and in Ray's writing. We hitchhiked over to the next town and made a call.

Coralee came through, thank God. She lent us the money to buy another engine for the Ford. While the car was being repaired, coffee and

boysenberry pie with ice cream restored us considerably. We were ready
to set out again.

Eureka, here we . . . come.

Our plans were set. We'd find another cheap apartment. We'd find
another baby-sitter. I would work at the phone company. Ray would get
another sawmill job for the summer and enroll in Humboldt State College's fall semester. Things would work out. Ray would get his degree,
keep on with his real work, and become a respected and successful
writer. And then I . . . I still wanted to be a lawyer.

Nor did we realize, yet, that we were enrolling semipermanently in
the school of hard knocks. Tough times were something both our families knew about, but what Ray and I would face was of a different order.
In the sixties we would have to deal with the refraction of our hopes and
dreams through the lens of the astonishing social changes about to occur
in America. That heady mix was liberating for some, psychologically
unmooring for others, and not infrequently a bit of both for most of us.
Along the way, as in many American families, there were survivors and
casualties.

Ray and I were survivors at heart. "If we didn't laugh, we'd cry."
That was what we said, half in jest, half as a self-protection incantation.
Oh, we both feared—and courted—our personal slings and arrows. Ray
was only twenty-two; I wasn't yet twenty. We were still forging the values of our married life, finding a frame of reference that could give us
bearings in a changeable world. It's much too pat to look back and declare, as some would have it, that Ray was already overburdened and
hindered in his writing development by his family. To the contrary.
Without me and Christi and Vance, without our extended families on
both sides, Ray might have had more financial freedom, but at a terrible
cost of lost psychological stability and support. What we gave him, for
better or worse, was the place to come home to.

When he ventured out, either in the workaday world or in his imagination, Ray knew what he was up against. He was basically a nobody
from nowhere, and if he had talent, he was well aware that most great

American writers had hailed from the older, established parts of the country, had passed through the halls of Ivy League colleges or the like, or had come from accomplished, educated families. Obviously that wasn't his background. He needed us, then.

He had his family to fall back on, always, and he had me. That was Ray's ace up his sleeve. At first our young family wasn't a weight, it was an anchor.

This was when Ray still believed—when we both believed—that no matter how poor we were, we'd be rich in spirit, and that's what counted. So you see how in tune we were with the sixties zeitgeist that would soon come blowin' in the wind. He later wrote: "We thought we could bow our necks, work very hard, and do all that we had set our hearts to do." This retrospective passage from an essay in his book *Fires*, written in the early eighties, goes on, "But we were mistaken."

But perhaps not. Maybe the fault was not in our stars. For me, I wanted something to start in my life that would propel me toward the goals I still dreamed about. Perhaps the next town, the next situation, would be where I could get started. I hadn't changed. I had grown up fast, if you like, and I was steadfast in wanting it all, my life with Ray, my children, education, a meaningful profession. As might be expected, the "way the world is" had more to teach me. In that sense Ray was right: We had been mistaken. Doors didn't always open with hard work. Opportunity was elusive, fickle, quick to evaporate. "Carver fear" was not illusory. And I was a woman, with a woman's circumscribed opportunities.

In 1960 we were, they said, the weaker sex, and most men agreed. I believed what I'd learned in church, to love thy neighbor as thyself, but I simply never understood "as thyself." For years and years I only heard "Love thy neighbor," and that "neighbor" was Ray Carver. When I finally heard "as *thy*self," it rose into my consciousness like a revelation. I had to teach myself, force myself, first, to love my own self as much as I did my significant other. I think for many, many women, that became as the sixties rolled on a stubborn *cri de coeur*: I matter, too!

. . .

FINDING A PLACE to live in Eureka (teasingly, "I found it!" in Greek)
was not so easy. Finally we got a converted apartment on the upper floor
of a house. We were exceedingly leery of again living up a flight of
stairs, but at least the staircase was inside the house and had a banister.
That made it safer for the kids.

On the other hand, Gertrude, the landlady, lived on the first floor,
along with her husband and two teenagers, a boy and girl. "That's us in
a few years," we joked. They were a nondescript couple. She favored an
ugly cotton housedress and had an evident limp. He was bald, with a
perennially grouchy expression as he read the local rag of a newspaper.
When we took the apartment, Gertrude offered to baby-sit the kids.
Dropping them off downstairs would be a great convenience. I didn't
have the heart to ask if she could keep up with two active toddlers with
her apparent handicap.

I immediately started work at the telephone company. In those days
the job of a long-distance operator was pretty much the same anywhere.
But I was a lot happier in Eureka. Confident, already experienced, I did
my job excellently from day one. It was a better group of women, too.
No more nights with the likes of fat Maxine and fat Joyce.

Ray got a job at the Hansen-Pacific mill in Fortuna, a few miles outside Eureka. Our two paychecks made us feel like real people again.
(Well, if we didn't laugh . . .) The mill abruptly declared bankruptcy.
Ray had seen only two paychecks. Management begged the employees
to keep working, claiming they'd eventually be paid, plus a big bonus for
sticking by the company.

Ray chose to stay. Under a new partner's name, the mill went on op-
erating. But no money for us for a while. There went our summer financial goals up in smoke. Or, I suppose more aptly, sawdust.

THE FIRST TIME I went to pay Gertrude that summer, I was shocked
to be handed an itemized list of "expenses," in addition to the baby-
sitting charge. It was, among other things, fifteen cents for a slice of
toast. "But I feed them every morning before I bring them," I protested.

"Well, that's just it. We're still eating when they arrive. So naturally they want some. So I have to charge you more."

That time I paid. But I soon noticed that Vance and Christi were clinging desperately to us when we dropped them off. They had always been comfortable anywhere with playmates, toys, and loving care. Every day I went to work sick at heart. And I knew that canning Gertrude would cost us the apartment.

Two weeks later the bill had food charges almost as high as babysitting. I tried to talk things over with Gertrude, explaining that my husband didn't have a paycheck right now because of the mill's financial troubles. I brought up my concern about Vance's nasty diaper rash, and said I hoped he was being changed frequently.

With that Gertrude got very angry and defensive. "Well, I change him and wash his diapers all day long." I thought she was lying.

"Look," I said. "I wish I could be home with them myself. Of course, I do want them to have good snacks and frequent diaper changes and—"

"Well, get someone else, then." Gertrude suddenly looked like a witch. "And while you're at it, find another place to live. I don't need your insults. And don't bring them kids back, either."

"Why, you freak! You're throwing us out just because I asked you some questions?! Fine!" Gertrude had gone white. I had hit a nerve. At the same time I was horrified with myself for saying it. I was angry, yes, because I felt that she was abusing my children's well-being—and our pocketbook—but I should have held my tongue.

That outburst, as I tearfully explained to Ray later, had cost us the apartment. "Don't worry, honey," he said. "I heard about a street of houses, all owned by one man. Clyde at work says there's a vacancy. I'll see about it first thing."

In Eureka think Greek. As in philosophy. "First the idea, then the manifestation. That's Plato," I reminded Ray.

"Maybe so," Ray said, "but let's nail this house down right now. Several other people want it."

We took it. Already we were on the move again, if only to another part of town. But that meant another round of packing, hauling boxes, unpacking, getting the kids settled in. I crossed my fingers that Artino Road was going to be a good place for us.

EVENTUALLY, IN OCTOBER, Ray got his back pay from his summer mill job, but no bonus. (. . . we'd cry.) By then I was refining my own opinion of management. I had jumped through the hoops necessary to become a phone company service representative. The work was less repetitive and more prestigious, but the arrogance and coldness of the company was self-evident. Most definitely it was a monopoly. You got your phone from us or you did without.

I was on the job in October when, as directed, I personally wrote off bankrupt Hansen-Pacific's $100,000 phone bill. The same day I was told to get tough on a single mother with an overdue bill. Her $12.86 bill was due by the fifteenth. If the bill was not paid, the phone would be disconnected. She had a little boy with heart trouble; the phone was his lifeline. Well, my coworker at the next desk, a policeman's wife, had the right company attitude. When I expressed my reluctance to "get tough," she said, "Don't they hand you a line, though?"

I decided to spill coffee on the bill and rub it until no one could make out the due date. Then I called the young mother and made a deal. She could make partial payments on her bill. Without fail, she did. But for me the shine was permanently off the Ma Bell logo.

At least our family was thriving in the little two-bedroom house on Artino Road. It had a sidewalk where Christi and Vance could ride their tricycles, and the neighborhood teemed with other children. Miraculously (or thanks to a Platonic materialization), a good baby-sitter was right on the other side of our backyard fence. She was a grandmotherly white-haired lady, with a sweet smile. I could relax about the kids' care.

All the ticky-tacky houses on the street were cheap, and the landlord, Gino Artino, was very busy with other businesses. He owned two liquor stores, and over each a blinking orange neon sign blasted ARTINO'S LIQUORS. He had more money than he could spend in five lifetimes. As for his private little kingdom out on Artino Road, he made it clear he didn't want to be bothered with the householders' problems.

That was fine with us. We thought we'd found a better sort of land-lord, and what with the other pluses, I put up with the mildew that grew halfway up the walls whenever it rained—and it rained virtually every day. Daily I quietly cleaned our shoes and took Clorox to the walls. But it was a small price to pay, especially considering what our schedules were putting us through.

Ray had begun attending Humboldt State that fall just up the road in Arcata. He also worked part-time at Simpson's mill in Eureka, on the night shift. It was a dangerous job. He operated "the hog," a machine that chewed up everything fed into it—including the occasional errant worker. Ray stirred the feed—raw pieces of wood—in the hog's hopper with a big metal pole to prevent clogging from uneven distribution.

Unemployed for several weeks after giving up on bankrupt Hansen-Pacific, he was grateful to get the job. But he wouldn't get home until af-ter midnight, when he'd eat dinner. Then he'd have to leave for school at 7:30 A.M. He only got some writing and studying done by hanging out at school between classes. I worked until 5:00, then picked up Christi and Vance from their baby-sitter's. After I fed, bathed, and played with them, I put them to bed, another lonely evening of reading and waiting ahead of me.

AT HUMBOLDT, RAY studied writing with Dr. Richard C. Day, a pro-fessor of English and a writer. Unlike everyone else we knew, including John Gardner, Dr. Day had actually *published* a short story. That proved it could be done by someone you actually knew, a living, breathing writer. Dick Day—as we soon knew him—had studied alongside Gard-ner at the Iowa Writers' Workshop. Both were awarded PhDs for a cre-ative thesis consisting of original writing, something Iowa had pioneered.

Dick made the literary life come alive as a folksy network of cama-raderie, yet with an overlay of glamour and serious elegance. It was cul-ture in progress. More than ever Ray wanted to join that world. He also told me how young, handsome, and smart Dick was. I thought, Seeing is believing. Which I soon did.

My, this dark-haired man *did* look like Cary Grant! He was wearing a cool, buckskin-colored suede jacket when we met. And there I was in my office clothes of the day—gold sweater, tight skirt, and black three-inch heels. Not exactly the demure wife that a lot of professors thought suitable in those days, I realized. Thank goodness Dick Day was anything but staid himself, and I liked him immediately.

Dick seemed modest and shy. You couldn't imagine him telling students off the bat as Gardner had that he assumed they knew nothing worth knowing. Yet both men had an unfeigned sincerity and a lot to offer a committed student like Ray. You couldn't miss how passionately Dick Day cared about writers and writing. He created an almost religious awe around the study of creative work. Ray shared that faith, and it was not surprising that they became lifelong friends. Gardner had helped Ray immeasurably by teaching him how to edit and rewrite his work; but Dick gave Ray his unshakable respect and encouragement for the talent Ray possessed.

Professor Day commented years later: "Creative writing teachers know when they undertake teaching, that in their entire career, they will only have one real writer who becomes published and well-known. In my first semester teaching writing, I picked up Ray Carver's story, 'The Furious Seasons.' I realized first shot out of the barrel, I had my writer."

For class Ray had submitted the story he'd originally drafted the previous year in Gardner's course. I was able to attend the Tuesday-night session when Dick read and discussed "The Furious Seasons." He pointed out its strengths and compared it to other classic short stories. Dick was certainly capable of being critical and analytical, but his aim that evening was to laud Ray's writing. We went home high on his unabashed enthusiasm.

ONE DAY I had an insight—not without irony—that it was actually a good thing that we were poor. I had to work. And until I could go to college, working was the one thing that forced me to use my mind and stay engaged with the greater world. Nonetheless, when I did get a vacation—Ray had classes, so we couldn't go anywhere—I had a wonderful time just staying home in our little house on Artino Road. I pretended I was a "normal" wife and mother, right out of the women's magazines.

I washed on Monday, I ironed on Tuesday, I waited up for Ray and heated up his dinner when he got home. For Christi and Vance I was there to put a Band-Aid on an "owie." I read them stories before naptime. I baked cakes, the kids helping me. Ray could hardly wait to see what new treat awaited him each night. Together we were able to sit down and share the news of the day. Along with, say, a batch of brownies.

It was fun for two weeks. Then, unavoidably, I had to go back to work.

Except for children, we didn't have much in common with the neighbors. In the house across the street were two women with a raft of kids. Their boyfriends came and went in pickup trucks, Bobby Darin loud on the radio. They liked to roar by, kicking up gravel. But it was the first neighborhood where our kids could play outside with other kids. For Halloween I dressed Christi and Vance up as clowns, and along with several other mothers and children, went trick-or-treating. I felt proud to be part of the group, such as it was.

One of our neighbors was a longshoreman who beat up his wife when he got drunk. She seemed to live exclusively in her nightgown, and except when he was beating her, was a loud, aggressive woman. They fought and shouted, week in and week out. We tried to ignore them.

But our best response was probably the day Ray had about had it with the old Ford. The balky car was doubly irritating since we were still paying back Coralee Holt for the engine replacement. That day it didn't start—again. Ray went and got a sledgehammer and, yes, began to beat on the car. The neighbors stared in disbelief. I tried to explain. I called out, "Ray's just trying to destroy the Black Hole of Calcutta!" Now they looked uneasily at me.

I guess we were really starting to fit in.

THE ELECTION CAMPAIGN was in full swing. We watched the presidential debates on our little black-and-white TV in the living room. Nixon looked like death warmed over, his pancake makeup as thick as an elephant's hide. We'd seen pictures of handsome John Kennedy before but hadn't directly witnessed his charisma and facile mind. He was an exciting candidate, and for born-and-bred Democrats like us, who had grown up under the eight long years of the Eisenhower administration, this was a breath of fresh air. Ray could vote for him, but I was not legally old enough. (Yes, in 1960 the voting age was twenty-one, changed to eighteen by the 26th Amendment in 1971.) How nonsensical.

We followed the news carefully. On election night we watched the TV coverage of the results. "Hooray for Cook County!" as the tally pushed Kennedy into the winner's column with the electoral votes of Illinois. Our man had squeaked in.

The next morning we were in an exalted state, like the high after a great party. President-elect Kennedy appeared on TV with Jacqueline, his beautiful pregnant wife. Despite his lack of sleep and likely exhaustion from campaigning, he seemed full of vigor and excitement. That day we couldn't have been more pleased to be Americans.

"You know, Maryann," Ray said, "this is it. This is the best political situation we'll ever experience in our lifetimes. No one else is going to look like this president and his lady. And no one is going to be that eloquent and humorous. This is a very special time."

Shortly after the election the Kennedys had a newborn son. "John-John," as he was immediately dubbed, would join his older sister, Caroline, and parents in the White House come January. His father was getting ready to launch the New Frontier. It was exciting to wonder where our new president would lead the nation. Surely somewhere better than the dull, drab, anesthetized world of the fifties.

OUR FIRST Christmas on Artino Road was to be very special. Ray and I were high on each other and on life, and we wanted to share that good feeling with our families. We wanted everyone to come to our house.

Ray's mom and dad and James came. My mother, too. She brought Amy, who brought along her serious new boyfriend, Harry Oliffe. (Oh,

Dick was long gone, on to fresh conquests, no doubt.) Even my cousin Irmagene showed up, all the way from Pasco, Washington.

Everyone had the Christmas spirit, eager to make the holiday wonderful for the kids. (Christi had just turned three, Vance was two.) Both were getting acquainted with Santa Claus, their stockings hung in anticipation on a mock fireplace. What better diversion could three careworn grandparents ask for?

The year had not been kind to the Carvers or to my mother. In the Christmas pictures C. R. and Ella look sad and deflated. He was thin, ill, again unable to work. It was impossible to get him to smile, despite his heart being in the right place. He simply couldn't. This was the man whose chuckle and broad smile had struck me as much as his good looks when I first met him.

As for my mother, her second marriage was history. At fifty-four she was alone, sad, and afraid. Clarence was still her boyfriend but nowhere to be seen. He hated Christmas. He took it as a mandatory time for gifts, and he couldn't afford any. Mom was also broke. Her Washington State Teachers' Retirement Fund money was gone, having financed the relocation to California and the Paradise house. Mom desperately wanted to buy Christmas gifts for her children and grandchildren but couldn't. I knew she'd rather be taken out and whipped than show up empty-handed. Her sad countenance said it all.

What Ray and I frankly couldn't do was take these heartaches too deeply into our hearts. We had to work hard to stay on track ourselves. We were determined to celebrate the holidays. It was a break from the routine, and we savored the fun we were having. We partied exuberantly, played cards, went Christmas shopping, went to a movie. With our younger company, we hit the cocktail lounge that winked and served Amy and me, enjoying the Christmas decorations as we relaxed and laughed and played holiday songs on the jukebox. We just couldn't give up Christmas.

Harry was the newcomer to our family scene, but I quickly came to like him greatly. After he and Amy arrived, he apparently noticed our

It's a family Christmas, always a special day for us.
Artino Road, 1960.
USED WITH PERMISSION OF THE ESTATE OF AMY BURK UNGER

broken-down, old-fashioned, inadequate percolator. He slipped out that night and came back with a nice Pyrex coffeemaker, a model that perked twelve cups. Accompanying the "people's coffeepot" were eight big white coffee mugs. "Merry Christmas," he said.

Later, when Harry saw that we needed a turkey, ham, pies, and whatnot for a proper holiday feast, he and Amy went to town and returned with a hundred dollars' worth of groceries. We now had chips, dips, cookies, cakes, fudge, pop, and beer for the friendly poker games at the kitchen table. Amy, the actress of the family, was riotously funny. She insisted that she was "Big Lou from Chicago," making bets and chewing on a big cigar. "Big Lou bets five dollars," she growled, pushing her matchstick chips into the pot.

Harry was such a kick to have around that I had to overlook his one transgression. He was sleeping with Amy in the same house as our mother and Ray's parents. When I tried at first to get them into separate rooms, he refused. "Making love to Amy was like the first time," he explained. "There's no way I could be in the same house and not be with her. I'll have to go to a motel or back to San Francisco."

I couldn't insist further.

It was a little mind-boggling that Harry was widely known in the Bay Area as the "beatnik cop"—a result of his undercover police work. By the time he was twenty-five, he had also been a Europe-based skier, drummer, and rally sports car driver. No wonder Amy had fallen hard for this guy.

What a Christmas we had! It was a joyous and happy celebration, a tonic for our spirits. Harry was a charming addition, and I suspected Amy wanted to make him a permanent member of our unholy, poker-playing, life-affirming Carver congregation.

THE NEW YEAR got off to an auspicious start. On the cold morning of January 20, Ray and I stayed home, glued to the TV. We had to watch the inauguration of John F. Kennedy, live from that other Washington. Walter Cronkite on CBS provided the running commentary. The president-elect wore a black top hat, a broad smile on his face. Jackie was behind him. She looked gorgeous, young and classy in a light-colored coat with a fur muff and a matching fur pillbox hat. What a great outfit.

"Aren't they a pair?" Ray exclaimed.

We watched every minute, hating to break away even to dash out to the kitchen for coffee. When old Robert Frost, white hair blowing in the cold wind, stood with Kennedy and read a poem, we got tears in our eyes. Imagine—our gorgeous new president invited a poet to participate in his inauguration. Unheard-of. For the first time in our memories, the arts had been openly honored by an American leader as integral to American life, not as a throwaway gesture.

For the first time we heard, "Ask not what your country can do for you—ask what you can do for your country." We were willing. We'll be glad to do our best, Mr. President.

Ray will become a great American writer. I will help him, just as Jackie answered that her first responsibility as first lady was to take good care of her husband and children. I'll continue to encourage and support

Whenever we could, Christmas brought us all together—my
younger sister, Amy Burk, with her fiancé, Harry Oliffe.
Artino Road, 1960.
PHOTO BY MARYANN BURK CARVER

Ray. I'll be the best helpmate a writer ever had. Yes, Jack Kennedy, out
here on Artino Road in Eureka, California, we're with you. We're a new
generation, ready for that New Frontier.

THE SEMESTER BEGAN at Humboldt, and Ray was back to the usual
round of classes, reading assignments, and term papers looming ahead.
School was endlessly time-consuming. Other than his creative writing
class, he found his courses at Humboldt less enchanting than those at
Chico State. The newness of college had worn off. He realized that the
Humboldt instructors were competent, but the required subjects were
mostly not very relevant for him.

What was important was writing, his short stories. Between school
and the mill job, he was always trying to squeeze in some time for creative work. Ray read avidly into the night, losing sleep to keep up with
other contemporary writers. He read Martha Foley's *Best American
Short Stories*, little magazines, and novels and poetry from all over the

world. These weren't works assigned in any class, but self-directed reading that was vital to nurturing his own vision. As for his part-time mill
job, it was a total waste of time, strength, and energy. He did it simply to
feed the family and pay the bills.

Which is why I worked, too. But I was growing increasingly fed up
with my full-time job at the phone company. I was putting in long,
alienated days strictly for the money. I desperately wanted to go to college. I envied Ray his course assignments—which he would gladly have
tossed aside if he could have spent the time writing.

Yet, as winter ebbed, we knew we had no other choices. Ray still had
another year to go before he had a degree. In the meantime each payday
couldn't come soon enough. By the time we paid the baby-sitter, the rent
and utilities, bought groceries, and put aside our weekly gas money, we
were broke. There was never any money left over to go out on the town
or see a movie.

Worst of all I barely saw Ray during the week. I hated it. For me his
company was better than anyone else's in the whole world. Weekends
were the only time we could be together, sleep a little later, have a big
breakfast with the kids.

Snug at home on Artino Road, Ray had coined a phrase: "They can't
get us on the weekend." We repeated it often, a small way to encourage
each other. "They" were the bill collector, the landlord, the bullying
teacher, the boss—all the authority figures we had to deal with daily.
They all seemed implacably determined to push us farther down when
we were barely clinging to the lowest rung of the ladder of success.

IN 1961 THE pill became available. What a relief. We didn't have *that*
worry every month. Obviously we had trouble enough feeding the children we already had. And the adults. It was a birth control revolution.

Free at last, no joke.

8

ARCATA

We soon moved seven miles north (up curving Humboldt Bay) to Arcata, our familiar college town. We had two reasons for the move: Basically I couldn't take Eureka anymore and Ray, as it would turn out, couldn't take farm life up near the Canadian border. That "explains" why we would leave Eureka in the summer of 1961 and go on a fourteen-hundred-mile "detour" en route to Arcata.

It wasn't meant to be a detour. But it was providential because it gave me a chance I badly needed. Let me put it this way—one day I was on my 10:30 a.m. coffee break when something in my soul quietly snapped. I was sick to death of selling phone equipment to people who didn't need it, followed by hours of bill collecting. As I sat in the employees' lounge, trying to read Dostoyevsky's *The Idiot*, my stomach was upset and my head ached from the stress. I thought, There *has* to be a way I can get my education. I just can't wait any longer. Wasn't I the girl who once wanted to learn "everything under the sun"?

Putting aside my usual stoic comportment, I told my supervisor that I was ill and had to leave. Immediately. That day in early May, I drove straight to Humboldt State. In lieu of a high school transcript, I had the registrar call Saint Paul's and get an academic report verbally. As soon as he heard my SAT scores over the phone, he winked and said, "I can admit you today based on your scores alone." The registrar next sent me to

It's a Carver clan—Ray at far right, his brother, James, behind him,
Vance on his grandfather's shoulder, and Christi in Ella's lap.
PHOTO BY MARYANN BURK CARVER

the financial aid office, where I applied for a scholarship and a thousand-dollar federal student loan.

Miraculously everything just fell into place. I could get a loan. I could start college in the fall of '61. There was a nursery school for Christi and Vance. And the nursery school owner knew of a wonderful old two-story house, available in late August. The old house and nursery school were both close to the college, and everything was in the heart of picture-postcard-charming Arcata.

Late that night it was fun to see the look on Ray's face when I told him all I had accomplished from eleven to five, when he thought I was at work.

"You were actually admitted to the college and got a federal loan approved in one day? I don't believe it. Things never happen that fast for me!"

"Well, you aren't as pretty as I am," I said. We both laughed. I felt absolutely elated to have an option, a plan in place for me, if for some reason the real plan didn't work out. Yes, we already had one. Did I forget to mention that?

But our original plan stood: When the semester was over we were moving to my dad's farm in Washington. My fantasy option evaporated and I chalked it up to a bad day at the office, even as I took comfort in the realization that I *could* go to Humboldt. Just not right away. Or I could go somewhere else. I was certified "college material."

Free of monthly rent and his job at the mill, Ray could devote all his time to writing. If all went well over the summer, as I was sure it would, we'd settle in for at least a year. My dad was welcoming us with open arms.

Up until that morning I was as enthusiastic as Ray, if not more so. I adored my father, and returning to my childhood home would bring me back to the roots I sorely missed in California. Until my little epiphany in the employees' lounge, I hadn't given a thought to any alternatives. The dominating goal in my life had been to help Ray Carver become a great writer, even if that meant postponing my college education or giving up any job the world had to offer—anything short of starving the kids. But this move to Washington had something in it for me, too, and might be a chance for us to get *out* of the financial quagmire.

Ray always felt I'd have plenty of time. He was certain he would die young, and never wavered in that intuitive belief. That made me want to give him everything he wanted as soon as humanly possible, although I couldn't abide the thought of growing old without him. Besides, the first half of 1961 had been so unsettling that subconsciously I must have been longing to go somewhere familiar and comforting. The high note of JFK's inauguration had made the world feel a more hopeful place. Then the family events of the spring yanked me all over the emotional map. It had been one thing after another.

FIRST, IN APRIL my mother got married for the third time. She and Clarence went down to Mexico with Coralee Holt and her husband, Harry. They wed the very day that Jerry was in court for the granting of a final divorce decree.

Her seventeen-year marriage to Les was over. The divorce was pretty ugly. Employed at the best restaurants, Jerry had developed a drinking habit, hitting the after-hours watering holes with her friends. That's how she met Gordon Davis.

Les was increasingly angry and frustrated, and resorting to physical battering, though they still kept it hidden from the family. He fought bitterly to keep his sons. Evidence of her affair with Gordon weighed heavily in court. The older boys, pressed by the judge, chose to live with their dad. They didn't like Mr. Davis any better than the rest of us did when we finally met him. My poor sister lost custody of all three of her children.

My sister made a sad odyssey to California. She brought Gordon over to our place. I was appalled to see them in identical silly baseball caps topped with propellers! I knew Jerry was devastated, but I couldn't believe how drunk and dislocated my beautiful chic sister had become.

Ironically Jerry considered Gordon the love of her life. We couldn't fathom why. He was content to drink away his days, cracking his sour, unfunny jokes at other people's expense. Maybe she was looking for her lost youth—she had married when she was sixteen; Les was six years older. Gordon was five years younger. For Jerry he was a challenge, and she was set on marrying him.

The lovebirds next headed off to Redwood City, just south of San Mateo, where Amy and Harry were living. They had rented a beautiful home on Emerald Lake, a mother-daughter on two floors. Kindhearted Amy offered them the lower unit.

Jerry went right out and found work to pay their share of the rent. She had always shared her resources with us, but now she needed a place to land. We had to help her—we were Burk sisters. But it was tough being a foursome in the house. Harry agreed grudgingly. He hated to share Amy, to lose their privacy. I imagine he quickly realized that he was dealing with a couple of heavy drinkers. Jerry and Gordon couldn't even come up with a table and chairs for their unit, yet no matter, the liquor flowed.

While Jerry's life was crashing and burning, the senior Carvers were Ping-Ponging back to California. This time it cost James his high school diploma. They left Yakima six weeks before his graduation. I loved James, his sweetness and humor, and begged them to reconsider. Let him stay with his aunt Von until June and graduate. But Ella and C. R. insisted he come with them. They were headed to a new town where James would have no acquaintances. In their usual distress, they depended on their younger son—to work some menial job and help support the family financially and emotionally.

Then, on May 11, Jerry called me at the phone company. What she said was as unexpected as anything I ever heard over a telephone line. "We lost Harry," she said. *What?!* Oh my sweet God! Harry was lost— he'd been shot, murdered.

Harry had taken Amy home after dinner out. She had to get up early the next day to start a new job at Burroughs Office Machines. He dropped her off, promising to be right back, and went to his old place for some reason. When he walked into the darkened apartment, Sally was there. She was Harry's separated wife, as we found out. She fired from the couch. It was Harry's own gun, one he'd used undercover and hadn't taken with him. Perhaps left for her protection.

Amy spent an anxious night wondering where Harry was. When she saw the headlines of the San Francisco morning papers, she had her terrible answer: BEATNIK COP MURDERED BY WIFE. Reporters tracked her down and took pictures—the pretty, blond, nineteen-year-old "other woman." Her photo was plastered on the front pages the next day.

Shocked by the horrible news, Ray and I took off to help, even though we could hardly afford to. Our regular baby-sitter kept the kids. I felt so sorry for Amy. She was crushed, heartbroken. Amy had been madly in love and had lived with Harry for more than a year. She kept thinking, If only they'd been by themselves, they wouldn't have gone out. He wouldn't have gone to the old apartment.

We set up camp inside the house, while the press snapped pictures outside, and prepared for Harry's funeral. At night somebody tossed rocks with ugly notes through the living room windows. We gave up and slept mostly in the daytime in shifts.

The rest of the country celebrated Mother's Day. Jerry cried for hours after a huge pot of blue hydrangeas arrived from her sons back in Yakima. As for Gordon, he was happily cutting out clippings on Harry's murder from several newspapers. This was the first time he'd ever been remotely a part of anything that made the news.

The photographers had a heyday at the funeral, too, snapping picture after picture: Amy collapsing in tears. Sally's parents came—I was stunned they showed up. At least the authorities didn't let Sally out of jail for the day. Amy wore a slinky, posh suit of Jerry's and looked like a fashion model. She wanted to look wonderful for Harry. Well, the press enjoyed the scene.

To see Harry, only twenty-six, lying in his coffin, small and lifeless and nothing like the man we had known—that had a profound effect on Ray and me. ("Harry's Death" is the short story Ray wrote, inspired by Harry Oliffe's death.) Harry received a military funeral, gunshots cracking as he was lowered into the ground. There were so many simple white crosses in the cemetery, identical white crosses, that I wondered how we'd find Harry's grave if we ever came back.

Harry was only three years older than Ray. His death had come suddenly and unexpectedly, and Ray pondered that in earnest. He decided he had to get on with his own life immediately. To do only what was important. That meant writing, and to heck with spending even one more year in classrooms, never having the time to do what he really wanted.

HOME IN EUREKA, I had started daydreaming of my dad's farm. "Live on the fat of the land" became our new motto. On the farm Ray could write full-time, and I could spend my days with the kids. Vance was just learning to talk in sentences. I could be there for every next development in my children's lives. I could cook and bake, which I loved to do because Ray appreciated it so much. I saw myself able to bake homemade bread, do my household tasks, and still have time to make everyone a hearty lunch.

And my dad—I could truly spend time with him. I had left the farm with my mother after the divorce and only saw him—and those acres of trees and green lands—during summer visits.

All the Burk daughters idolized him. Dad was thought of as a local

John Wayne for the selfless acts he performed in the community. If his car was stopped, the police officer would recognize him and let him go. I myself was at the farm when the game warden came to see him about a deer shot out of season. We were standing in the barn where said deer hung above us, dripping blood.

"I'm not going to look up," the game warden said. "But Val, you've got to be a little more careful. I realize you've been hunting here all your life, before the laws were passed, but you have to appreciate my position. I'm paid to uphold the law."

Then the game warden and Dad, old school pals, went into the house for lunch. What's for lunch? "Beefsteak." My father laughed uproariously as he served up the venison.

He was a jack of many trades. He could log and dairy-farm, raise racehorses, harrow a field of strawberries. Everything he did he did well. What he couldn't do was tolerate laziness or dishonesty. Then his notorious temper was likely to flare.

I wrote Dad and proposed we come and live with him. We were fed up with schedules: fed up, period. I painted in words the pictures Ray and I had imagined. Of raising beef cattle and tending the vegetable garden. Of salmon from nearby Puget Sound, of oysters and clams off the beach. I had convinced myself that with just a little labor, we'd be living off the fat of the land.

But I didn't stop there. Winter nights we would all play cards and have neighbors drop by. I'd serve fresh cake, hot berry pies. We'd play with Vance and Christi, and with Dad's daughters Valla and Annette. (One day Ann, Dad's wife, would flee the farm as my mother had, worn out from the dawn-to-dusk workload.)

My dad wrote me back. Of course we could come live with him. All Ray and I had left to do was pack our things, load up the car, and point it in the heavenly direction of Canada.

ONE FURTHER INCIDENT certainly had me itching to go. As the days counted down, I came home one evening as usual. Ray was at work. I was reading the paper, taking it easy, when I heard a knock at the door.

So I went and opened it a crack. It was Mr. Artino, the landlord. I opened the door.

"Is everything all right here?"

"As well as can be expected," I said. I hadn't changed out of my office clothes: turquoise Pendleton straight skirt, sheer nylon blouse—lingerie visible underneath, very fashionable at the time—and black leather high heels.

"Well, I'm just checking. I had to come out to fix a hot-water heater and it seemed a good time to stop and say hello."

"I'm glad you did." No sooner were the words out of my mouth than Mr. Artino clamped a thick, hairy hand on me.

"What the *hell*?!"

"You know, if it would make things easier, you don't have to pay me any rent." He was staring at my breasts under the sheer blouse. "Hardly anyone else out here does." He nodded in the direction of the longshoreman's house.

Before he could brag any further, I said quickly, "Well, I'd much rather pay my rent. Which, incidentally, isn't due until next week."

Mr. Artino had a leering smile plastered on his face. Maybe he was so used to simply having his way with other ladies on the street that he found a little resistance irresistible. I fixed him with what I hoped was a first-rate version of the evil eye.

"Listen, creep, if you think I'd let you chase me around my kitchen table for this squalid, mildew-ridden, little piece of trash house, think again. How dare you! Please leave right now!"

To my amazement he did exactly that. But I was shaking as I locked the front door shut behind him. Didn't he realize I had my kids in the next room? Or, worse, maybe he did. Well, good riddance, and good riddance to Artino Road, the sooner the better.

I saw our landlord again before we left, but Ray was there. Of course, I told Ray what had happened, but by then I found it more humorous than threatening. Artino could tell Ray knew. He was barely able to look us in the eye or get a word out. Not with my virile young husband standing there staring him down.

. . .

MOVING DAY. U-Haul packed, kids in the car, the phone company already a dimming memory, we headed off to Washington. Seven hundred miles later . . . we were lost.

Not seriously. But I had gotten confused. We had driven through Northern California, Oregon, and most of Washington uneventfully. Past Bellingham—where I had been born in Saint Luke's Hospital—we only had seventeen miles to go. Any farther north and we'd be in Canada.

Leaving the paved highway, we made a turn onto a dusty gravel road that led to my dad's place. That was when it hit me: I hadn't spent time on the farm since I was fourteen. Seven years ago. My mental map was a bit hazy. "I think you can reach Burk Road by turning off Badger Road onto Markworth," I directed Ray. "But I could be wrong."

I knew the worst that could happen staying straight on Badger was it would bring us to the little country store. I could get reoriented there. As a young girl I had ridden my horse down to buy licorice and Nesbitt's Orange Pop. (Later I added Pall Mall cigarettes and hair spray to my shopping loot.) Soon enough we did come to the store. Ray stopped the car, decided to go in.

It used to be clean and thriving. Now, in '61, the store was dusty and the shelves were almost bare. Ray bought some cold cereal the kids liked and a pack of cigarettes. When he got back in the car, he was fuming. The proprietor, missing teeth, in a dingy undershirt, and reeking of BO, had quibbled over a penny Ray was short. It was like a warning shot across the bow. He ranted to me: "It's ignorance in the air. It's in the water. Soon it will be in the blood." (When we opened the cereal it had little bugs in it.)

I reassured Ray that my dad's place wasn't anything like that. He'd love the big white two-story 1920s-style farmhouse. He'd see. My dad and Aunt May were going to have a big welcome mat out, and I'd bet the table was loaded with good things to eat. The fat of the land was waiting for us!

• • •

MY AUNT May had stood firmly behind my dad all his adult life. She was the aunt I doted on. I was her "girlie," her namesake. Her real name was Mary, and I was often called Mary, so that made us a pair. Aunt May never married. She stayed on the family farm to take care of her parents; she taught school. And worked as hard as any man. Morning and night, she milked a herd of cows. Every week she wrote for five local newspapers.

My father and Aunt May were partners, though neither was going to admit it. My dad worked around the clock to take care of both his land and hers, while she held all the cash. When his grocery tab got too high at the little country stores, she'd pay it off. (She was always afraid his debts would besmirch the family name.) She lived on Burk Road, named after my grandfather. He was a pioneer from Germany who settled the family's original 160-acre homestead in the 1880s.

Also nearby was my dad's oldest sister, Aunt Elsie. She and her husband, Glen Pettit, had a big yellow house in Custer, with spectacular flowers of every kind. Her angel food cake always took first prize at the Western Washington Fair. In the Pettits' estimation, no one else in the family measured up. Aunt Elsie had frowned on my dad's divorce and his living with Ann before they were married. I was pretty sure I'd never measure up, either.

But I sure gave it my best shot at Dad's place. I labored the way a farmwife does, from early morn to late at night. There were three full meals to be cooked and cleaned up after. The kitchen floor needed mopping at the end of every day. Clothes, sheets, and blankets awaited their turn in the wringer-washer. Then there was the shopping and baking and baby-sitting. I was so tired at night that I fell into bed and went into an instant stupor. Forget reading a word of the novel I'd begun.

My first response had been simple joy at being back in my childhood stomping grounds, but soon I had to face it: Things were very slow on Dad's farm. I'd never in my life seen it like this. Even the quality of

Dad's thoroughbred horses had deteriorated. I suddenly understood that life at fifty-nine wasn't as easy for him as it had been at thirty-nine or forty-nine. Equally evident, after my family had settled in, was that neither of us had much cash in our pockets. Even on a farm there are things you have to go out and buy.

"Are you as broke as I am, Deedle?" Dad asked.

"Yes," I said. "Getting here took all the money we were able to save. We had to take the money and run while we could."

As for Ray, he felt displaced. This was my familiar territory, exhilarating to me, but he found it alien and dispiriting. They say it's impossible for two women to share a home, but the two most important men in my life weren't doing any better. Ray was used to being king of the walk wherever we lived. Here he clearly wasn't.

With all his time free to write, and a room to himself to do it in, Ray found his creative imagination knocked out of the box. He had to face it. His belief that he could write anywhere *if only he had the time* was simply untrue.

Eventually Ray wrote a story based on the move to the farm ("Cartwheels," also called, "How About This?"). But in the meantime, there we were, a few sharp, unpalatable truths spiking our summer balloons of heady optimism.

IN LIFE FEW moments are as truly abrupt as when your husband announces: "*We* are moving." That's what Ray said to me one morning after we had been at the farm about six weeks. Unbeknownst to me he had already written his dad to borrow money to get us back to California. It had come the day before.

Dad and I had been savoring our time together, just as when I was little. We loved each other as deeply as ever. But he took the news of our impending departure intelligently and stoically. He didn't say anything, just nodded his head when I explained that Ray had decided to finish college. We were heading back to California.

Remember our liking for inspiring mottos? I had a new one: You always hurt the one you love. Sound familiar?

· · ·

SEVEN HUNDRED more miles later, welcome to Arcata. Our rented house was far and away the best we'd ever had. That blue-green, two-story Victorian at 1590 I Street was like a child's dollhouse wonderfully enlarged. For years afterward, whenever I dreamed of halcyon family days, that was the house we were in. Ray confided that it was the same for him.

The first floor had a large kitchen, dining room, bathroom, living room, and a huge study at one end, perfect for Ray. Upstairs there were four bedrooms and a bathroom. Our master bedroom had an old-fashioned slanted ceiling and a large walk-in closet.

Christi and Vance each had little rooms so high up they could look over the rooftops to the tall steeples of the tidy churches. They could see our garage below where they rode their trikes and played, and the backyard with the garden and a riot of flowers. They felt immersed in nature. Once they broke the windows in the garage—to our profound exasperation— because they wanted to let in the rain and wind.

But if there was a room Ray found irresistible, perhaps except our

Our house in the college town of Arcata from 1961 to 1963.
PHOTO BY MARYANN BURK CARVER

bedroom when I was in it, it was his study. He showed it off immediately to anyone new to the house. Best of all he loved to write there. I can still picture him sitting in that big square room with the high ceiling, and through a window, the backyard profusion of peonies, crocuses, the snowball tree, tulips, daffodils, primroses, and rhododendrons.

In his study he had a huge bookcase filled with his favorite books, and a large oak desk. There was a leather couch along one wall where friends would sit and visit with him. It was a room for writing—and for talking about writing.

His friends the poets Jon Remmerde and David Pierce had also transferred from Chico. These three musketeers of literature had lofty ambitions. Why couldn't Humboldt State College make a name for itself in literary circles? Toward that end Ray took on the editing of the student magazine, *Toyon*. To keep the quality as high as possible, he wrote several entries himself under pseudonyms and dismissed any notion that the work of as many creative writing students as possible should be included.

That was Ray in action. The end in mind justified virtually any means to achieve it. His talent and charm often led others to believe he was actually right.

THAT FALL I was a college freshman. At last. Just being back in school was a shimmering joy. In my excitement my heart sounded so loud to me that I wondered if my classmates could hear it. Here at last. Here at last.

Yes, wasn't this the world I had trusted in? I was twenty-one, married to the man I loved more every day. We were both students, sharing a life, no longer stranded with jobs at opposite ends of the day. The kids had a wonderful nursery school nearby and a safe yard to play in. We were a part of a college community, not commuters, making new friends with people we felt were our peers. It kept on getting better.

Even work wasn't so bad. I was a waitress at Sambo's Pancake House out on Highway 101 in Eureka. I had the two-to-ten-p.m. shift, four days a week. Knowing the kids were with their dad, I could go off to work lighthearted. With tips I was making ten dollars an hour—and those tips were mine immediately. What a relief to have cash in my purse when we needed it, instead of always being short until the next payday.

Ray worked at the new college library, chiefly with David Palmer. Dave was a first-rate reference librarian and a poet. His wife, Charlene, was also a poet, and an excellent oil painter. The Palmers came to Humboldt from Berkeley and were very hip, quasi–role models for us.

David took great pride in knowing how to look up any kind of information, and enthusiastically showed Ray and me the process. Maybe it was all the hours Ray spent there, but he seemed especially alert and knowledgeable at Humboldt, informed about everything that mattered. He could wear the best clothes he had, rather than a grungy mill outfit, and sit warm and dry at a desk, a wealth of reading material always available. At the library Ray always smiled openly and quickly when I visited. That was a good sign. Ray actually *liked* his job.

Our other stroke of fortune was the new boarder in our house. We had persuaded Amy to come and attend Humboldt, too. She was slowly recovering from Harry's death. We wanted to shield and comfort her.

My sister, the family actress, became the star of Humboldt's major college drama productions: an adaptation of Henry James's *The Turn of the Screw*, Brecht's *The Good Woman of Szechuan*, and of course Shakespeare. Playful eyes on Amy, the drama professor and director, Jerry Turner, would quote from *Antony and Cleopatra*: "[O]ther women Cloy the appetites they feed, but she makes hungry Where most she satisfies" (2.2). High praise indeed coming from Jerry, who was also the director of the Oregon Shakespearean Festival at Ashland for twenty years (1971–91).

With Amy around to help out, we managed to have a social life again, despite all the hours we put in working and studying. Dick Day, Dave Palmer, and their wives were the mainstays of our set. At our house close to the college, we had as many faculty at our parties as students. The I Street house also became a hangout for Amy's drama friends, who liked to pour in after rehearsals.

Down at the Keg, a student dive, Ray, Dick, and other friends hung out over draft beers. They talked about Swiss novelist and playwright Max Frisch, Henry Miller, and the old standbys—Hemingway, Faulkner, Steinbeck, John O'Hara, Robert Penn Warren. Dick could take up a whole evening speaking about Ken Kesey, or people he knew from the Iowa Writers' Workshop like Ray B. West, Bill Knotts, "Curt" Harnack and his wife, Hortense Calisher, and Ed Skillings.

They also discussed the wild literary scene in San Francisco. An older generation of writers, the so-called Beat Generation, frequented poet Lawrence Ferlinghetti's bookstore, City Lights. The notoriety of Jack Kerouac's *On the Road*, published in 1957, had propelled this loose group of freethinking, freewheeling artists and individualists into a public attention they largely held in contempt. These writers were still on the cutting edge in the early sixties, but there was a sense that their creative high was running out . . . or was it the Benzedrine?

We'd head to San Francisco when we could. It was an eight-hour drive. You went down through the redwood groves and little towns of Scotia, Fortuna, Pepperwood, until you got to the wine country around Napa, and finally on down into the city. We'd visit City Lights and take in the neighborhood: loud, joyful music coming from shop doorways, irreverent posters hanging in the stores, bars with old wooden furnishings serving Irish and Venetian coffee. We went to clubs like the hungry i and the Purple Onion, featuring avant-garde comedians like Mort Sahl and Dick Gregory doing their acid commentaries on social and political life.

Back in Arcata we literary aficionados excitedly discussed just "who was who" on the West Coast and "what was what" in contemporary literature. Something new was faintly in the literary air.

THE 1961 FALL semester bustled away in a lovely whirl, and by Christmas I'd say things were looking up across the board. I was part of the college scene, at twenty-one, a coed. Surprisingly Mom's marriage to Clarence was thriving—the first year of nearly forty they had together— and her bills were paid off. This year she could buy all the gifts she wanted. Ray's family was better. His dad had rebounded with steely determination. They were living in Eureka, and he was temporarily employed at a mill.

C. R. was able to host the family Christmas gathering, buying food, liquor, and gifts. He was laughing again, chuckling as he lined up pop, candy, and gum in a long row for his grandchildren. He loved seeing their eyes widen as they waited to dive into the bounty he was providing.

AS 1962 CAME waltzing in, I found out that I had won a scholarship that paid for my tuition and books. My late-night hours of study in the kitchen and many glued-to-the-books library sessions had paid off. My grades were excellent, a 3.89 average. The two years I was at Humboldt, I was always on the President's Honor Roll.

My second semester I took Introductory English and History, plus two upper-division courses: Aesthetics with Dr. Clarence Howe and a course on Shakespeare taught by the formidable professor Dr. Reginald White. My adviser had suggested that these courses might be out of my league. I let him have it with my "life CV" to date, implying that I was old enough and prepared enough to take any course. "Every semester I'm in school may be my last," I pleaded.

He acquiesced, readily sympathizing with me. Telling the truth worked! I couldn't get over how humane and reasonable the ivory tower was, compared with the so-called real world. This beat pounding the streets practically begging for work.

As an upperclassman, Ray took an independent study course reading Russian literature with Dr. Thewall Proctor. Proc, as everyone called him, was a Russian-language instructor—and fencing teacher. He loved acting and actors and appeared in many ambitious productions himself. Gay—and in those days necessarily in the closet—he often came to our house to visit Amy. He adored her and sensitively provided diversionary trips to San Francisco when she needed them.

Ray went through all the Russian masters—Pushkin, Turgenev, Gogol, Tolstoy, Chekhov, Gorky, and Dostoyevsky. In their discussions Proc was amazed at some of Ray's original insights. Enthusiastic, he encouraged Ray to attempt critical essays and he would try to get them published. But

Ray wasn't interested. Writing was the primary act; criticism was secondary. (Later in life Ray disciplined himself to write book reviews and essays, much as he'd done to turn out papers for his academic courses.)

One night Proc told me, "You won't be working so hard forever, you know—the way you are now, Maryann. Your main job in the future will be to organize literary soirées and get-togethers, which is your forte anyway. The presentation of your sweet hospitality will become your enduring pleasure and legacy."

Smiling at that pronouncement, I could see it all. Our ultimate family motto: A walk in the sunshine. That's what we'll ultimately have. With our constant penny-pinching, I thought of Ray's glorious gesture of defiance: He'd wad up a rejected page into a ball even if it had only a few lines on it and throw it aside, until the study floor was a sea of discards.

Slowly "the Humboldt stories" (as we privately called them) emerged. Written at Artino Road and I Street, they included: "The Night the Mill Boss Died" (later titled "The Ducks"); "Pastoral" (later "The Cabin"); "Sometimes a Woman Can Almost Ruin a Man" (later "What Do You Do in San Francisco?"); "The Father," "The Hair," and "Mine." Along with "The Furious Seasons"—Ray's first published short story in *Selection 2* (Winter 1960–61)—these were his earliest truly polished works if yet unpublished.

Nothing was as exciting for me as Ray saying, "I've got a draft of a story to show you now, Maryann!" All the magic in the universe gathered in his study when we read and analyzed the first draft of a story or poem, our cups of hot coffee together on the floor beside us.

THE PACE OF our lives ramped up again in the spring semester. On weekends, I was now working mornings at Sambo's, starting at 5:30 A.M. Often I'd stay up all night on the principle that there was no point in going to bed at 4:00 only to get up at 5:00. Yet Ray had to take another part-time mill job to keep our rickety finances stable, while he seemed to have more things than ever going on at Humboldt State. We went nonstop—studying, working, writing, caring for the kids, seeing friends, partying, deflecting flirtations.

Ray with the kids, dressed in "twin" outfits from their grandmother Ella.
COURTESY OF JAMES CARVER

Oh, well, let's get at it: Flirtations. It was a perennial mystery to me that it was so difficult to be an innocent friend with a member of the opposite sex. Cerebral friendships always seemed to degenerate into sexual situations when that was the last thing I wanted. My preference for men sprang from the different way they thought. They seemed more able to take risks and think for themselves. Men were more original, less petty and constrained, I thought. Didn't every man agree?

I certainly found Maurie's mind superior. He was Jewish, maybe the best student of philosophy at Humboldt. I enjoyed his incisive remarks in class and afterward over cups of coffee at the cafeteria, when we discussed philosophical questions. He came to dinner at our house, but Ray was oddly curt and dismissive.

One evening Maurie and I were talking in the study at the house when Ray walked in. We both got a classic case of the stammers. Let's face it, when Maurie and I were together, we fell into a sort of mental lust that might conceivably have gone further. But it never did. What might have happened if Ray hadn't come home early, I'm not sure. I was glad to see him, though. It snapped me out of the dreamlike state I had fallen into. With Ray there, all lust disappeared. I never felt with Maurie that—unnerving-to-me—physical quickening again.

I was not without women friends, however. I cherished them. My Arcata friends were smart and confident, usually attractive. One in particular became a lifelong friend, Bonnie Day, Dick's wife at the time.

When I first met her, before she had her kids, Bonnie was as slender and tiny as a child. Yet she had the oldest, wisest eyes imaginable. She was an "old soul" before I knew what the expression meant. Dave Palmer would affectionately roll her name over his tongue, Bonnie Day, Bonnie Day. He said her name was a found poem, that Bonnie herself was a kind of living poem. Many thought she was. Ray and I never met anyone more consistently and sincerely considerate of other people.

One morning Ray moved aside our white organdy kitchen curtains and saw Bonnie skipping down the street. She wore a yellow cotton sleeveless dress, her waist tiny, the color high in her cheeks, her black hair glistening. I never forgot the tender look on Ray's face. "It's Bonnie," Ray said softly. "It's Bonnie Day. She's skipping down the street." He got up to open the door for her and welcome her in for coffee. She was a shining, magical, joyous sprite, a muse, and the friend I would turn to when my own days grew less fair and bright.

RAY WAS ON a personal roll. Simultaneously he got word that a story and a poem were accepted for publication. From Utah came the news that "Pastoral" was to appear in *Western Humanities Review*. His poem "The Brass Ring" had been accepted by *Target*, a little magazine published in Arizona. The envelope with correspondence from *Target* enclosed a check for a dollar.

When news of Ray's double publication got out on the grapevine, we entertained people dropping by to congratulate him for three days before our lives returned to anything like normal. We were incredibly high and happy the entire time. We didn't mind telling the story over and over again, certain now that Ray was going to be published in the greater world. This was just the beginning.

Was there anything Ray couldn't do? The next thing the Humboldt campus was abuzz about was Ray's first play. *Carnations* was inspired by the likes of Antonin Artaud and influenced by the Theater of the Absurd playwrights that Ray had been reading and studying in Jerry Turner's class. He missed work to advise the student director, who—although well meaning—was at a total loss. Ray felt he was having his own minor existential crisis: his night mill job or a decent production of the play.

His friends and I all suffered along with Ray on the night of the performance. One scene has the solitary, despairing narrator sitting at a simple little table in a room. Suddenly he jumps up and tears down the set walls imprisoning him, only to lapse into more despair: "I must take some action." Some in the audience laughed uproariously while others were mystified. I was out in the hallway, much too nervous to watch. Afterward we had drinks with our good friends to celebrate the performance being over and behind us, thank God.

(Ray wrote one other play at Humboldt. *The Man Who Died* was an adaptation of a D. H. Lawrence story. I thought it was terrific, but Ray put it aside. I didn't have enough energy left to give him the boost of enthusiasm he needed to overcome his smarting sense of letdown from his first play. He didn't seek a college production.)

The next remarkable thing Ray did was rent a room for himself in a big old house a few blocks away. He wanted to work at night, totally undisturbed, he explained. I was surprised. That gave way to almost-rage as I realized I was supposed to baby-sit the kids and then occupy our empty bed. Didn't he have a perfectly good study at home, one I busted my rear end to pay for? "Well, if things have come to this," I said as snottily as I could, "better I'm twenty-one than fifty-one. The nice thing, though, is I'll never have to worry about being taken to bed again." Ray turned pale at those words. I carefully committed them to memory, in case I ever needed to repeat myself.

The novelty of his rented room wore off quickly enough. When it came right down to it, Ray didn't like to be alone. And he couldn't afford the rent. He moved his writing paraphernalia back home. I gave him back the key he had given me to his place.

WELL, RAY DECIDED to attend the summer session so he could take the science and PE classes he needed to graduate. That would let him finish his undergraduate work by the end of the current year, the sooner the better.

Of course before the 1962 summer session began, we moved out of the house. It seemed like a good idea at the time. (And then we would move back *into* the house, because, among other reasons, it was now spotlessly neat and tidy.) I guess I better explain. Our friends spent three days and nights helping us clean, pack, and load up boxes, plus our camping gear, in the car and U-Haul. Ray and I were very tired from final exams and what we called "work, work, work." We thought if we could just quit punching a time clock, everything would be all right. We'd go and camp in Richardson's Grove, a favorite spot for the kids, with no jobs, no housework, no damn time clock. Bliss.

Before we even got as far as Eureka, though, I turned to Ray and said, "I hate like hell to admit this, Ray, but this is a terrible mistake. I have to tell you that." I hadn't given the landlady notice or quit my job, either. Maybe on some level I knew that I should wait before burning any bridges. Ray must have been thinking the same thing, as he turned the car around without a word of protest. Months of life ahead in a tent would never do for us. While Ray did the summer session?

People heard we came back. Ray and I laughed at our folly—our friends had made all that effort for us. Our friends laughed, too. A few more drinks and a party would get under way, and before long it would be another "remember the time when . . . ," classic in the making. We were the Carvers. Honestly, people expected this sort of thing from us.

Now we were set for the summer. Ray could work at the library, attend his classes. I would work full-time at Sambo's. We'd all pitch in and baby-sit the kids. (Amy was leaving, not fully healed from Harry's loss but wanting to pursue a professional acting career.)

My God, we really needed a vacation. How could we manage it? The answer, unexpectedly, came from my tips jar.

First, though, I was oddly dispirited on my birthday. Twenty-two. For the first time in my life, I wasn't thrilled to be another year older. I could legally drink, I could vote, and I already smoked and drove. So, another birthday? What gain? To be a year older and working at Sambo's, one day like the next?

That evening we visited the Palmers, then came home for birthday cake. I was still pretty blue. To distract myself, I suppose, I decided to empty out the tips jar. Ray's eyes almost popped out. He couldn't believe all the change stashed in the jar. He and the kids wanted to count it.

They got out muffin tins and heaped up coins, twenty dollars a tin. Vance was rubbing his eyes but stuck to the task; Christi counted out dimes faster and faster. Finally I'd had enough. I went upstairs to lie down. I read a book—after setting the alarm for an ungodly early hour. I had to work again.

Ray came to bed, his face flushed and excited by the final tally. Half asleep, I whispered, "Let's go on vacation as soon as we can. Let's take off. Travel the Oregon Coast. Make our way to Seattle. The World's Fair." Let's spend all that tip money, I was thinking, and suddenly I was very happy.

WE DROVE HIGHWAY 101 north. We first stayed at an old inn in Brookings, Oregon; visited Olympia, Washington, the state capital; and rode the Monorail from downtown Seattle to the heart of the World's Fair. What a blast! Then we headed another hundred miles north to see Dad and Aunt May. We left Christi and Vance with them while Ray and I crossed over into Canada and visited Vancouver.

Back at the farm, the last day of our visit before we hit the road for home, my dad had a doctor's appointment in Bellingham. It was only the third time in his life he'd seen a doctor. Dad had decided to get a physical and apply for early Social Security at sixty-two. Logging and running the whole farm operation by himself was getting lonely and tough, especially in the wintertime.

I decided he should wear a nice shirt to the doctor's. I plucked a wrinkled one out of a pile of clean clothes and started ironing it.

Dad caught me at the ironing board and said, "Don't bother with that, Deedle. Give it to me the way it is."

He smiled as he watched me put a perfect crease in one sleeve, but he was fidgeting noticeably. I was halfway done when he grabbed the shirt off the ironing board and put it on. He was back in control, the way he liked it.

"Dad, give me that shirt back! It looks worse than if I'd never touched it."

"I told you so," he laughed. He went on buttoning the shirt.

"C'mon, Dad. It'll only take a second to finish. You can't go to town that way!"

Dad looked into my eyes, his expression amused as he gave me a big kiss on the cheek. He headed out the kitchen door. "A hundred years from now, Deedle, what difference will it make?"

SOMETIMES YOU THINK life is about to slow down a little and then it does the opposite. August gone, our vacation over, the fall of 1962 barreled in. We never stopped running. Ray was in his last semester, after successfully completing his summer classes—thanks in part to a friendly professor of science—and I had signed up for a full course load. I took political science, a course called History of Political Theory, and three classes in history, philosophy, and literature.

That October the Cuban missile crisis erupted. The boys in my political theory class—I was the only woman—were revved up—not that they were in line for military duty. The Russians pulled out their missiles. Life went on.

BEFORE WE KNEW it Christmas and family gatherings flashed by and Ray finished his course work. In January 1963 he received his BA from Humboldt State College. That promptly led to a new dilemma.

I had my spring classes at Humboldt. Ray had found a job at a university biology library in Berkeley. Obviously this was the wrong time to pull up stakes, especially with the kids happily in the Arcata nursery school. Instead we'd reluctantly live apart for a few months, traveling back and forth when we could, until I could join Ray when school was out for the summer.

In Berkeley the most glamorous thing Ray had to report about the biology library was that he was working with Eartha Kitt's son. But out on the streets that spring and summer of '63, it was a restless, hip America. Mario Savio reigned on campus, and "free speech" brought hundreds, even thousands, to hear him and others speak. What they had to say was startlingly different from the mass media. It was a mistake to send "advisers" to Vietnam. Hadn't we learned anything from the French?

Visiting Ray, I listened spellbound to radical speeches. I couldn't get enough of Telegraph Avenue, where Black Muslims spoke of Malcolm X and Elijah Muhammad on a street lined with cool jazz joints and folk music bars. There were foreign-film cinemas; bookstores and record shops; clothing stores with wild, colorful outfits; and everywhere you looked, these ultraliberal young people.

June couldn't come fast enough for me. I wanted to get back to the happening scene as soon as I could.

BERKELEY WAS A place where everyone seemed to be doing things they'd never done before. One Friday, Ray came home a little late from work. He looked different but very happy. Everything made him laugh, and, man, was he hungry. First he ate almost a whole pan of brownies, and then he tied into the spareribs. All before dinner.

"What on earth has gotten into you, Ray?"

He confessed to smoking a marijuana cigarette. He gave a ride to some guy he worked with at the library, who invited him in for a smoke.

"Oh, I see," I said, not seeing at all. I hadn't tried marijuana, but I knew it was supposed to turn you automatically into a heroin addict practically overnight. Much to my relief, nothing happened to Ray. Well, we were learning more and more that the "establishment" wasn't necessarily telling the truth. A lovely, exciting summer in Berkeley was all to the good. But what were we going to do next?

Dick Day had been writing to everyone he knew that the Iowa Writers' Workshop would be missing out on a special writer if they didn't get Ray Carver. But it looked as if Ray was in fact going to miss that boat. We were basically broke anyway. How would we pay for more school? If we didn't laugh, we'd cry.

Then, unbelievably, there it was. A letter for Ray. Admitting him to the University of Iowa Graduate Program in Creative Writing and awarding him a thousand-dollar stipend.

9

IOWA CITY

We were on our way to Iowa. Immediately. We had never seen the American heartland, or even been curious about it. Our destination, Iowa City, was reputedly the "Athens of the Midwest." There, they said, was a place where writers and writing were of paramount importance.

Berkeley long behind us, we drove endless miles with the kids through Nevada, Utah, and Nebraska, onward toward someplace called Des Moines. From that city it was going to be a hundred miles and more farther east to the university.

We were not out of the Nevada desert when I said to Ray, "You know what I realize already? The revolution is *not* just around the corner. Back in Iowa, I'll bet the prettiest girls in town will be twirling batons as they strut in short skirts, leading the local bands to the city park for an old-fashioned Fourth of July picnic."

In Berkeley there had been a cloud of propaganda from proponents of radical change. I suspected that what we'd been hearing had absolutely nothing to do with what was going on in the rest of the United States.

How right I was!

Iowa City turned out to be a little oasis, surrounded by acres and acres of farmland. In the lush, green summers, cornfields and hog farms were the two most visible parts of the landscape. In the long winters, the same landscape and the now treacherous roads were frozen under sheets of ice and snow.

When we arrived, in August, it was hot and muggy. The talk of the natives was of tornadoes and the necessity of storing two weeks' worth of supplies against the dreadful winter ahead. That was the summer Jackie Kennedy was pregnant, and so was everyone else in Washington who could manage it. Martin Luther King, Jr., marched to the Lincoln Memorial, and on August 28, 1963, said to his fellow Americans, "I have a dream." It was the largest civil rights demonstration in U.S. history. In Iowa I promptly came down with a wicked summer cold.

I took antibiotics until side effects caused me more misery than the illness. I quit the pills and gratefully went back to bronchitis, convinced anyway that my discomfort was largely a metaphysical response to the American heartland. Coming from Berkeley, I felt I'd fallen into a time warp and wound up in the early fifties, or maybe it was the forties. The locals seemed so dowdy and old-fashioned. Did all the women have to wear cotton housedresses and pin-curled hair parted on the left side? Was it was some de rigueur style?

As I recuperated, I was reading Nikos Kazantzakis's *Report to Greco*. The narrator's head swells to twice its normal size—I could relate—on a journey to Russia, but it dawns on him that the root of his bizarre incapacitation is "soul-sickness."

Right.

I knew I had to marshal my own inner strength and positive energy to deal with our sojourn in dismaying Iowa. I cautioned myself, Don't look at the map and see how far away you are from family and friends. Hopefully I'd also stop coughing soon.

No matter what, we were here for a reason. Ray enrolled in the two-year MFA program of the Writers' Workshop, his stipend money in hand. I enrolled in undergraduate classes at the university, a schedule of philosophy, French, history, and Russian literature. And started looking for a job.

· · ·

THE WAGE SCALE in Iowa City was very low—when any jobs were available at all. After much effort I landed a waitressing gig at the University Athletic Club, a private country club frequented by both businesspeople and University of Iowa faculty. As for housing, we had landed temporarily in the Hawkeye Trailer Park. We had a makeshift trailer that cost too much money for what it was.

That was where Christi started kindergarten; naturally, a milestone in our family life. She went off to Mann Elementary School with a new, soft permanent that made her look just like Shirley Temple. No little girl was prettier, we thought. Every day she came home happy and confident. Christi plunked down her drawings for us and wide-eyed Vance to see and sang the new songs she was learning, "Itzy Bitzy Spider" and "I Went to the Animal Fair."

Cheaper housing opened up through the university. We jumped on it, even though it meant moving again, but I cried the first time I went to our assigned unit. The housing for married students was in converted Quonset huts, relics of World War II. I sat on our double bed, deposited in the living room, and looked at the cement floors and the high little windows. There was a small heater that smelled of oil fumes. I felt incarcerated. In the kitchen all the cupboards were open, bare, splintering.

Christi had to change schools. A cruel prank by two local kids left her so badly shaken that I felt she never recaptured her original enthusiasm. These two kids ran off when she was walking with them to the school. Christi was left far behind. Terrified, she ran after them, desperately afraid of being lost. Her tormentors sped out of sight. She gave up hope. Then, somehow, she spotted her new school.

That evening my little five-year-old was sick with fever. Her temperature shot up alarmingly, 102, then 106. She was delirious. Utterly traumatized, I ran for Ray. Christi was lying in our darkened bedroom. As we came in she shrank back in terror and uttered a little scream.

Ray instantly realized how we appeared, backlit in the doorway. "Put out that cigarette!" he said to me sharply. "See how we must look to her?

Like a couple of ghouls. And you, smoking a cigarette! We're terrifying her."

"I'm sorry. I'm so sorry." I didn't know I was smoking. Crying and distraught, I said, "Oh, Christi baby, it's Mama and Daddy. We love you. We're going to put a blanket around you and take you to the doctor."

We brought her to University Hospital. The excellent staff began emergency measures to bring down the fever. They gave her antibiotics, cold enemas, and applied cold cloths. It was touch and go, but finally the fever broke. Thank God, she was going to pull through. She was going to be okay.

I had only been going to classes for a month, but in the wake of Christi's illness I decided to drop out. I had to give her the best care I possibly could, nurse her back to full health. My job at the club I couldn't quit, but the rest of my time I'd devote to Christi and Vance to reassure them and give them confidence in this alien Iowan environment.

I had no regrets. But I missed school dreadfully, the activity and mental stimulation, a sense of moving toward a degree and my own career. Instead I slogged on with the tiresome work at the club, took care of the kids, and tried to support Ray with his own difficult transition to the environment of what everyone called "the Workshop."

YOU'D THINK A self-important outfit like the University Athletic Club would be a better place to work than a Sambo's on 101, but you'd be wrong. Here condescension smacked you in the face. In my black-nylon-and-white-apron waitress costume, I was required to play servile help to the haves of Iowa City. You had to watch your step, too. Any rule infraction could get you bounced out the door, with no union protection or other recourse.

I put up with it for one reason. On Big Ten football days I made as much as three hundred dollars in tips.

The liquor would flow. Live music filtered in from the ballroom. Mammoth sides of prime rib were wheeled in, one after another, and left on display in the dining room next to an ice swan carved by the master chef. (It was usually melting by midevening.) The staff worked like crazy until the diners thinned out, when we could stand respectfully in the background like Cinderella's shadow.

Thankfully I found an ally, another waitress. Rose had been a stripper and go-go dancer in Kansas City. (She proudly showed me pictures of herself dancing in a plastic cage in a getup of feathers and sequins.) At thirty-four she had married a nice hunk of a guy who took her away from all that and brought her to Iowa.

Rose had seen better days. Her front teeth had cavities that cried out for care. She was a lot sturdier than in her dancing days, and her hair was obviously dyed jet black. She couldn't utter a grammatical sentence. But Rose was unfailingly good to me.

She taught me little tricks about preparing butter and relish dishes when I set up for dinner. She taught me how to close up. She saw to it that I did things right so I could hold on to my job. And she understood how badly my family needed the money. She knew what that meant.

And what were the UAC's patrons like? Some were decent people, particularly some of the university professors. But a lot of them . . . they had no use for the rest of humanity.

IT WAS A day in late November. I'd gotten my paycheck, and the whole family went off to Woolworth's to buy Christi a child-size umbrella. Ray liked the plaid one, so Christi did, too.

Back home, the kids turned on TV. The soap opera *As the World Turns* was surreally interrupted by a bulletin slide and Walter Cronkite's voice saying: "In Dallas, Texas, three shots were fired at President Kennedy's motorcade in downtown Dallas. First reports say President Kennedy has been seriously wounded by this shooting."

"Oh, no! Our president, our president!" Ray and I said it together. We hung on to hope, we sat frozen in front of the TV until the greatly saddened newscaster intoned, "The president is dead."

That night the staff hoped UAC management would close the place out of respect for our slain president. But it was business as usual on

November 22. I was scheduled to work, so I had to. I had to watch people eat heartily and dance as usual. Several of us, waitress-flies-on-the-wall, saw a table of fat cats lift their drinks to toast the new times. One of them expressed regret that they hadn't gotten Jackie, too.

That was the American heartland attitude to me. Raise a toast to Mencken's boobs and philistines.

HIS FIRST SEMESTER, Ray was assigned to Professor R. V. Cassill's fiction-writing class. Tom Doherty and Joy Williams, Ray's friends, were classmates. Cassill loved Tom's and Joy's work and sent their stories to the *Saturday Evening Post* and other places in New York where he had connections. Before coming to Iowa, Ray had published more work than any of the new students, but he was quiet and inconspicuous in class. Cassill didn't seem to be aware of him.

Ray thought Cassill was brilliant when he lectured. I went with Ray the day Cassill discussed Thomas Mann's *Joseph and His Brothers*. He was persuasive, and I was very taken with his philosophically subtle argument that "Joseph's tragic flaw was that he had no tragic flaw."

Near the end of the semester, Ray turned in a story, a course requirement. Cassill really disliked it. He thought Ray's work was unjustifiably pessimistic. "Life couldn't possibly be that grim, could it?" he commented with dry sarcasm.

Ray felt he had to stand on principle. The tone and the events were true. He wasn't revising the story to suit Cassill's viewpoint. But he was hurt and angered by the negative response. His other teachers—John Gardner, Dick Day—had loved his work even if they made critical comments, so this blanket criticism was something new.

Cassill, on the other hand, felt it was his job to red-pencil student ideas and conceptions as readily as he ticked mistakes in syntax. If a story wasn't true to life, he wasn't buying it. For him a story of a relentlessly grim world, of characters buffeted by circumstances beyond their control, was apparently unthinkable. Or perhaps he simply wasn't going to put up with a student who didn't willingly play the game and placate the professor.

The upshot: Ray got an "Incomplete." Dick had warned him about the Workshop: "With all the backbiting and competitive infighting, one has to be careful not to come out of there with a ragged asshole." No kidding. But what was the family that had given up everything for Ray to study at the Workshop going to come away with?

It was a sad, depressing time. We had loved President Kennedy and his beautiful young family and couldn't see how our country could ever be happy or innocent again. In our own little world we didn't have the money to go west for Christmas.

A NEW YEAR began in freezing-cold Iowa. For his second semester, Ray drew a wonderful teacher. Call it Irish luck—Bryan McMahon was on leave for a half year from his secondary-school teaching job in county Kerry, and clearly enthralled by the opportunity. Probably in his mid-fifties, he was the author of a volume of stories, *The World Is Lovely, The World Is Wide*. Like a father to his children, he told his ultracompetitive graduate students that this world could use every one of them. There couldn't be too many good writers. He suggested that they needn't try extinguishing one another.

Professor McMahon was very supportive of Ray. He invited us out to drinks at the Colonial Inn, a restaurant outside Iowa City. Warm and cordial, he complimented Ray on his pretty wife, which made me feel special and genuinely welcome. It was a pleasant contrast to the typical attitude at the Workshop. Wives were basically undistinguished nonentities, and if you weren't some sort of artist, intellectually worse than useless.

At student dinners and parties I didn't like the put-downs. I was presumably a nobody. Not an artist, not creative—just a parasite on the Great Man. In a couple the male was automatically assumed to be the writer. (Our friend Joy Williams was a rare exception.) Women writers weren't encouraged, nor did they put themselves forward. Everyone *knew* that as soon as a woman married and had children, her talent would shrivel and she'd gratefully step into the background.

No one at these cocktail parties and gatherings gave writers' wives any

credit. But they worked so that their husbands could write. They kept the children quiet. They edited and suggested and consoled their Great Men through years of rejection slips and meager income. When and if the good times arrived, they could only watch as superficial friends surrounded the newly acknowledged Great Man, eager to take him away to bigger and better things.

If I hadn't liked many of the grad students I met, at least I was happy to know the neighbors. Celia and Adrian Mitchell lived in the housing unit in back of us. They were not students. Adrian was a British writer and had a one-year teaching contract at the Workshop. As for Iowa, when the year ended, the Mitchells could hardly wait to sell their belongings and return to civilized society in London.

They were witty, fashionable, sophisticated people, whether discussing their politics as committed socialists or the really proper dress for a faculty dinner party. Adrian preferred his tuxedo and lustrous black shoes. Celia ought to come arrayed in one of her innumerable elegant "terrace gowns." He had been a reporter on Fleet Street, and Celia was a professional actress, working with the likes of Kenneth Tynan.

On their rare evenings at home, they had us over to listen to Adrian's vintage jazz collection. It was there, too, that we first heard of the Beatles—before they were on *The Ed Sullivan Show* or known at all in the United States. Adrian's last reporting assignment in England, prior to coming to Iowa, was to write a contemporary music piece. He had made a trip to Liverpool to interview "these four lads" in a new rock and roll group. The band's music joined elements of Little Richard and Elvis and something it was hard to put your finger on.

We found ourselves a little envious of the lives of our English friends. This had never happened before. We were untroubled by the philistines who had money but lacked any sense of art or culture. We had something better: genuine ideals. Yet here were Adrian and Celia, also dedicated to the arts but still able to travel, dress well, and lead a glamorous life—to have it all.

We liked them a lot. Celia made me laugh and expanded my vision of life. I told Ray one evening after a visit with them, "I feel like a naive American character out of Henry James. Celia's disdain of Iowa was infectious, however, and I wondered how we were going to prevent a further deterioration in our own attitude. We still had a year and a half to go.

NEAR MIDNIGHT THE telephone rang.

It was a dark, cold Iowa night, January 21, 1964. Christi and Vance had long been asleep, but Ray and I were up. All the lights were on to give us some illusion of warmth.

Ray answered the phone. His face was intent as he listened, but he didn't say anything more except good-bye. He turned to me, somber and grave. "Maryann, your dad died." He waited to see how I was reacting. I wasn't. "Honey, it's your dad."

"What?" I couldn't believe it. It was impossible. *Impossible*. My dad? He was the strongest person I knew. How could he die? "Who called?" I was shivering uncontrollably.

"Western Union," Ray said. "They read me a telegram from Aunt Elsie." I must have looked bewildered. "God, honey, I don't know any more than what I've told you." He opened his arms, and I went into them.

The next day, as early as I dared, I tried to reach Aunt May. I called her person-to-person at Aunt Elsie's house. I hated to phone there, but where else could she be? There was no other relative close by. Aunt Elsie

had disassociated herself from my dad since he and my mother divorced. That had been nearly two decades ago.

When the phone was picked up, I heard the long-distance operator
ask for Mary Burk. Aunt Elsie replied as if still composing telegrams in
her head: "She's not here. She went to see dead brother at funeral home."

"Dead brother." Those two words in Aunt Elsie's cold, heartless tone
made Dad's death a reality, all those long, long miles away.

I had to make plans to travel back, to go and see him. I was both saddened and angered by our financial constraints that locked me into help-
lessness. Only Aunt May could possibly come up with the money I
needed.

THE BURK SISTERS were scattered. I was in Iowa. Amy was in Sausalito, living with her actor boyfriend, Michael Wright, on a houseboat.
They were drama students at San Francisco State. Jerry, traditionally so
capable when the family distress flags went up, was living over in Anacortes, a small, peninsular town in Washington. She had married Gordon, had an eighteen-month-old son (her fourth), and was pregnant
again. Her hands were beyond totally full. She had just moved into a
new apartment, so she didn't even have a number I could call.

I spoke with my mother. She and Clarence were living in San
Bernardino, east of Los Angeles. We tried to formulate some sort of
plan. I had better bring the children with me. If I took the train to save
money, I could leave the kids with her and fly from L.A. to Seattle. From
there I . . . well, I'd sort it out later.

It's funny how in the middle of a personal calamity your ordinary life
spins on unabated. For that matter, why doesn't the whole world come
to a stop? You'd think it would if it had any decency. I must have been
running on adrenaline fueled by shock, because I went right on dealing
with the normal demands and problems.

As we awaited Aunt May's return phone call, Ray and I were figuring
out what to do about his term paper for World literature. I had been envious as hell when he first showed me the list of authors and works to se-

lect from. Discuss one. Ray had waited and waited to do the paper.
When the deadline got short, he was hot on a new story and didn't want
to stop. So we had a wild idea, something we had never done before: I'd
write the paper.

I had almost finished a first draft on Ray's choice, *The Notebooks of
Malte Laurids Brigge* by Rainer Maria Rilke. We decided I should stay
in Iowa another day, possibly two, to finish the draft before I left for
Washington. We'd been talking about the book every night—Ray had
read and enjoyed it—so that would leave him with only minor edits to
do and typing the final version.

The phone finally rang again. It felt close to historic when it was Aunt
May on the line. She never made long-distance calls—they cost money.
A stamp for a letter was reasonable. This was the one undeniable excep-
tion to her rule.

Oh, she was unbelievably sweet! She knew about our financial situation and didn't expect me to have the money to come west. She didn't
quibble a second about the amount I shakily asked her to wire. (At least
I got in that the train was so much cheaper than flying.) And it was her
gift, not a loan—something she didn't approve of.

Now I just had to get through the rest of this ghastly day.

I tried to concentrate on mundane tasks. Going to the grocery store
was sheer agony. When I returned, Ray asked, "Honey, how can I help
you?" I couldn't say anything. I just shook my head, my eyes glazed and
stunned.

"Would you like me to make love to you?"

I had never seen him look so sad. I was fragile and stricken and
couldn't imagine sleeping with anyone. But he was so sincere and concerned, and trying to help me, that my heart was moved. He had to be
the sweetest husband in the world. How lucky I was.

I nodded yes.

Then I went over to the couch and sat down. I watched Ray gather up
the kids. Gently he put on their hats, coats, mittens, and boots. Then he
took Christi and Vance by the hand and led them over to a neighbor's
house to play. I couldn't trust myself to speak as my dear little family

trudged out into the bitter cold. I thought I might just break down right then.

When Ray got back, I was still frozen on the couch where he'd left me. He pulled me up, led me into our bedroom with an arm around me. We lay down on our bed. We looked into each other's eyes.

Afterward I cried and cried until the front of his undershirt was entirely soaked.

THE TRAIN LEFT from Marion, thirty-five miles away. We drove to the station through a blizzard, seeing no other cars on the road. I don't know how we made it, but we did. Good-bye, Ray. Bye, Daddy! Bye, Daddy!

On board I came out of my fog of grief long enough to realize that I had two energetic children with me and a long ride ahead. In the little train compartment I diligently read story after story and contrived games to play. By the time Vance and Christi were asleep, I was exhausted.

The porter was a kind elderly black man. He asked if there was anything he could do to make me more comfortable. I blurted out that my dad had died. Sympathizing without intruding, he offered to watch the kids if I wanted to take a break and go to the club car.

I did.

It was late. There were seven or eight attendants, all black men, in the club car. I drank Johnny Walker Red on ice, the barman's service attentive and tactful. I finally began to relax. Maybe I could make it through this after all. As the train rolled on in the night, one of the men picked up a guitar and sang the blues like Muddy Waters.

After three long days, my mother was waiting for us at San Bernardino. She took charge of the kids, then shepherded me to the helicopter terminal for a hop to the L.A. airport. As I went up the steps of the 'copter, she handed me a sympathy card with the handwritten message—"I love you, he loved you, we loved you."

In Seattle, Amy's boyfriend picked me up. A big man, Michael handled my luggage with ease. I asked him to take me directly to

Aunt May's. As Michael drove north, he filled me in on develop-
ments.

Jerry had gotten the news from the local sheriff, who had come bang-
ing on her apartment door. She had already been to see Dad at the funeral home and had temporarily closed her restaurant—Dad had bought
it for her. Now she was at the Anacortes hospital in labor.

Michael and Amy were going to stay on with Aunt May and tend to
Dad's animals, farm equipment, and machinery.

The "little girls," Valla and Annette (now thirteen and eleven), were
with their mother.

We drove up the long driveway off Burk Road and parked in line
with the big maple tree. Aunt May greeted us as we were getting out of
the car. She had on the rubber barn boots she always wore to do farm
chores. "Maryann, Maryann." Her voice broke in a sob. "I . . . without
you." I went and embraced her, something unheard of among the older
generation of undemonstrative Burks.

She was soon more her normal self. "If only the neighbors had got me
when they found your dad passed out in his car." She was in despair. "I
could have gone up there. I would've known what to do! I was right here
at home when it happened. Mrs. Liffengren is a nurse—they went and
got her. She said Val had a strong pulse. If they'd just come and gotten
me!" She shook her head repeatedly.

That night we went over to Gillies, the funeral home in Lynden.
There was a line outside. So many people had come to see Dad that there
wasn't enough room inside. That said something about Val Burk.

I went in. My handsome, always-animated father was lying still on
white satin in a cheap gray coffin. He had been the humorous and hu-
manizing force in a cold, unfeeling family. How horrible to think that
the final rites for this witty, wonderful man would be largely dictated by
that hard-hearted bunch.

It suddenly came to me when I'd last seen him alive—two summers
ago when we visited the World's Fair. I ironed the shirt he didn't want
ironed. Who'd care in a hundred years? he had said to me with a wink as

he went out the door for a doctor's appointment. Oh, *I* would, *I* would. I was sure of that.

The funeral was the next day. We sat in Gillies "family room." Four of the Burk sisters were there—Jerry was still in the hospital with her new baby, Vawn Burk Davis. The older generation was out in force, headed by Aunt Elsie and Aunt May. The service was stiff and formal, as I expected.

Aunt May had engaged a local Baptist minister, not that he had known the deceased. He recited some dry facts about my father's life and named the Burk sisters and brothers—my dad was the youngest of the five. Then he launched into a fire-and-brimstone sermon: "We have this sinner, Val Burk, struck down in his coffin here in front of us. Why? Because, brothers and sisters, this man was never seen in church. He was never seen reading the Bible. He—" I stopped listening to this ignorant, uneducated, sleazy son-of-a-bitch country preacher.

Then it was over.

I was worn out from a tumult of emotions—not something Aunt Elsie approved of. I went back to my father's cold house. Aunt May had gone over to her farm to do chores. It was empty, except for the dogs. Some huddled in a corner while others went around in anxious circles. They had loved Dad, too.

THREE WEEKS LATER Val Burk's five daughters gathered at Aunt May's place. There was a square white box with farmer string wrapped around it. Like a gift. Together we all walked out to a grove of fir trees behind the pasture where Dad had spent so many hours with his horses and cattle. No authorities were consulted. We knew Dad did not belong in a graveyard in Lynden. He belonged on the land where he had lived his life. And there we buried him.

I flew back to California.

I COULDN'T BELIEVE the warmth of the California sunshine. It seemed chimerical, the San Bernardino orange trees shimmering in the light. I was overjoyed to see Christi and Vance and my mother. I was even glad to see Clarence.

My third evening at Mom's, Ray called long distance. "Maryann, if you don't get on the train tomorrow and get back here, I'm going to get into somebody else."

After we hung up, I tried to calculate. How long had I been gone? *That* many weeks? A month? The calendar was a product of human artifice, cold rationality. It couldn't account for what the passage of time felt like. An eternity in a heartbeat.

But it was time we headed home. My God, to Iowa. "Mom, I've got to leave tomorrow."

My mother strongly objected. She thought I was very run-down. "I'd like so much to have you stay awhile."

"No, I've got to go. I've been gone a whole month. I won't have a home if I don't get back to work and start paying the bills."

The next evening the kids and I left on the train. So long, California; so long, sunshine. Snow and ice, that's what we had to embrace. Well, actually I wanted to embrace Ray.

Back at our place my husband was in the middle of a story. He had given it a title: "Will You Please Be Quiet, Please?" He was excited, working hard. Ray had never before written about a powerful wife betraying a hapless husband. As the winter went on and on, he wrote by day in our bedroom, unless he was in class or at the library. At night he wrote on the kitchen table.

Sitting at that table in the fall he also wrote "Sixty Acres," imagining what it was like to be a humiliated American Indian, unable to protect his land, family, and heritage. There were more stories in the works, like "The Student's Wife," which he wrote during spring vacation—perhaps distilled from my routines and moods? He was just in this amazing creative ferment.

After that awful January, though, I think the Workshop steadily lost its appeal. Ray didn't want to do anything but write. Every job, every hour in a classroom was a distraction. To teach writing would be no different. Every lame attempt to earn a living, to put food on the table, came down to the same thing—less time to write. When Ray was at his desk, he was in command; when not, he felt the world was crushing the life out of him.

I should have been the one in graduate school. That would have made a lot more sense. I loved going to classes. I wouldn't have minded a TA's job. But things were as they were, and I was always in a rush. Get the chores done, prepare dinner, wash the clothes, read to the kids, cuddle them. Go to work in the evenings. There wasn't even time for me to mourn my dad properly or someplace where I could cry alone in peace. Every room in our two-bedroom apartment was constantly in use.

I dreaded another year in Iowa as much as Ray did, although I mouthed the logical arguments. What about the investment we had already made in time and money? Another year, and Ray's graduate degree would be the ticket to a good job at a college. That was the plan.

Right?

The winter finally called it quits. The native Iowans seemed to congratulate themselves on how miserable it had been, as if putting up with the ridiculous climate proved their superior fortitude. But our logical arguments utterly collapsed on a pleasant evening in May. Ray was getting caught up in the "movin' on" spirit of those who were leaving the Workshop and university. "The thrill is gone. I just want to leave, like everyone else I value and trust here. I'm tired of this godforsaken country and I'm tired of going to school."

"Oh, I know," I said, "but one more year, just one more year, would make all these school years—"

"I can't do it," Ray said. He meant it.

I didn't have any fight left in me, not when every fiber in my being wanted us to leave, too.

Every U-Haul trailer in town was booked. Signs sprouted with bargains: MOVING SALE! DOUBLE BED, 2 SINGLE BEDS, WINGBACK CHAIR. BOOKS. BABY FURNITURE. MUST SELL! Everywhere we looked in our neighborhood, people were packing and getting ready to move.

So let's pack up our dishes, bedding, and books. Time to hitch up the U-Haul to Old Faithful, our '53 Chevy, and put up some for-sale signs

of our own. The Workshop semester was over, the course work completed. The Carvers were going to be traveling. Iowa, keep your little
stipend. It's too little, too late. So long, Finkbine Park, city of tin huts.
We don't live there anymore.

California, *here we come!*

10

SACRAMENTO

We arrived in downtown Sacramento late in the evening. We had never been to the latest apartment Ray's parents were occupying, so we had to search out the address. After a week on the road from Iowa, the city felt ominous and sinister, neither familiar nor friendly.

It was our destination, basically, because we had nowhere else to go. In our haste to leave Iowa, we had somehow neglected to fashion a new workable plan for our lives. We had simply driven west, prepared to deal ad hoc with what came next. Naturally we were sure we'd come up with something as we usually did. I already had ideas in mind.

The restless Carvers were in Sacramento because C.R. was shortly expecting a settlement for his disability from the state, presumably Workers' Compensation. He had been answering doctors' questions— "Who is the president of the United States?"—for years. He claimed once to have stated honestly what he saw in an inkblot, and that, he believed, held up the settlement for another year and a half.

They were huddled in a small, dark apartment in a city where they knew no one and had no other purpose except to wait out the doctors and the state of California. Ella was in her usual working mode—land a job, stay with it awhile, become disgruntled, quit or get fired, then find another and go through the same routine. James was caught in the same pattern. He worked when he could find work, but nothing was heartfelt, nothing was a step to something better.

At the apartment door we put Christi and Vance in front of us. C. R. and Ella hadn't seen their grandchildren for nearly a year. To our shock they weren't particularly overjoyed to see them. Or us.

Ray immediately realized that his dad had *gotten* his settlement and was afraid we'd come to help spend it. Whatever it amounted to—we never knew—Ray's parents acted as if it was the last money they'd ever see. (Which may have had some truth to it. Ray's dad was only fifty-one yet unlikely to ever hold a job again.)

But there we were, so they invited us in. We were family, and that was that.

The next morning something happened that convinced me we had better move along soon. Vance threw a temper tantrum because there wasn't enough milk for his cereal. I was so proud of him. Somebody was reacting honestly to how unwelcome we all felt. James had gone out for milk but got only a quart, hardly enough. Grudgingly Ella took a quarter from her purse and sent him out again. But, brother, I got the message.

I went to the bathroom and cried. We were broke from the trip. My dad had been unhesitating in his generosity. I wished we could get in the car and go see him. New tears erupted as I realized that was never going to be possible.

Ray came into the bathroom and tried to comfort me. He looked so agitated that I somehow pulled myself together. I didn't want to make him feel any worse. I'm sure he was thinking of all the times his folks had stayed with us and we shared whatever we had. We never held anything back.

"What's on your mind, Ray?"

"We made it through the year, Maryann. We made it back west."

"I was just thinking—" I broke off and smiled at him.

Okay, get on with it. I'd hoped to have a day or two before I started job hunting, but now I changed my mind. I spoke to Ray as calmly as I could. "I want you to take me out to Davis. I'll look for a waitress job."

We left the children in the apartment and headed out. I wanted a job over in Davis, which is close to Sacramento, because that's where I planned to go to college next.

I got a job at Mandy's, the seven-to-three day shift. The place was a madhouse. I'd have to hustle my buns, but I'd do it. They gave me a uniform to wear, accessorized with an apron and a little cap. Tomorrow I could start bringing people their coffee, plates of eggs, hamburgers, and french fries. Then my family could eat. Saved by the hand of Providence one more time. The first thing I was going to buy when I got a paycheck was a gallon of milk.

THE SUMMER BEFORE, I had been planning to attend Berkeley, but we went off to Iowa. As I had been accepted, I assumed Davis would admit me, since they were both University of California schools. Davis did; I could begin in the summer semester.

Unexpectedly we also scored student housing. We gladly left C. R. and Ella's dark apartment in Sacramento and relocated to a two-bedroom unit in married-student housing. It was on the edge of the campus. There was luxuriant green grass right outside our door. The kids were happy. Mandy's was two blocks away.

We lived among top students who were studying to be scientists, doctors, and engineers. Unfortunately we likely couldn't stay past the summer. I realized that there was no way I could handle tuition at Davis and support the family. It wasn't like Berkeley, where I would have gotten a break as long as Ray worked in the biology library.

There was one other factor working against us: Ray had no luck finding a job. None. Or, as I started to think when the euphoria of being back in California faded, he had no luck finding a job he'd *accept*.

A motor inn wanted to hire him as a desk clerk. Ray had told the manager he was happy to take the night shift, thinking it would leave his days free to write. But after Ray got back from the interview, he started worrying about the responsibilities. He didn't want to get caught up in anything that might pull him away from writing. He just wanted a paycheck. Ray wrote a note declining the job and then had *me* deliver it.

Saved for one more day. His personal integrity was intact; his life was still his own.

My mother got a lead on a good professional job, one for which Ray's hard-earned college degree actually qualified him. It was a teaching position—English and drama at Willows High School. She had worked in Willows, about thirty miles southwest of Chico. Initially Ray said he'd love to teach there. Then, when he heard more of what the job called for—two play productions in addition to five classes—he had second thoughts.

Both of us were awake all night with the jitters. How could he turn this down? We'd been back in California two months. Ray had pounded the pavement and discovered just how much an AB in English was worth in the real world. Not much, apparently, and not an academic door opener that a Writers' Workshop MFA would have been. And if he didn't take it, what would we tell my mom?

This job was heaven on earth as far as she was concerned. It gave you standing in the community, with security for years to come. This was a job with three summer months off with pay, not to mention school holidays that amounted to another month. Four *paid* months a year to write, for Pete's sake!

Ray had nothing else. The logical thing to do was to teach at the secondary level. Ordinarily a teaching certificate was required, and that took a year and a half more of college to obtain. But Mom's old friend Coralee Holt had pulled some strings. As secretary to the superintendent of schools, she filed the papers to obtain a provisional teaching certificate for Ray.

Poor Coralee Holt, that formidable, efficient woman who once rescued us when the Black Hole of Calcutta blew its motor, was about to be disappointed and disillusioned. As was my mother. Ray decided not to take the job.

That night we lay in our student-housing double bed in the hot bedroom, talking and anguishing. "Well, that's it," I said with sour finality. "Cut your losses and explain it that way. Better than your breaking down under the strain."

A telegram went out to Coralee in the morning declining the job.

I knew Ray was having a case of the heebie-jeebies. However, explaining this to someone like my mother, who considered teaching a noble profession, or to other hardworking folks like Coralee, was not going to be easy. Look, okay, Ray is a writer, with a trunkload of idiosyncrasies. He had to do things his way. That's the way writers are.

But for the first time people who knew Ray would start to look at him differently. Not as a talented kid anymore, indulgently allowed his missteps, but as a grown man of twenty-six with . . . problems.

Secretly I wished that Ray had felt able to take the Willows job. We didn't need to be in a big urban center. A small community where we could put down roots would have been wonderful for me and the children. I could have commuted to Chico State. One reason I was determined to finish college was to get the opportunity of professional work. I knew in my heart of hearts that I wouldn't have turned down Willows, no matter what.

If only *I* could have accepted the job instead. I knew I could do it. If only Ray had been able to handle it long enough for me to finish college. Then I'd have taken over the lion's share of the economic burden. I'd have been happy to do it forever.

Ray didn't think he could teach high school for even a day. So no use trying. Well, I was the one who'd championed him and admonished him to be true to himself. Hadn't I?

WHEN YOU TAKE a wrong turn on the highway, it's not out of the question to turn around and go back. But life doesn't work that way. You may think you've chosen the right course, but when you realize that you're not getting where you want to be and another choice might have been better, it's usually too late. There's no going back.

Without money for tuition, we had to leave the ivory tower of Davis's student housing at the end of July. Farewell to the neighborly chat of art, politics, and literature. The rented house I found for us was large, unfurnished, and shockingly expensive.

Our furniture consisted of a table, chairs, and three beds—we couldn't afford anything more. We stuffed our clothes onto shelves, hoping to get dressers one day, and sat on the rug in the empty living room because we had no couch.

The first day I had off from Mandy's, I lined up my next job. It was a lunch gig at the Pine Cone, a restaurant in Sacramento. Ray kept looking for work. It seemed that daily survival was becoming our one overriding issue.

Before, we'd had goals—like Ray finishing college—that made hardships seem tolerable. Now, instead of making progress, we were treading water. I had a fading vision of my future, of a financially secure life. Maybe we weren't heading off life's good highway—though I had my doubts—but it felt like we'd tossed the map out the window.

So why exactly had we moved to a costly house with a big backyard? Because of a dog. Really! (Okay, also a better place for Ray to write and probably a bit of my own suppressed desire for some decent housing.) A poodle, the most brainless little female puppy imaginable. She was a mass of white fluff and curls. Christi and Vance fell in love with her instantly. And where did she come from? A gift from Amy when she visited us at Davis—knowing full well the college housing rules: no pets. (Yes, the antiauthoritarian attitude of the sixties was flourishing in our family.) And we couldn't say no to a gift.

Mitzi, as the kids named her, did give them something to do from morning till night. They played endlessly with their dog while Ray and I feared she would drive us nuts. Every time she barked, we saw ourselves tossed out on the street by the campus police.

Now the dog had a great backyard. But what she liked to do was pee on the carpet in the living room. We'd harshly chase her out with a broom if we caught her, but she didn't seem intelligent enough to learn. Ray and I got instantly depressed every time we looked at the pee-stained carpet in the empty room. What would we tell the property management company after I'd sweet-talked them into letting us have the place?

Given all the stress it was understandable—but excruciating—to see that Ray couldn't seem to write, either. In the blazing heat of a city where

Christi and Vance with their less-than-well-trained poodle, Mitzi. Matheson Way, Sacramento, California, 1965.
PHOTO BY MARYANN BURK CARVER

we didn't know a soul except for his family, his energy was focused on getting a job. Anything. So fate obliged him, with a little twist of mockery, perhaps. He landed a job at Weinstock-Lubin & Co., a big department store.

As a stock boy. He would work "in the bowels of the store," down in the basement. Among his duties: the assembly of toys and other merchandise.

What a nightmare for Ray! Neither of us was mechanically gifted. Yes, we had fantastic discussions of current events, movies, and popular entertainment, history, and literature. We always had a huge stack of books we were reading, and more waiting. But when it came to assembling or fixing things, use this punch line: It took two of us to change a lightbulb.

The money from two jobs was enough to squeeze out the second month's rent. It was due. I took care of the kids by day, and Ray took care of them at night, saving the expense of baby-sitters.

On the brighter side, the Pine Cone job was turning out better than I expected. The restaurant, owned by Paul and Aldo, actually had two operations going. One side of the building was the pedestrian Pine Cone, serving mediocre American fare, but the other was a truly gourmet restaurant, the Flambé Room.

The two partners wanted to jettison the Pine Cone side of the business as soon as they could. (It wasn't long before they moved to a handsome, mostly brick building, a perfect setting for showcasing the best Continental cuisine in Sacramento.)

Paul was the handsome, dark-haired chef, French, trained in Paris, cosmopolitan and suave.

Aldo was from Italy, the perfect, charming maitre d'. At the tables, he prepared—what else?—flambé dishes: steak Diane, crêpes suzette, cherries jubilee, and other specialties.

They both liked me. I found their effusive attention and compliments captivating, and I started to look forward to going to work. By my twenty-fourth birthday in August, I had been promoted from waitress to hostess and cocktail server. Shifted to evenings, I served customers in the bar waiting for dinner in the Flambé Room. The hours would fit nicely into a class schedule—I had a glimmer of hope.

Mercifully the blazing summer was almost over. The kids would start school soon, Christi in first grade, Vance in kindergarten. I resolved to attend Sacramento State College that fall, *somehow*. Ray was stuck in a menial job and I felt abysmally sorry for him. (His poem "Looking for Work" describes this time.)

Right again—if we didn't laugh, we'd cry.

AS THE HOSTESS of the Flambé, I was the first person to greet arriving guests. I'd take their names, bring them drinks while they waited to be seated. All the waiters were men, so I obviously stood out. My job was only busy when the dining room was busy, which was about four hours a night. Then I could relax.

Aldo and Paul started inviting me to eat a late dinner with them. I certainly couldn't refuse the gourmet meals. They had seen something in me. Yes, I knew I was pretty. But I wasn't city elegant and sophisticated—a woman like my sister Jerry.

But their interest opened up possibilities for me. On a payment plan, I bought a new pastel silk sheath with matching sandal heels that showed off my figure to maximum advantage. The increase in tips paid for the dress and more. I had already learned it didn't hurt to admit I was a college student. Everyone knew students had to take any sort of work that fit around their classes. The customers encouraged me in my studies at Sacramento State—and tipped me better.

The restaurant trade was a world of its own. Those in it loved it, and I learned why. The guys at the Flambé were proud to know their counterparts all over town. When they weren't working, they frequented the other local bars and restaurants, leaving lavish tips. Gossip abounded. There were after-hours parties capped by breakfast, after which everybody went home to bed. I was only passing through, but I began to feel as if I genuinely belonged.

That summer and fall I was delighted to be back in the classroom, where life made sense. Many students had a greater goal in their lives than working a job and carousing on weekends. It was also a haven from the world beyond California that seemed to have gone haywire.

President Johnson announced that he was creating a Great Society. It did not feel great. It felt controlled and arrogant. As he and Barry Goldwater squared off in the presidential election, many spoke about voting for the lesser of two evils. I was too young to be able to vote for Jack Kennedy. Now that I could vote, I had a choice of shades of moral grayness, pick one.

Ray's workdays consisted of unpacking boxes and stocking shelves in the department store basement. He managed to sidestep assembling items, but that was about his only spot of luck. I wished he could just stay home and write. But we couldn't make it on what I was earning. It took two paychecks. That was the very practical math we could do in our sleep.

One night Ray came home looking gray-faced and sad. "What in the world happened to you, honey? You look as if you are going to cry?" I gathered my big guy in my arms and gave him the biggest hug I could.

"I got fired. Handed a pink slip. For stealing cookies!"

I heard Ray, but didn't get it. Cookies? Like a lunch-box snack?

"And the best part is, I never went near the damn cookies." It seems that in the basement there was a big barrel of very stale Hydrox sandwich cookies. Somebody had started helping himself. Yuck. But since management couldn't figure out who it was, they just fired everyone in the stock department.

"Well, shit," I said, "it was a terrible job for you anyway." I was furiously thinking, How in hell are we going to pay the rent and live? But I was ten minutes late getting out the door to my job, so I left it there. All I could do anyway was reassure Ray. He'd find something else, and things would be all right.

But he didn't find something else. Again Ray went out every day to find a job, and every day he came home with nothing. Except alcohol on his breath. Coming home, he started having a couple of drinks. That was new.

One morning I took a good look at Ray's wan, depressed face. "You look at a breaking point. Don't go out there today. Go back to bed. Take a good book with you and just sleep and read. Maybe you'd even feel like writing a poem, or starting a new story."

"Fine chance of that."

"Well, take time out. Step back from everything. Get a new perspective. It's critical that you . . ." I was running out of ways to say the obvious.

Shortly after, Ray started to insist on driving me to work so he could keep the car. That meant taking Christi and Vance with us, dragging them away from playing with our brainless dog or the other neighborhood kids. It meant I had to call Ray when I was done, as it was unpredictable when business at the Flambé would slow enough for me to leave. And I had to wait for him to come pick me up.

I didn't want to upset Ray when he felt miserable and defensive. I wanted him to feel totally loved. As gently as I could, I tried to ask what was going on. "Why do you need to keep the car at night, honey? You can't really go anywhere or do anything when you're taking care of the kids."

"It just makes me feel better not to be stuck, not to be stranded. I even kind of like the routine of driving you to work and picking you up. It makes the night go faster."

"Okay," I said. But I wanted to add that we desperately needed even those four or five dollars that Ray had gotten in the habit of borrowing—from my tips—for a double whiskey at the bar before he escorted me home.

For the first time ever, I wondered how we were going to make it. Not next year or next month, but next week. I was doing all I could. What if it wasn't enough? My God.

The date of the rent payment came and went. There was no way we could cover it. A week passed before the management company called us. I told them, "We should definitely have the money this week. For sure by this weekend."

"All right, Mrs. Carver," the male voice said. "I'll note the records. If you have it in by this weekend, there won't be a problem, but we can't let it go beyond that."

"I understand. By this weekend. No problem."

Grasp the only straw left. That was what we were being forced to do. "Ray, you've got to go to your dad and ask him to break into his settlement. We've never asked them for anything. We need help. If they come up with three hundred dollars for the rent, I can pay the power bill. We got an overdue notice yesterday."

Ray looked at me. "You know how they are about that settlement. I'll ask. But I don't count on them for anything."

"They have to help us," I said. "We have nowhere else to turn."

When Ray came back from his folks' place, he looked haggard. And angry, sullenly so. Acidly he told me what had happened. "They pointed out I should have taken that scholarship at Iowa and stayed another year. Or I should have taken the desk clerk job. He couldn't afford to carry us, Dad said, when I was passing up work."

Well, hang on for the next curve life throws you, I told myself. I didn't have to wait long. I came down with a killer cold. It went straight to my chest, and I knew it must be bronchitis. I'd had it before.

Somehow I went to work the next night. I shivered with fever and chills as I waited on customers. When I phoned to get picked up, Ray didn't answer—no one did. I was panic-stricken. All I could think to do was to call a cab and rush home.

Ray came in about a half hour later, carrying one sleeping kid at a time into their shared bedroom. It was obvious he'd been drinking. He didn't look at me as he explained he'd been over at his folks'. Since they didn't have a phone, he couldn't call.

"Jesus, Ray," I said, "I don't mean to complain, but you knew how sick I was."

"Sorry," he muttered as he shambled into the kids' room. He moved Vance into bed with his sister. Then he stretched out on our son's bed.

"What's the matter with you?" I asked. "Come to bed with me."

"I'm fine here, thanks. I'll talk to you in the morning." He turned over, pulled the covers over him, and closed his eyes.

Man, oh man. I made myself a hot lemonade, took aspirin, turned the heat up, pulled on a flannel nightgown I hadn't worn since the cold of Iowa, and crawled into our big lonely bed. What is happening to us? To Ray? Is he cracking up? Why can't he find a job washing dishes, washing cars, anything? I would. I wouldn't be proud.

And what was he thinking? Dragging the kids out on a school night just to amuse himself, then drinking too much and driving. In seven years of marriage, it had never been like this. We were always united. This was truly frightening, because I felt we were breaking apart. I shivered with chills and fever, and then I sobbed.

The next night Ray took me to work, promising he'd have a good night with the kids and be down to pick me up promptly. "Please," I said, "I spent almost all day in bed and I'm no better. I don't know if I can—" No, we needed the money.

To my surprise, before I finished my shift I was called to the phone. It wasn't Ray but James. "My God, what's happened?" I asked in a panic. "Has something happened to one of the kids? To Ray?"

"No, no, Maryann, nothing like that. Ray asked me to call you and ask you to get another ride home."

"What?" I asked. "Where are the kids?"

"They're with us, over at our place. Ray figured since it was Friday night and they didn't have to go to school in the morning, it would be all right for them to stay over."

"Oh, he did, did he? Well, tell me this, James. I mean, level with me. Where the hell is Ray and what is he doing?"

"I don't know, Maryann. He just told me to call you when he brought Christi and Vance over. I said I would."

"James, where is Ray? Don't bullshit me. I don't buy it! Where is Ray?"

"Well, he told me he had to go out to Davis. He might not be back in time to pick you up. So I should call."

"That's okay, James. I don't mean to put you on the spot. I'm just furious at Ray. He knows how sick I am, and damn it all, he pulls this shit."

"I'm sorry, Maryann."

"Well, for God's sake, take good care of my babies until I can pick them up. Kiss them for me, will you?"

As I hung up the phone, I tried to figure out what was going on. Davis? Do you suppose Ray had gone out there to see that rich girl? He had met her at a bookstore when we were living in student housing. She was an art major, and he had teased me about her. I'd passed it off as Ray's normal kidding around.

I was oblivious that I was crying as I went back to work. Aldo and Paul were at their table, ready to eat, but they could no longer discreetly ignore me. Aldo got up and came over.

"What happened, baby? Is your family all right?"

"Yes and no," I said. "Ray can't come pick me up."

"Have dinner with us. Come on, now. Have a nice glass of wine, a bit of steak. You'll feel better. Sit down and relax. You don't have to do any more tonight."

I tried to joke with him. "You're so sweet, Aldo, even when a person's not a paying customer."

"You're pretty sweet yourself, Maryann." Paul came over, and Aldo explained how I was stranded. That's why I was crying.

"I can take her home," Paul said.

I was too sick to eat or drink. "I just want to go home," I sniffled.

Both were nice men and made me feel happy and cared for—though I didn't feel as close to Paul. They worked hard, made money, and then the rest of their lives automatically fell into place.

I got my coat. Feebly I said I could take a cab, but I hadn't made much—only eight or ten dollars. I wasn't getting tipped as usual because I wasn't my usual vivacious self. It made a difference.

"No, I'll take you," Paul said. "It will be my pleasure."

So off we went into the night in Paul's black Porsche. The next thing I knew, he zipped into a parking place in front of a nice apartment complex, the kind with a swimming pool and Jacuzzi. "This is where I live." Paul smiled. "Let me make you a fruit plate and a hot brandy. You need to sweat that cold out of you."

"Oh, I have to get home."

"Well, your children aren't there. Your husband isn't there. You might as well have a drink with me. I'll play you some nice music. Some French music. Some little songs from Paris."

"Do you have some Edith Piaf?"

"Yes, I have some Edith Piaf." He jumped out of the car, came around and opened the door for me. Ridiculously gallant.

"You shouldn't make me laugh," I said, laughing.

"Why not?" Paul asked, oddly serious. "A pretty lady like you should be laughing all the time. You shouldn't be crying. You should be happy."

"Oh, I am happy," I said.

"That boy you're with doesn't know how to take care of you. He doesn't try very hard. He's more interested in having a drink, reading a book, keeping life as easy as he can for himself."

"No, that's not true. Ray is a great writer. He's going to be famous someday."

Paul's apartment was nice. Like him—relaxing and mature. A man's place, with hi-fi, TV, leather furniture, thick carpets. I hadn't seen a bachelor's pad like his. He fixed me a hot drink with lemon. It felt good to relax and feel a little warm inside. The French music was fine. By the end of a second drink, I was starting to feel fuzzy. I was so tired.

Just then Paul reached down and kissed me. "I've waited and waited for you. I wanted you the first time I saw you."

"You must stop this," I protested.

"Why? Don't you like it?"

"I'm married. I love my husband. Please let me go!"

He took me home. Our car wasn't there.

I got out of the Porsche. "There you are, *madame.*" Paul spat the word out before he sped away in his fast car.

RAY CAME HOME eventually. The next day I went around to my instructors at Sacramento State and had them sign me out. "Why?" the sympathetic ones asked. "Why are you doing this?" The semester was nearly over. All my papers were written. I was carrying A's in every class.

"Economics," I said. "My husband lost his job."

The next day the power company turned off the electricity. We realized we were beaten. There was nothing left in the tips jar. We packed up the kitchen by candlelight. The last thing I put in the last box were the kids' school lunch box Thermos bottles.

Ray and I became oddly mellow and sweet with each other. The poignancy of our last day together made any recriminations pointless. We were going to have to part temporarily to survive. Each of us would go to the only people in the world who would take us in.

I was taking the children and heading to my mother's. Ray would bunk with his folks. They had room for him. He could continue looking for a job in Sacramento, still the best bet in that area of California.

I asked him about the girl, the art student. He admitted looking her up. The night he failed to pick me up, he saw her. Yeah, she was rich. She wanted him to go to Europe with her. I just looked at him. I felt sorry for him. He obviously didn't care about her and wouldn't be taking off to Europe. He had just been desperate, that's all. I understood what desperation was now.

We made our escape from the big house with the stained carpets. Ray drove Christi, Vance, the dog, and me to my mother's house in Paradise. She and Clarence were living there. Mom was overjoyed to see us, of course. She was looking forward to Christi's upcoming seventh birthday. The one Daddy wasn't going to be at, for the first time in his life. Ray had to turn around and drive straight back to Sacramento. His folks were expecting him.

The first night back in Paradise, I lay in bed shaking. I couldn't get warm and couldn't lie still. I missed my husband. I wanted Ray there. The situation was insane. "By God Almighty, I'll forgive you, if you forgive me," I wanted to tell him.

MOM URGED ME to stay on with her in Paradise, enroll the kids in school, and live happily ever after. Clarence was obviously of a different opinion, but he kept his mutterings behind their bedroom door. School Christmas vacation was nearly here, so I held out. I refused to treat our "visit" as anything else.

I wanted to tell the kids that Mama and Daddy will rescue you. We'll do it. You'll see.

In the meantime I found child care and took the bus to San Francisco to see Amy and her boyfriend, Michael Wright. I found them in the apartment they rented after abandoning the Sausalito houseboat—well, it sank and they lost all their belongings. They had missed the spring semester at San Francisco State helping out at Dad's farm after his death. From their perspective it was a hell of a year, too.

Michael had been drafted. He had absolutely no intention of going to Vietnam—or anywhere else for that matter. He liked his life as it was. He had a beautiful, fun-loving girlfriend—my sister—and he loved acting in local productions of Shakespeare. He and Amy were deeply engrossed in selecting a back brace that he'd strap on before going off to boot camp. He was determined to pass go and then proceed immediately to sick bay.

Their friends Buddha and Sheilah lived with them. They were proto hippies and would-be revolutionaries who later held notorious love-ins in Golden Gate Park. Also hanging around in Michael's final days of freedom was Amy's pal Little Jimmy, nephew of the historian Charles Beard. Happy-go-lucky Amy was working as a cocktail waitress at the No Name Bar in Sausalito when she didn't have class.

I never went near San Francisco State. Every day I struggled to find a place for me and the kids, and a job to support us. The little pills in my pocket—mild tranquilizers prescribed by a doctor in Paradise—eased

only slightly what I was facing daily. I had to put my family back together again.

WE WOULD TURN things around and go forward. I wasn't going to
second-guess the past. Money had opened the rift in our lives, but I
wasn't going down into the valley of marital discontent. I didn't want to
see what else might be there.

In Mill Valley, that quaint, fanciful village, I found a temporary
apartment that appealed to me very much. One weekend Ray came to
see me. It seemed safe and right, though none of our real issues were resolved. I kept focused on finances and how we'd pull it together.

I received an unexpected gift from friends of Amy's—a copy of the
Tao Te Ching with a bus ticket to Sacramento tucked inside. And a
twenty-dollar bill. I called Ray. He said he'd be waiting for me. I could
stay with him at his folks' place, sleeping on quilts on the floor as he did.
I didn't care.

He met me at the bus station. On an impulse I asked him to stop at
the best nightclub I knew of, a place on Auburn Boulevard. I went inside. I felt six feet off the ground when I got back to the car. "I got a job.
I start tomorrow night. I'll have some money of my own."

A few nights on the job, and I had enough money to make a payment
on a motel unit with a kitchenette. It was big enough for us and the kids.
We went up to Paradise and got them. Thank you, God, I thought, as
we all slipped into clean, fresh sheets on two queen-size beds. Ours.
Rented for a week. A new beginning.

We had some income. We made a plan: rent a house in Sacramento as
soon as possible and go from there. It was Christmas before we knew it.
We proudly loaded up the car with the kids and presents (bought at the
last minute) and drove to Paradise to celebrate. "To eat, drink, and be
merry," as my mother liked to say.

We had made it through another year.

I was more aware of myself as a person in my own right, an individual, not always half of the couple called Ray-and-Maryann. I began to
be better attuned to my own consciousness. To the need to protect and

nourish my inner being, even if that meant keeping some feelings and insights to myself.

A FEW WEEKS later we found a house. It was on Matheson Way in Sacramento—tiny, but we could make it work. Ray had a job. He was now an employee of Mercy Hospital in the housekeeping department.

On the day shift, he really had to work—mop floors, clean bathrooms, whatever the head housekeeper wanted. The eight hours of his shift were rigidly allocated. Ray was lucky to get a half hour to eat lunch or five minutes to sneak off to the bathroom for a cigarette. But he stuck with it. In a year he had won a transfer to the night shift, a very different story.

It was a gravy train.

Ray immediately felt at ease. He worked with a guy named Ross, a good-looking, married college student, originally from Arkansas, no less. They could have been cousins. Once Ross had his MBA, he planned on a career in hospital administration. Their usual night routine was to dispense quickly with whatever chores were left over from the hard-driven day shift, then settle back to watch Johnny Carson until it was safe for one of them to leave early. They would cover for each other as needed.

Usually Ray just wanted to get home to his writing. When he was working on a story or "a batch of poems," as he called them, his imagination was totally focused. He hated to do anything else, unless he genuinely wanted to. Then he'd go out to dinner, read a book, see a movie, play baseball with the kids. Odd as it might seem, working the night shift bolstered his energetic return to writing, disrupted since the move back from Iowa.

WE FASHIONED A life in Sacramento. From '65 to '67 we slowly attained an unconventional but reasonably prosperous state. We moved over a street to Larkspur Lane, into a lovely house with a lot more space. Christi and Vance stayed in their schools and kept the same playmates but had nice big bedrooms. There was a large and pleasant kitchen and living room.

My marriage was healing. Ray and I were more in love than I could imagine—and passionate lovers, no matter what else was going on in our lives. I thought what we had would always be enough.

LOOKING FOR SOMETHING other than hostessing in a club, I answered an ad in the local paper. On January 15, 1965, I first went out into a neighborhood with my Parents' Cultural Institute kit in hand, ready to knock on doors and see if I could make a living as a salesperson. I was sure I could do it.

The institute was the education division of Parents Magazine Enterprises. They had created an instructional program of materials, sold on an easy installment plan, for mothers concerned about their children's education. I knew I'd love to have their books, a library of reference volumes and a set of classics. That's probably why I was so effective at selling the program. I became a master at staying and visiting with a customer after the sale, calming any anxiety she might be feeling. My plans stayed sold, and my customers were happy.

Soon I was a manager, responsible for a team. "Mac's Movers" was my group, and move we did. From our base in Sacramento, we went to Modesto and Stockton, and sometimes as far north as Chico, laughing and listening to hot new tunes in the car like the Rolling Stones' "I Can't Get No Satisfaction," the Beach Boys' "California Girls," and Herman's Hermits' "Mrs. Brown, You've Got a Lovely Daughter." We sang along at the top of our lungs.

It kept getting better. I was promoted to regional manager. The company gave me a car—a candy-apple-red Pontiac convertible that went faster than the wind. It was like nothing Ray or I had ever owned. (It's immortalized in an image in Ray's haunting story "Are These Actual Miles?") Unbelievably money was rolling our way.

We hired a housekeeper, Mrs. Benson, who looked after the house and the children if I worked late. She was a wonderful, grandmotherly person. Freed from most domestic chores, Ray could write while she did the cooking and cleaning.

As regional manager I reported to the San Francisco office. Werner Erhard was the executive in charge. He was twenty-seven, handsome and poised, clearly a young man on the way up in the world. He'd come to Sacramento periodically and solve problems or pump up the flagging enthusiasm of sales reps. (His ability to connect with a group of people flowered fully in his creation of est [Erhard Seminars Training], that briefly spectacular form of mass-group awareness for a price, a half dozen years later. The first est event was held in October 1971 in San Francisco, of course, with nearly a thousand attendees.)

RAY WAS MAKING progress as well. During those three years in Sacramento, he worked on various stories, including "Sometimes a Woman Can Almost Ruin a Man" (later titled "What Do You Do in San Francisco?"), "The Idea," and "The Fling," as well as such poems as "Trying to Sleep Late on a Saturday Morning in November" and "Highway 99E from Chico."

In the fall of '66 Ray decided to sign up for a poetry-writing class at Sacramento State. It was at night, so Ray had to make a deal with Ross to cut out from work. As it was an undergraduate course, the credits were meaningless for a graduate-level student. But Ray took it solely because it was taught by the poet Dennis Schmitz. He admitted later that he was looking for a kindred spirit, and hoped that Dennis, who wasn't much older, would become a friend.

They did become friends. And we hit it off with Dennis and his wife, Loretta. They were parents of a growing Catholic family of three girls and two boys. She was an Italian girl from Queens, and her table typically overflowed with several kinds of pasta, meats, and lots of garlic bread. We gathered around for many evenings filled with raucous laughter and camaraderie.

Dennis was the author of *We Weep for Our Strangeness* and other outstanding books of poetry. He was a wonderful influence on Ray. The new poetry Ray wrote scintillated with laconic passion. He also made friends with some of Dennis's other promising students like Gary and Lucy Thompson.

It's hard to say exactly what had changed, but Ray's writing was reaching some sort of critical mass. He was someone other writers knew about, even if readers were mostly unaware of him. Ten years of effort had brought him to the point where he might be on the verge of finding a wider audience.

In 1966 he got a letter from the editor Martha Foley. She had selected "Will You Please Be Quiet, Please?" for *The Best American Short Stories 1967*. It was Ray's first major exposure on the national literary level. We went out to celebrate, just the two of us. We didn't take along any of our usual drinking and partying friends. We danced. We had dinner. We talked. We looked at each other with love and enchantment, and as Ray put it, "It's an amazing life, an amazing life."

MY SISTER AMY literally brought "amazing life" into the world in '66. She gave birth to her daughter, Erin. She married Michael and joined the ranks of a growing phenomenon—the hippie mother. More than ever we were the people she looked to for support and reassurance as she pursued the actor's life in Hollywood.

I REACHED THE high point of my career with the Cultural Institute. I was one of the three top sales producers on the West Coast. In a ballroom of the San Francisco Hilton, full of Parents' employees from all over the country, I was awarded a TV set and a cash bonus. My

speech was well received, and I was told I looked great in a black sheath dress and a short hairstyle à la Audrey Hepburn.

After the conference Werner asked me what I would

My sister Amy and her daughter, Erin Michelle Wright, born in March 1966, during the time we lived on Larkspur Lane, Sacramento.
PHOTO BY MARYANN BURK CARVER

like to do next. He told me I should think about designing my next job.
I came up with what I wanted to do—become a traveling representative
who would introduce our employees to cultural activities and entertainment. If they were marketing culture, they should know something
about it.

Ray didn't like the sound of it. I knew that lately he had begun feeling restless and in need of some kind of change. He complained that my
current job kept me away from home too much. "What about the kids
and me? I'm tired of this whole merry-go-round. It's time we do something else, get back to who we really are and how we've always lived."
Meaning, starving artist with a family?

I remember looking at my face for a long time in our bathroom mirror. Damned if I do, damned if I don't. Ray and the kids *were* my life,
but I loved my job. Moving again, as Ray hinted he wanted to do, made
me feel very uneasy—even though I might be able to go back to college
and finish my degree.

"Take your choice," he said to me bluntly another night. "Your marriage or your job." That had an effect, all right. It threw me into the first
prolonged sales slump I had ever had. Desperate to write an order, I
couldn't write any. Other reps' orders fell off, and the weaker reps began
to quit. A week or two without a check and many people find they have
second thoughts about working on commission.

For me personally the money tap had run dry. Nothing seemed to get
it going again, try as I might. In the spring of 1967, we had slid into a
deep, deep financial hole. Ray had a new answer. We'd declare bankruptcy. He was getting a lawyer.

"No, no, Ray," I said. "We'll pull out of this. I'll start writing lots of
orders."

"Well, it's time to move on, that's all," Ray said. "The lesson for you,
Maryann, is there are some battles worth fighting and some that aren't."

I threw in the towel. With bankruptcy looming, I learned we had better sell my red convertible as soon as we could. We'd have to let our
housekeeper go. As quickly as we had become accustomed to things like

two cars, charge cards, and trips to Reno, those good times were over. We'd run out of road. Our successes were like the freshly built freeways in California that ended abruptly at concrete barriers, while the builders waited for next year's appropriations to come through.

The next day I answered an ad in the paper to manage an apartment complex. There was a three-bedroom apartment free, plus salary, and it had a swimming pool and cabana. The kids would like that. I was hired on the spot. I quickly wrapped up my job at the Cultural Institute. I could cut my losses when I had to. (Ray's story "The Bridle" came from this experience.)

Ray engaged a lawyer with glasses as thick as Coke bottles to file our bankruptcy petition. But he had another plan as well. Of all the jobs he'd held, he most enjoyed working in libraries. He would become a reference librarian like Dave Palmer, our librarian and poet friend in Humboldt. That meant Ray needed to take graduate courses in library science.

Where? The University of Iowa, he explained. I hated to admit it, but it made some sense: Better the devil you know. And graduate credits were not necessarily transferable elsewhere. Besides, I had matriculated at Iowa and could certainly return. By hook or by crook, I'd go to school, too, and finish my degree.

In the spring of 1967, Ray went to Iowa to "seal the deal." He was accepted into the Master of Library Science program. A course schedule for the fall was drawn up. His adviser actually joked that Ray's reference letters from Professors Day, Palmer, and Schmitz were so laudatory, perhaps Iowa ought to send a plane to fly Ray in.

Our actual plan was slightly more modest. Ray would get settled in Iowa before he sent for us. I would bring in what money I could from the apartment-complex job, dispose of most of our belongings, and pack just our clothes, books, and dishes.

Before Ray left Sacramento we took time to celebrate our tenth wedding anniversary on the seventh of June. We made it count.

I found that managing the apartment complex was no longer fun with

Ray gone. As soon as I began cooking dinner, inevitably some tenant was at my door bugging me about some minor problem. I began to get annoyed; I wanted to wind things up and hit the road to Iowa.

One Saturday morning the phone rang before I was quite awake. One of the tenants again, I thought. Calling about a leaky faucet or a balky garbage disposal or, sorry, they had to vacate on short notice. Please go away.

The phone kept ringing. Sleepily I picked up the receiver. It was Ella.

"Mary," she said, sounding miserably distraught, "Ray died."

"What?!" Instantly my mind was racing double time, my heart was pounding. I thought, Oh my poor little children! Not Daddy.

"What should I do, Mary? Should I call the coroner?"

Wait, Ella was calling from her place. It wasn't Ray. It was his father.

11

PALO ALTO, ISRAEL, PARIS, HOLLYWOOD

Ray dropped everything and came home. We met up by serendipity in the Sacramento airport—I wasn't sure of his exact travel plans. He hugged me hard. Then we went out to his folks' current place in Crescent City, a coastal town about eighty miles north of Arcata.

Gathered together, Ray, his mother, and James were seemingly immobilized. I grabbed the car keys and headed for the door, saying, "I'm going to go see Raymond." This stirred Ray. He was strong now, and he wanted to go see his father. The two of us went over to the mortuary.

After Ray saw his dad, he brought his mother and James to view the body. C. R.'s restless travels were over. But Ella and James were still in a state of shock, faced with the unthinkable. The heart of their world was gone at only fifty-three.

After his dad's death on June 17, Ray did not return to Iowa. He scrapped his goal of becoming a librarian. As you'd expect of a man like Ray, there was no great outward display of grief, but he was deeply affected. He and his dad had been very close in their own understated way. Now Ray would never have the chance to say good-bye. Life, as any Carver could tell you, was like that—though only Ray could craft it into luminous, compelling words. Yet after the dislocations of the last six months—my job change, bankruptcy, the abandoned relocation to

Iowa—and C. R.'s unexpected death, we settled into our next situation with surprising effortlessness.

I think it was through Curt Johnson that Ray got a lead on an editorial position at Science Research Associates (SRA) in Palo Alto. (Curt first published Ray's groundbreaking story, "Will You Please Be Quiet, Please?" in his small literary magazine, *december*.) He applied for the job, had a charming, successful interview, and was hired.

To get us set up, I did something I'd never done before, no matter how tight a jam we were in—I borrowed money from my aunt May. Three hundred dollars. But my vibe was we had to land somewhere safely and quickly. With the loan money we rented a house at 886 Loma Verde, Palo Alto. Like that the other pieces of our lives fell into place. Ray started his first white-collar job; I went back to college full-time. The kids went to a decent school. We found new friends, mainly through Ray's job.

The previous residents of the house had converted a portion of the garage into a playroom. It was carpeted, painted, and equipped with in-wall heat. We made it Ray's study. He was delighted to have a room in close proximity to the rest of the house, yet one that gave him a psychological sense of privacy. After days working as an editor in downtown Palo Alto, he spent many productive evenings there "fiddling with his pencil," as he liked to put it.

Ray was now regularly sending out stories and poems, and by the following spring was frequently in print. Mail from little magazines and literary journals stuffed our mailbox as often as ad circulars. Curt Johnson flew out to San Francisco and visited us in the Loma Verde house. We drank bourbon, served good food, and invited SRA friends over. The party was on again at the Carvers'.

IN SEPTEMBER I started classes at Foothill Community College in Los Altos. The beautiful campus had won many architectural awards. Set high in the hills of Los Altos, south of San Francisco, it had an excellent reputation as a preparatory feeder to Stanford. The instructors took greater personal interest in the students than they could at the big schools with huge student populations. It was more like an extension of a very good high school. I did well there.

From my speech instructor's pool of four classes, I was selected to participate in the speech competition. My research topic, "Murray the K and the New Left," tried to penetrate our turbulent, interesting times, exploring everything from contemporary music to Vietnam to the New Left politics of the young generation. Protests against the Vietnam War were growing more violent. In my view and that of my friends, it was necessary.

At Foothill I finally made the decision to major in English. I probably had greater aptitude for philosophy and history, but my choice had been crystallized one day in the process of "dissecting" a poem. The class experience took me beyond analysis to artistic enthrallment. As usual I wanted to have it all. (That happy semester I pulled a 4.0 and was on the honors list.)

Ray was thriving at SRA. He was learning to be a specialized editor. His job, basically, was to read stories, articles, and poems to identify works that were "grade appropriate" for SRA's graduated reading program, used throughout public schools to this day. His eccentric reading background was a great asset to him, as he brought in obscure stories by Chekhov and de Maupassant. Ray's immediate boss, Dick, whose area of specialization was French literature, actually bought several of Ray's own stories and poems to include in projects SRA was producing.

What a change from the days of custodial duties at Mercy Hospital. He was among bright, enlightened people who were pursing fresh educational ideas and concepts. These were people who got more out of their work than a paycheck.

IN THE FALL OF '67 we went down to Big Sur for a weekend. A number of friends had places there.

There was an outdoor pavilion lit by lanterns in the huge trees, the cliffs and the majestic ocean beyond an illusory arm's-length away. Esalen Institute was around the corner. Ray and I danced and danced to Morrison and the Doors. Light my fire. And Van Morrison dancing in the moonlight.

Ray at his editorial post at SRA, as corporate as he could stand. Palo Alto, California, fall 1967.

PHOTO BY MARYANN BURK CARVER

There we were, dancing under the stars on a warm California night, turned on by each other's bodies in our jeans and sandals.

"I'm so in love with you," I shouted over the music to Ray.

"I'm so in love with you," he replied, as Jim Morrison's voice took us higher. Then we drifted off to our double sleeping bag and another bottle of wine.

The next night we all went to Nepenthe, the residence Orson Welles built for Rita Hayworth. It was now a restaurant. Our friend Eve graciously paid for the entire evening. We watched all the lissome young lovelies dance, not a trace of a bra under costumes of Indian prints, blouses, long skirts, or their hippie dresses. It was the perfect time to be young and dancing the night away on the patio.

EARLY IN '68, when *The Best American Short Stories 1967* came out with Ray's story, "Will You Please Be Quiet, Please?" it was time for a celebration. First Ray and I went out alone to have dinner and dance to "our" music. The following weekend there was a party of the entire SRA office—staff, spouses, and other friends. Ray's story was the buzz of the evening.

Everyone had read it, and some asked me if it was true. Had the events in the story really happened? "I'll never tell," I'd say, no matter how imploring the questioner. What is art without mystery?

IN FEBRUARY I transferred on to San Jose State. (Foothill was a two-year community college and I wanted a regular four-year degree.) I wormed my way into a full class load, despite restrictions put in place due to overenrollment. Compared to Foothill, it was a huge, ugly, impersonal institution. I felt sharply alienated for several weeks and longed for the days in Sacramento when I managed a successful office, drove a red convertible, and drew a big paycheck. But Ray was right; we had moved on. So I hung in there.

On a spring day I spotted a notice outside my adviser's office promoting a new opportunity, the State College Study Abroad Program. I asked the receptionist about it. "Here," she said, "I'll give you the paperwork. Take it along and fill everything out."

I couldn't believe it: The program could, in some cases, send the student's family abroad, too. I was seized with ambition. I put my name down on the application list and submitted the paperwork as fast as possible. I checked off three places I wanted to go, in order of preference: Florence, Italy; Uppsala, Sweden; Tel Aviv, Israel.

Ray and I had always wanted to travel—now might be our chance. After I turned in my application, I was closely questioned. Ray and I had to take psychological tests. We held our breath.

AROUND THAT TIME Curt Johnson brought Gordon Lish over to our house to meet Ray. They were both textbook editors, working across the street from each other. Something just clicked between the two of them.

The bond endured after Gordon went back to New York. He had sat in our living room with Barbara, his current girlfriend, and claimed his former wife had tried to run her over. Ray and I were taken aback. That story—true or not—coupled with a sheriff after him for outstanding child support, had sent Gordon ducking out of Palo Alto in a hurry. To New York.

He landed a job as fiction editor at *Esquire* magazine. Working untold hours a day, he read more manuscripts than anyone thought humanly possible, soon establishing himself as "Captain Fiction."

As the "big brother," Gordon thought himself admirably suited to take charge of Ray's literary career. He was in a position to tell Ray where stories should be sent and what the titles should be. He even floated overbearing suggestions about Ray's personal life.

Gordon altered some of Ray's stories, often in ways I didn't agree with. But I realized how much he loved Ray's work—and wished he had written the stories himself.

He smilingly told me that "Will You Please Be Quiet, Please?" did not end the way he would have it.

"The good thing is," I said, "it's not your story. It's Ray's."

On balance, for the good work Gordon did as an editor, Ray was deeply appreciative. He often agreed with Gordon's edits, and what he did not like could someday be restored. What counted for now was getting his work published. You had to believe that Gordon Lish's sway with agents and publishers excused a lot of his idiosyncrasies.

THE STUDY ABROAD program accepted us. But, as we were given a choice, where should we go? The stipend for study in Israel was five hundred dollars more than those for Italy or Sweden. In those days if extra money was offered us, we reflexively grabbed it.

We were going. I collected a mystical, magical five-thousand dollar check. Happily, SRA granted Ray a one-year leave of absence. Then, using Mom's JC Penney credit card, we got ourselves outfitted. Christi had new dresses, sleek and slim, and for Vance, a three-piece suit, with vest, white shirt, and tie.

June was here, the semester was over, and we sang along to "Up, Up and Away (In My Beautiful Balloon)" and couldn't stop laughing. It was a good time, a rare time. We were going to ride high above the discordant world.

First our group flew United Airlines to Kennedy Airport in New York. (I was the escort leader.) Pitching in, Ray led the brigade of students, most younger than we, across the airport to the international terminal. On to Orly Airport, Paris. Sleepy with jet lag but full of anticipation, we boarded an El Al flight bound for the Promised Land.

It was a year after the Six-Day War. In less than a week Israel had shown the civilized world—and the uncivilized—what Zionists were made of. Now here came the Carvers, gentiles from California.

We had promises of a villa on the Mediterranean; Ray saw himself writing and basking in the sun. But once we cleared customs in Tel Aviv, our local escort herded us to a battered jeep and deposited us at the Sharon Hotel. We didn't know what had happened to our villa, but we made the best of it.

The hotel suite was spacious, with a balcony looking out on the sea. There were two queen-size beds taking up most of the room, yet enough space to wheel in a table covered with a starched and ironed white tablecloth. Along with the evening meal, the table had silver candlesticks that matched the silver goblets. The white candles were lit. Even as Ray and I lifted the silver plate covers, ready to break bread and divide all this beautiful bounty among the four of us, we began to wonder just who was paying the tab? No one had said anything as we checked in.

I had no idea if the hotel would present us with a preposterous bill that would eat up most of the funds we needed to last a *year*. Could it be that this luxury was courtesy of the program because we were a family? Or because I was a leader? Or was it an amazing early nod to Ray's importance in the world of letters?

Better not to ask. And we didn't think anyone else in the hotel had a clue. Most other people we talked with in the next few days read their Torahs or Bibles as if they were just last week's newspaper. The answers we needed weren't likely to be found in Scripture.

So we didn't know who was footing the bill. Or where we were supposed to live. Or when my classes started—the reason I was here in the first place. Thanks to the anxiety, we had a hard time enjoying the opulence of our accommodations.

And what about the American school in Tel Aviv that was promised to have places for Christi and Vance? We were baffled and bewildered. When I called the Israeli host university for more information, I got nothing—and I was pretty good at extracting info from a bureaucratic fog. No one knew anything. People they suggested I contact knew even less.

I was supposed to learn Hebrew at an *ulpan* (a school for intensive study of Hebrew, especially for immigrants). In a troubled tone, I'd tell the latest official I reached on the phone that I certainly didn't want to start late. No problem, no problem. We'll let you know. (Ray was also going to take a Hebrew class, one of the program's conditions for his inclusion.)

Ray was becoming annoyed and complained privately. Finally he couldn't stand the limbo at the hotel any longer. On his own he found a third-floor walk-up apartment for rent that belonged to a conductor of the Israeli Philharmonic. It would do, even though it had only two small bedrooms. And we knew what it cost.

After a few days in Israel we began to get the picture of what our year was to be like: not exactly as advertised. At last I did get some information and got started. Ray promptly dropped his class at the *ulpan* so he was free to take a bus downtown every day and buy supplies. There was no easy cruising down the freeway to the supermarket here.

I went to class six days a week. I did oral Hebrew drills. And I studied on my own, hours and hours. Atypically I was lost in a linguistic maze. My home life suffered as I studied endlessly, just in case hard work was the key. Unfolded laundry was scrunched in the living room furniture, and the kitchen sink overflowed with soiled, tomato-encrusted plates, unheard of in my kitchen back home.

Ray and Christi were not warming up to Tel Aviv. Vance and I had a more innate curiosity about people and their customs. We were torn, annoyed that so many "promises" were wishful thinking by the Israeli hosts of the study abroad program. Yet we became friends with some very special people, like our neighbors, Sima and Schlomo, who lived across the hall from us.

And we remained fiercely pro-Israel. Even when we indulged in some tart comments on the Israeli way of conducting life's little unavoidable daily transactions. But I think we—and particularly Ray—might have weathered a longer stay if, on top of everything else, Amy hadn't showed up with her two-year-old daughter, Erin.

As long as planes could fly, Amy was always glad to pick up and go. Better yet if she had relatives where the plane touched down. So there she was at the Tel Aviv airport.

Ray went to pick her up.

"Oh, Ray," she said first thing, "let's duck into the restaurant here and get a cold Coke with ice."

"Ice!" Ray ranted, much to Amy's bafflement. "You've got to be kidding! There is no ice! We've been sold down the river!"

And that was only the beginning. Amy explained she needed to leave Erin with us because she was joining Michael in Spain. He was acting in a movie being made there. Then, if I didn't mind, could I fly with Erin to Rome where Amy would collect her?

Even the Middle East wasn't far enough to get us away from my family. Ray was fuming and growing increasingly dissatisfied. Amy had badly fanned the flames. And when exactly did our kids start school?

RAY DECIDED TO take a bus trip through Greece and Rome, retracing Lord Byron's travels. I didn't blame him for going, but I always liked to share his extraordinary experiences.

Departing with a load of guilt in his mental luggage, he was gone barely more than a week. He made it to Rome, then turned around and headed right back to Israel. He had sped over the Hellespont and in Greece tasted as many wines as he could at local village celebrations. The old god Bacchus still had his devotees—and it was quite Byronic, I thought. Ray was working on poems, too.

Around the first of October, Ray had an ultimatum: Go home, or stay and be a student without a family. He was in full "good parent" mode and had decided his children should be out of this dangerous land. Hadn't an extremist set off a bomb in the bus depot our children passed through every day? Six people were killed. As a result they were taking two buses to reach the city of Jaffa and their Scottish-run, English-language school.

We knew that bombs turned up in theaters, airports, and in bus sta-

tions. Tragedy is everywhere. I had gotten that much out of Jewish history, soaking it up at the source.

I think Ray understood that this year abroad was significant for my
postcollege opportunities, especially for graduate school. I had already
given up a lot. I'd wanted to be an attorney, and at Humboldt had taken
some prelaw classes. But that dream had been put aside for the good of
the family. I had to drop out of Iowa. I couldn't afford Davis. I'd had to
drop out of Sacramento State. Then, after the move to Palo Alto, I finally completed three undergraduate years. I won the honor of studying
abroad.

Now, after four months in Israel, I was supposed to give it all up because my husband was homesick and restless?

My stomach was tied in knots. Ray not only feared for our safety but
also worried that our money wouldn't last the year. He claimed that we'd
spent a disproportionate amount in four months, even if all our expen-
ditures were justified. (We had not been frivolous. However, to pay rent
and buy edible food took what it took.)

He had a "carrot" as well—a booking on a first-class cruise ship. He
had told the travel agent that he was a writer, a journalist, and wangled
a special rate. All I had to do was say the word and we'd go cruising—
from Haifa through the Greek islands with stops at Rhodes, Athens,
and Corfu; debarking at Venice. Then we would rent a car and drive
through as much of Europe as we could before flying home from Luxembourg.

Ordinarily I'd have been thrilled. But I hated to be a quitter. Ray,
contrarily, made his favorite point, that there are some battles not worth
fighting. Responding to my obvious reluctance, he said disdainfully,
"I've decided lately that we're going through life like transients."

"What?!" I was pretty mad. I listed all the times he had turned our
lives upside down because *he* felt we had to move on. Nobody had mar-
shaled us out the door as much as he had.

"Well, I'm changing my mind," Ray said. "If we can just get home to
the United States of America, I think I'll weep with gratitude."

"Yes, I see you clutching your *Life on the Mississippi* out on the balcony like a baby blue security blanket. But for eleven years we have been pursuing college educations!"

I suddenly grasped how emotionally deadened Ray had become. He had lost much of his spontaneity and natural sense of fun. I realized that he was ignoring his profound grief over his father's death, damaging himself, hardening his carapace of cynicism.

No one had spoken of his dad in the year and a half since C. R. died. The Carvers had clammed up, unlike the emotional members of my family who wept openly for lost loved ones and recalled them in stories and reminiscences. In the Carver family the pain was so great that they were mute.

In that moment my heart went out to Ray.

We'd go home.

As I packed up for the umpteenth time in our marriage, I wished that Ray could weep for his father. Perhaps that might restore his spirit of compassion and cause him to step back from a bleak, self-centered orientation in his inner life. Like his mother, I thought, it was so hard for Ray to be fulfilled. He'd want something, get it—and not be satisfied.

But he was who he was. And I loved him to distraction.

THE GOOD GREEK ship *Pegasus* was not winged, but it was a marvelous way to see the Mediterranean. As promised, it was indeed first-class, and after our chaotic time in Tel Aviv, we enjoyed the perfect mix of energy and lassitude of shipboard life. As we made the various ports of call, we went ashore and packed every minute with as much as we could take in.

Rhodes, Athens, Corfu—onward. Don't look back. Keep your memories of Israel alive. Someday in my eighties, when so many things would be lost, I wanted to be able to say to myself, Imagine, when I was young and lithe and lovely, I skipped my way through the Holy Land and stared in awed amazement at the place where the Christ Child lay.

As we steamed into Piraeus, the harbor of Athens, the light from the city was as translucent and crystalline as Henry Miller proclaimed.

Rereading the *The Colossus of Maroussi* before we went ashore for the obligatory yet stunning tour of the Parthenon, I was amused and impressed with Henry's way with words. He must have known that we are made of light. Forget the textbook's water, muscle, and bone—our real essence is light, as a walk in Athens will attest.

WE DISEMBARKED IN Venice. Farewell *Pegasus*. The next stage of our trip was by rental car. We planned to drive to Florence, then on into France and up to Paris. A few days in *la cité*, and then off to Luxembourg and a plane to L.A.

Not that there was a place to come home to—we had sublet the Palo Alto house. Amy wanted us to come live near her. She was looking for something in Hollywood.

Venice was a kaleidoscope of colors. Color everywhere. In every clothing store, in the vegetable stands where red tomatoes, green peppers, purple eggplants, deep blue plums vied for attention. In our trusty guidebook, *Europe on Five Dollars a Day*, we located a *pensione* with breakfast included. The kids fed the pigeons in Saint Mark's Square, and Ray and I looked at the frescoes and Renaissance paintings and thought about life in the age of the Medici.

"I would have taken my chances," Ray decided, "to have lived in a time when a good artist could get a celebrated patron who lifted material worries and concerns from him. And left him time to paint or write."

"I'm sure you would." I laughed. "And you would have fared well, too, with palace intrigue and party politics. Machiavelli would have been your best friend, if that's what it took to receive patronage and popularity. You're lucky, too. It would all have worked out, without heads rolling or your manuscripts destroyed."

Ray ignored my remarks on his chances in the Italian Renaissance, other things on his mind. "I wonder what I'll be working at when we arrive back in the States." We hadn't planned far ahead. Just pack, get on the ship, leave Israel. "Well, let's enjoy ourselves in Europe. Let's have a vacation now."

"Let's," I said. "Let's not worry. We always get jobs and carry on."

Our drive from Venice to Paris featured must-not-miss American tourist moments. Ah, the magic of Florence. Then the quaint little country restaurant that charged prices right off Maxim's menu. They tried to clip us for forty dollars for bowls of soup and bread. We beat it down the road, then got lost, wound up back where we started, totally blew the schedule.

We had to have our car transported across the Alps by train. Reunited with our vehicle, we were on our way again. At nightfall we arrived in Paris. We'd made it. We weren't going to die without having seen the City of Light.

We did the standard sightseeing things with Vance and Christi—the Eiffel Tower, the Louvre, the Luxembourg Gardens. But the more Ray and I saw, the more we wanted to take the time to satisfy our adult interests. We knew the kids were getting restless and bored. Ray had an idea. Let's send them home to California ahead of us.

I was very unsure. Vance had just turned ten—on the *Pegasus*—and Christi wasn't eleven. They were too young to be flying on their own, especially all the way to L.A. Naturally, being their parents' children, they thought it was a fantastic idea. The lure of real hamburgers, TV, and being back in time for Halloween trumped the glories of French culture any day.

Ray had already made up his mind, I could see. "Let's call Amy and Michael. We had Erin for six weeks in Israel while they traveled all over Europe. Now it's our turn."

We worked out a plan like a military campaign. Amy would have to meet the kids. They would be under the strictest orders. Anybody deviating from the program would be shot at dawn. Well, no TV for a month.

I made the transatlantic call to my sister.

Amy was enthusiastic. She'd have costumes ready for the kids so they could go trick-or-treating. Even better news—she had a lead on a big house for us in Hollywood, right behind hers. She'd grab it for us before somebody else got wind of it.

At Orly I put my precious children on the plane for the thirteen-hour flight to Los Angeles, praying that nothing would go wrong. Christi and

Vance looked like miniature jet-setters, experienced travelers benevo-
lently tolerating this fussing couple who claimed to be their parents. I
went over all our instructions again and told them to let us know as soon
as they'd arrived safely.

While they were gone . . . *yippee!*

We went to the Jeu de Paume, the impressionist museum, and didn't
want to leave. For three days, we went back repeatedly and gazed at
paintings, together or on our own. Once I found Ray looking at van
Gogh's painting of his room at Arles, with its little single bed and red
chair. Ray was just standing there, silent tears in his eyes.

We bought wonderful French delicacies, pâtés, cheeses, loaves of
French bread, artichokes, olives, beautiful desserts, and brought them
up to our hotel room. When it rained softly, what a treat to stay in and
lie in bed and read a good book. We'd snack on patisserie goodies. And
make sweet love.

We went to the Rodin Museum and lost ourselves in the garden. We
found it difficult to leave. We saw Napoleon's tomb, massive and elegant, guarded by an honor guard in uniform. What amazed us the most
was the display in a glass case of the emperor's white glove. We couldn't
believe how small it was. Like a child's hand.

Voilà! Our vacation was over. We flew back on Icelandic Airlines.
There was a mandatory stopover in Iceland.

During the layover, I joked about trying a reindeer burger. We were
sitting in the airport bar, a clean, well-lighted place. All the bar stools
were taken and everyone stared at the television. Nearly broke, Ray and
I shared a cup of coffee laced with cream and sugar and sadly watched
the U.S. election reports. Richard Nixon was going to be the next president of the United States.

It made us feel doubly out in the cold. Our months in Israel had been
the American summer of the Democratic Convention riots in Chicago,
hard on the heels of Bobby Kennedy's assassination. And before that the
murder of Martin Luther King, Jr. Well, by all means leave Israel and get
back to a nonviolent, safe, and secure land like the U.S.A.

. . .

CHRISTI AND VANCE were happy in Hollywood. They got back in time for a great Halloween with Amy. Enrolled in a new school, they quickly adjusted. Compared to their last classroom in Jaffa, L.A.'s urban school scene was nothing they couldn't handle.

The night Ray and I got back, we feasted and partied at Amy's. Best of all, the house behind hers was ours. She had gone ahead and rented it for us. Our beds were already made up and waiting for us.

The next day I asked Amy to take me job hunting. Ray was going to join Amy and Michael in their theater hustle, selling programs for *2001: A Space Odyssey*. I declined to participate; a restaurant job was harder, but I'd find one fast and make steadier money.

The first place Amy took me to was a Hollywood institution—Edna Erle's Fog Cutter. The following night I was in a full black skirt, white blouse, and red vest serving up steak and baked potatoes, 5:00 to 10:00 P.M. My station was always full. That first night I went home with more than $50.

There was another good omen. About an hour after I started work, I walked up to a table and my customer was—Bob Hope. He was with another man, who enjoyed seeing my surprised reaction. Hope was tanned and looked far more handsome and youthful than in the movies or on TV. Welcome to Hollywood, Maryann.

Ray's attempts to hawk film souvenir programs was wryly amusing to everyone, except him. Amy and Michael were actors and were used to projecting their voices under public scrutiny. They were each netting $350 a week doing what came naturally—to them.

(This being Hollywood, they wouldn't have had the work if Michael's father hadn't been a union bigwig. Yes, the Theatrical Janitorial Union had jurisdiction over program sellers. The name cracked Ray up—besides, he had a "professional" interest, as he knew something about the custodial biz.)

We all joked about Ray's lack of barker skills. It was funny until Amy and I noticed that he had taken to carrying around a half-pint bottle of whiskey. We never saw Ray drunk from his daytime imbibing, but it was alarming. Maybe it was only temporary, something to take the edge off his nerves and his mortification when he had to shout out, "Souvenir programs! Get your souvenir programs!"

It was obvious to me that Ray would not be ending our "transient" days in Hollywood. This was no place for him to settle down and do serious writing. Though it was easier to earn a living here than in some places we'd lived, everything about the town was ephemeral and decadent. As much as we appreciated Amy and Michael's efforts to help us, and the fun we were having together, life as an extended party was not our style. Besides, we had two children on the verge of being teenagers. That was something to consider.

I was no more ready to embrace lotus land than Ray. Neither of us worked in the theater or movie business, as Amy and Michael did. It was only immediate necessity and family that had brought us here. One other reality: Ray was "three-oh"; I was twenty-eight. Any further time in college had to be aimed at eventual employment, not enriching the life of the mind, if we were ever going to settle down permanently. I hadn't forgotten his declaration in Tel Aviv.

HOLIDAYS IN HOLLYWOOD were, however, another matter. They turned out to be wonderful. And convenient. Nothing like living next door so nobody has far to travel.

Warming up for Christmas of '68, we had a great "dry run" at Thanksgiving. (Well, not that dry.) We were at the height of our gourmet cookouts craze. On Thanksgiving Eve, Amy and I chopped celery and onions in my kitchen for the dressing. We had one turkey to be stuffed with our traditional "German" dressing that our mother made (after our dad taught her): sage, bacon, onion, celery, egg, and giblet stock. The second bird was getting oysters, sausage, apple, and chestnut stuffing.

The dining room was filled with the usual cast of characters from Michael's theatrical crowd. Soon we could hear laughter and stories from the other room. Our thoughtful husbands came into the kitchen, bringing a joint for a puff and drinks for a sip. "Here they are," Ray said, "the Burk sisters, the prettiest ladies in town, slaving away on these turkeys."

"Whoa!" I said. "Being called one of the prettiest ladies in Hollywood is like being called the most attractive whore in Paris. But thank you very much, gorgeous husband."

"Why don't we take you away from all this?" Michael said, picking Amy up and effortlessly carrying her to the dining room. Ray slipped his arm through mine and led me away from the kitchen.

In the morning we laughed and laughed to see how we'd left everything—the celery and onions half chopped—as though there'd been a sudden evacuation. The repercussion from our dereliction of duty was that our feast with all our friends was rescheduled from two to five. A more civilized hour anyway, Amy and I pointed out. Especially when you wanted to serve white wine and champagne.

Which we most certainly did.

In December, Ray quit his job selling programs and went north to see how we could relocate. Enough of Southern California. His three hundred a week, though, was sorely missed. One week without it and I was scrounging. I offered to work any shift another waitress wanted off.

When I worked a double shift, I saved the extra tips. That money was going to buy Christi a guitar, the only gift she wanted for Christmas. I was determined to go to Penney's and buy Vance a pair or two of brown school pants. He was playing sports so constantly that the knees in all his other pants were shot. I had to hope relatives would buy him games and toys.

Ray was back in Hollywood on the twenty-third. He had run into car trouble and needed money wired to him, but otherwise there were no major problems. I was overjoyed to see his handsome, smiling face when he walked into the Fog Cutter shortly before my shift was over.

He had looked around San Jose and decided we should go back, carve out a life again, even if it would be tough getting started. Through Michael's father's union, Ray could get a job as a janitor, cleaning a bank or two at night. Hopefully he could get back to some solid writing by day, much as he had done in Sacramento when he worked at Mercy Hospital.

"You can go back to school, Maryann," Ray said. "I went to the college. I told them it was my fault you left Israel. They said with your grades, no problem. Just come in when you get back and figure out a schedule with your adviser."

And he had done more. At the college housing office, Ray learned there was a good chance we could get into Spartan Village. It would be a little two-bedroom place, but the price was right—$129 a month. It was close to the college.

He'd obviously done a lot of thinking. "Hell, it's going to be hard and dreary, but you'll get back in school. I love everybody here, but I can't get anything done in this three-ring circus—nobody's fault, mind you."

I couldn't have been happier. We weren't part of the Hollywood circus, just spectators for an act or two. It was time we left and made a home for ourselves again.

IF YOU DON'T know about 1969, go and read about it. Those of us who lived through that year can't forget it. In Hollywood we started off on a high note. The last day of December, Ray, Amy, and I were sitting on her vine-covered porch on Gregory Avenue, bantering about the choice of a family New Year's motto. We settled on "Things will Be Fine in '69."

I worked that night and made $350 in tips at the Fog Cutter. Enough to get Ray, me, and the kids out of town, to buy gas and food all the way to San Jose. Fine, indeed.

Shortly thereafter we moved into number 82, Spartan Village, San Jose State College married-student housing. We were willing to live austerely because Ray had to write and I had to get a degree. We went on working the menial jobs we knew all too well. I got a waitress gig; Ray, a janitorial job. Life as usual, but we brought a spirit to that little apartment that made us want to dance to the Beatles' latest hit or Motown pumped up loud.

Vance was doing pretty well, once he got past some altercations with a local Mexican gang that harassed him. Enter the Brown brothers, who threatened to "kick butt" if the Mexicans didn't cool out. Vance began to spend a lot of time at their house, eating chitlins and greens, pork chops, and sweet potato pie. He loved the food. And heavyset Mrs. Green (yes, the Brown boys' mother) adored the little blond guy that their black family all but adopted. The boys were all sports nuts and played at endless games.

Christi was another matter. For starters she was no longer Christi— she now insisted we call her Chris. She was moody, oh so much like her dad. She did not find joy easily. The circumstances had to be right for her to respond positively. In Sacramento she'd had close girlfriends, nice teachers, and a good overall experience. Iowa or Palo Alto or Israel had basically been miserable times for her.

A few weeks after we were living in the apartment, Michael, Amy, and Erin showed up on our doorstep. Erin was about to turn three. Michael had been reading Edgar Cayce and was convinced the coast of California was about to fall into the sea. Any day now. He and Amy had to get out. Did we have room for refugees?

RAY DID SOMETHING I never expected. He had lunch with his old boss at SRA. In February, Dick Fournier hired him back. That let me quit my oppressive waitressing job. It had been exhausting me.

For the first time ever, I was able to go to college and enjoy cooking dinner for my family. To study when I wasn't bone tired. But I worried, How could he write if he was spending his days over in Palo Alto?

Amy had been hospitalized, unable to cope. Michael had split to New York. Supposedly he was going to get settled, and then she would join him to do theater. Ray wanted to know why he couldn't wait for Erin's birthday. He saw two more mouths to feed, courtesy of Michael.

My poor sister realized that her life was crumbling. It would only get worse as the year went on. Michael had essentially abandoned her. She was one of those sensitive, openhearted people who couldn't take rejection. Amy just didn't understand—wasn't she pretty enough?

She recovered enough to attend the summer session at San Francisco

State, with assistance from me. Then she headed off to New York City to further her career on the stage and to work things out with Michael. By the end of the year their marriage was over.

Now both Amy and Jerry had gone through the trauma of ending a relationship central to their lives. Like our mother. Two out of three of her daughters with a failed marriage; I was as determined never to make it three out of three.

What a year. Ray and I were happy to be alive and working toward some better days, modest goals in a troubled time. He announced soberly that we should do nothing to ruffle the gods, not even a little. For the coming new year we simply would not have a motto.

1970s

Ray and I, in our private backyard on Wright Avenue.
Sunnyvale, California, 1970.

12

WRITING, TEACHING, DRINKING

Ray and I went into the seventies with what I thought was a solid marriage and family. During the first years of a difficult American decade—the unrest after the invasion of Cambodia and escalating protests against the Vietnam War—we were advancing professionally and personally. In the years 1970–73 particularly, I believed that many of our long-held dreams were coming true. Well, it's the old Chinese saying, Beware of what you wish for, you may get it—and it may not be what you expected.

Let me unknit the whole cloth of our experiences and show something of how Ray was transformed into "Raymond Carver, author," for better and for worse. And how I became the professional wife who couldn't rescue him. Though even as our relationship frayed, I never thought it irreparable.

But in 1970 we were still a young family with a future. I'll separate out some major threads of our lives—teaching, writing, drinking. Teaching had stabilized us and writing was boosting us up the economic ladder. Drinking made it easier to ignore the hard realities down below us should we ever lose our grips and fall.

A good way to thank your husband for a new outfit.
Christmas 1969.
USED WITH PERMISSION OF THE ESTATE OF AMY BURK UNGER

TEACHING

Spring '70

At twenty-five I had given up my adolescent dream of being an attorney. At twenty-nine I realized my plan of going to graduate school and
pursuing a Ph.D. in literature and humanities was not realistic either.
And Ray wanted to quit SRA and write full-time; there was no way we
could do that without income from somewhere. I decided I would qualify to teach in the California public school system.

I "drifted into" Professor Alice Scofield's Honors Intern Program.
This program allowed an exceptional student to become a teacher after
one summer session of education classes and student teaching. Rather
than apply to graduate school or take a career opportunity offered by the
campus recruiters, I thought, if I could begin teaching locally we'd be
able to live on my salary.

I would still have to attend a four-hour class on Wednesday nights
during the school year, and another full summer of classes after teaching

a year, but then I'd have a lifetime secondary teaching credential. A union card, so to speak. Given the choppy seas in our lives, I thought such a professional lifeline was the most intelligent choice. I had grown up watching my mother teach in various communities—though she seemed to like a change of scenery every two or three years. (Perhaps she got drained from the scrutiny a small-town teacher faced in those days.) Wherever we went, however, my mother was instantly employed. She was respected for the great teaching she did and her contribution to the community.

Summer '70

During my stint of mandatory student teaching at Prospect High School in Campbell, I became friends with my master teacher, pretty, red-haired Rita Wilkinson. Before I began teaching I had worried that I wouldn't know how to relate to high school students, as I was years removed from adolescent arrogance and silliness. Instead I found that I loved these students, and I loved teaching.

Ray and I went to a dinner party that Rita hosted. She told me that she and the principal had figured out a way to create a full-time position for me starting that fall. I had a job prospect! Then the old saw that it never rains but it pours . . . well, mostly it doesn't rain in California, but a second offer landed in my lap immediately.

Offer number two: teach English at Los Altos High School. Dr. Scofield had been asked to send out one of her top-notch students for an interview. She chose me. It was the plum of high schools in the area, with only four classes to teach per day, rather than five. The smaller class load let teachers do more intensive preparations. The school wanted to achieve maximum quality for the students, the children of parents who worked at Stanford and in Silicon Valley, the most expensive area in the entire state.

I hesitated, but after consultation with several people I took the Los Altos job. I would teach there for the next eight years.

WRITING

April '70

Less than a week after Ray and I returned from an SRA business trip to New York—I'll skip for the moment how I got to tag along—there was an emphatic knock on the classroom door of my French II class. Annoyed, the instructor went and opened it, even as a student went on reciting *le texte*. Ray stepped in.

The kids. Something must have happened to one of the kids! Ray had never before come to one of my classrooms. My brain was racing—whether in English or French, I'm not sure. I heard him telling the instructor, "I need to speak to my wife, Maryann Carver."

I leaped to my feet, out of my trance. "Ray, Ray, what is it? The kids?"

He took me out in the hall. "No, no, honey," he said, "I'm sorry I scared you." He grinned. "I was just informed that I'm going to receive a National Endowment for the Arts grant."

He thought I might like to know sooner rather than later.

I bounded over to him. Ray caught me in his arms, a happy light in his eyes. I wrapped my legs around his waist, my arms encircling his neck. I guess he knew how I felt about the news.

What impressed the kids was that this was indeed *news*. The local radio station most people in San Jose listened to had a newscast every half hour. The announcer read off the AP wire. So, every half hour that day, you'd hear: "Local poet and fiction writer, Raymond Carver, was awarded a National Endowment for the Arts grant for demonstrating outstanding excellence in his chosen field." Which the station underscored with a sound effect of a twenty-one-gun salute.

Usually that honor went only to sports heroes or the like. (The American track star Lee Evans was a neighbor in student housing. He was the athlete who held up his gloved fist in a gesture of protest at the 1968 Olympic Games in Mexico. A controversial figure elsewhere, he was a hero here.)

Vance and Christi—excuse me, Chris—were very proud and excited that their dad was in the same league as Lee Evans. They kept bringing in friends on the half hour to listen, over and over. And to hear the guns going off.

If winning NEA awards and the like were simply a matter of great references, Ray already had what it took. For years he had collected and preserved a file of "ready references" from friends, sparing them the bother of composing something new every time he needed application "ammunition." The letters could be used for school submissions, for grant requests, for job recommendations. Dick Day must have written fifty on Ray's behalf—David Palmer and Dennis Schmitz did the same.

Ray's notorious reference letters had, naturally, already become part of the legend. We used to joke about which "form letter" we should pull when Ray needed one, cracking ourselves up as we called out this or that number. It wasn't actually true, but it well expressed our attitude about bureaucratic paperwork.

Everything from Guggenheim award forms to applications for teaching positions at the Universities of California and Texas were graced with these first-class references from first-class people. After all, based on those sterling references, hadn't the adviser at the library school in Iowa joked about sending a plane out to fetch Ray?!

Spring '70

Ray's second book of poetry, *Winter Insomnia*, came out, dedicated to Dennis Schmitz. It was published by George Hitchcock at Kayak Books, a small press based in San Francisco. George was a friend of ours. (In a technical sense this was Ray's first book from a real publisher in the book business. His first book of poems, *Near Klamath*, was lovingly put out by Dennis Schmitz and the English Department at Sacramento State College, but that was hardly commercial.)

By this time Ray had pretty much established his compositional process. For starters he definitely needed the right sort of space to work in. He needed one that gave him a sense of isolation and distance from the buzz of the everyday world. (That particularly meant, as the kids got older, rambunctious teens.) Once he had his imaginative train of thought running, he hated for it to be interrupted; he didn't want to suspend his work and resume later as some writers apparently don't mind doing.

Ray sharpened his pencils before he began anything—but often enough used a ballpoint. He'd write in his small, illegible hand on a yellow legal pad or white typing paper. The important point is that he wrote a first draft of a poem or story, if possible, in one sitting. He wanted to push on while he was in the same mood and could hold the same "voice" throughout. However, most stories did take several sittings to complete, but he would keep at it, sleeping very little, eager to pick up where he'd left off.

After Ray got a first draft of a story or a poem finished, he was home free, so to speak. He didn't worry about how long a manuscript might sit in the drawer before he got back to it.

Revising, he'd use his typewriter for subsequent drafts until he was ready to put the finished piece in the mail. He always wanted to send something off to some little magazine as soon as he was reasonably satisfied—otherwise he might keep "fiddling" with it, as he called his interminable editing process. He was an absolute perfectionist about every word, every comma, every detail in everything he wrote. He'd laugh and say that he knew he was finished when he started to put back punctuation that he'd previously taken out.

Ray never cared how long the revision process took. He actually liked to put early drafts of his stories aside, so that when he took them up again, he had a fresh eye. He was a crack self-editor, objective and detached. If a story could be made better by cutting a scene he really liked or had enjoyed writing, he cut it. The effect of the whole story was more important, period.

I realized later that it was years before Ray could write several stories over the course of a summer or academic year. (For example, "The Furious Seasons" was Ray's entire class project during the second semester he studied with John Gardner.) Though he always told everyone he was a writer, he didn't believe that prolific output proved anything, one way or the other, and in his earliest years, it clearly took a long time for him to bring a story from first draft to completion.

He learned through repetition, not by analysis, and was modest about his technical skills. If his writing reads effortlessly, it is because of the work he put in to make it that way. Ray spent years struggling to compose short stories and poems in a period when a "real" writer was expected to produce novels—at least two or three—before being taken seriously. Short stories, never mind poems, were pleasant exercises that ought to make way for the magnum opus. But those were the forms congenial to Ray's concentration, talent, and heart, despite the pressure he felt to produce a "big book." He was compositionally a miniaturist in the sense of Japanese haiku or Persian painting of the thirteenth–sixteenth centuries. Or, if you like, the way a three-minute rock and roll song can seem to say it all.

Ray liked to claim that he hadn't written a novel because it was too difficult to tackle a long work in the midst of struggling for an education and supporting a family with young kids. Fair enough. With short stories and poems, though, he could have a sense of completion and exhilaration often; he didn't have to wait years to feel that fleeting satisfaction. And he got his work done. He had seen other writers and academic friends blocked, unable to write much, lacerating themselves as they struggled to meet the conventional expectations.

Later in life, when Ray had the time and financial security to tackle any project he wanted to, what did he do? He wrote stories and poems the way he always had. He never wrote a novel, despite other people's urgings. Look at what happened after he won the prestigious Mildred and Harold Strauss Living Grant in 1983. That triggered one of the largest batches of poems he ever produced. He had five years to write full-time, no distracting children around, no financial worries—he still chose to write short stories and poems. Really *great* stories and poems.

Summer '70

It made me uneasy from past experience when Ray took a room on Chaucer Street in Palo Alto. He wrote his story "Neighbors" there. (He told me he got the idea for it from the time in Tel Aviv when he looked after Sima and Schlomo's apartment across the hall for a couple of days.

Ray had watered the plants and "looked into things" in our Israeli
neighbors' apartment.)

After we settled in Sunnyvale, Ray launched into a different kind of
work. It was an adolescent coming-of-age story, strange and compelling,
with almost mystical overtones. But "Summer Steelhead" had nothing
overt or superficially shocking about it—that new-age style fashionable
at the time.

I had never seen Ray so excited and compelled to write. He worked
relentlessly on "Summer Steelhead" (which he later retitled "Nobody
Said Anything"). He barely took time to eat or sleep. After maybe three
hours of exhausted rest, he'd be right back up, pencil in hand, working
on the story until he got a first draft down. Then, as was his habit, he
went through many drafts, cutting and refining. The story moved ahead
from penciled longhand to typescript. After many further typed revisions, he called it finished—for the moment.

Ray and I had established a routine of how we interacted when it
came to his work. As much as I wanted to know what he was writing
when he was so excited and focused, I knew better than to ask even a
single question. A story in progress was off-limits, nor would I ask to see
it. I waited until he finished the draft and offered to show it to me. Then
I'd read eagerly.

I was always curious to see who the characters were and where they
were going. Typically I was held by the story's tension and Ray's subtle
humor, which I could detect and appreciate better than anyone. (Not infrequently I had witnessed the core incident that inspired the story.) But
transfigured in the telling, the incident was artistically framed to achieve
Ray's desired effect, as otherwise it would have had little more impact
than any random observation pulled out of our busy, chaotic lives.

To help Ray I'd first read as quickly as I could, letting it hit me as future readers might experience the story. Then I went back over it more
carefully, pencil in hand, looking at every word, sentence, punctuation
mark, and paragraph in terms of Ray's overall conception. Every nuance
had to work and contribute to the whole. Essentially my job was to give
feedback he could use when he began his revisions.

TEACHING

Fall '71

Ray accepted his first job teaching writing at College V, University of California, Santa Cruz. "Not bad for a boy with a BA from Humboldt State College," he observed dryly.

I helped Ray set up his first course plan. My suggestion was that he start by passing out a good Robert Coover poem that looked simple enough for anyone to write—a "list" poem. Then I helped him gather objects from our house that students would choose from to make a list and write their own poems. That activity, and some others that I used in my own classroom, got Ray launched. He also drew on his own experiences at the Iowa Writers' Workshop.

After a nervous beginning, he soon found his stride, a matter of getting some experience under his belt. In addition to reading and discussing the students' writing, Ray had them read authors he loved—Frank O'Connor, Flannery O'Connor, Chekhov. Teaching the great writers he really enjoyed kept Ray interested and gave him confidence. He wasn't concerned about a specific curriculum to cover. His students were there to write, and the reading was to stimulate their writing.

WRITING

Fall '71

Gordon Lish, Ray's good friend from their days in Palo Alto, was now the fiction editor at *Esquire*.

Ray sent stories to other magazines only after Gordon had seen them and made suggestions. For Gordon that was a license to take his editorial pencil to Ray's work. I felt that Gordon's m.o. was to make Ray's stories more hip, slick, and cool—rather than soulful and real, the way I liked them.

I must say, as the first reader, I resented it when Lish boldly changed the title of "Are These Actual Miles?" to "What Is It?" The new title seemed to have nothing to do with anything, except that it came from the text. The original title was subtle, compared with the bland, clueless one Gordon saddled it with. Ray's title caught the sense of off-center cruelty, the way the used-car dealer of the story asks the husband questions as he's buying the husband's wife's convertible. (Shades of my red Pontiac convertible that we had to sell!) Then the dealer wines and dines the wife.

Ray and I got into a real conflict over the title change. He accepted it to get the story published. I accused him of being a whore, of selling out to the establishment—and that maybe Gordon wasn't always acting in his best interests.

Don't worry about it, Ray argued, there's more where that came from. "It's a bigger sellout to let stories sit in the drawer." Success begets success, was Ray's attitude. Getting publication in a major magazine was worth the changes he had to make.

I cried, argued, and disagreed to no avail.

"Later on, honey, I'll get my stories back. If I put them out now and get attention in whatever form they appear, they're still my stories. No one else wrote them." He had a plan for what he'd do eventually. "I'll change them back, or use original titles if I want to, after they've served their purpose. Besides, I like some of the changes. For sure, they do improve the story. That's what a good editor does for a writer. That's what you do when you first read my stuff and bring your thoughts."

Ray made an additional point. "I'm not one for being too precious, the way some writers are. They are so concerned about being purists, their work sits around in desk drawers, rather than be contaminated or exchanged for filthy money. Then, for the lack of filthy money, they don't have the time to write any more stories."

I had to admit that Gordon did have clout. "Neighbors" and "What Is It?" were published in *Esquire*. I was ecstatic about the layout of "Neighbors" and thought the accompanying illustration positively inspired. *Esquire* was still in its large format, so it made quite a splash. It was a moment of triumph. Ray's first major publication in a big national magazine. And one that was "slick" but with a serious literary reputation.

Gordon was promoting Ray behind the scenes to *Harper's Bazaar*.

They took "Fat." He placed "So Much Water So Close to Home" at *Playgirl*. Nonetheless Ray also remained loyal to the little magazines that had regularly printed his poetry. Much of his fiction still first saw public exposure in these periodicals. We both read them extensively, at home and in libraries, keeping track of what authors were being published where, and who the editors were.

For the first time, with Gordon helping in New York, Ray had an "in" to some of the money markets, the magazines with mass appeal. The sort, I imagined, that busy people took on airplanes or bought to read in their hotel rooms. Doctors and dentists displayed them in their waiting rooms. People subscribed and had them lying about in their homes. His work was going to be everywhere.

Ray got the news that he was going to share the Joseph Henry Jackson Award that year. The award honored the "best writer in California." He was to receive a plaque and check at a banquet in the San Francisco financial district.

Winter '71

When we were living in a house in Ben Lomond (I'll come to how we wound up in Santa Cruz), Ray wrote a poem called "Country Matters." Soon after, Mr. Six, Chris's little dog, was run over and killed; Ray responded with another poem, the touching "Your Dog Dies." (Mr. Six was the sixth puppy of the litter, a gift from Amy.)

Those first two poems unleashed something in Ray, and he went into a frenzy of poetry composition. Poem after poem came out of his wood-and-glass study overlooking the mountain and the redwood trees. The worldview expressed was often bleak, but the spirit that drove it was fierce and kicking.

DRINKING

August '71

After we moved to Ben Lomond, Ray began to drink more than ever. I did, too. It never got out of hand as long as we lived there, but it seemed an acceptable aspect of our new and accelerated lifestyle. Both of us were working, teaching, and entertaining a lot. It seemed that every day we were drinking something. A bottle of wine with dinner, or cocktails with university people at some fashionable downtown Santa Cruz restaurant, or a casual beer with friends. We didn't think our drinking was a problem, not when we were both functioning well.

Ray often taught students old enough to drink. They thoroughly enjoyed the individual attention and laughs of a barroom session with Ray, away from university and classroom formalities. Then Ray would come home and have two or three drinks with me before dinner.

The kids found the new ritual of a cocktail hour at our house boring. Well, it wasn't for *them*. I wanted some adult sophistication in light of our new positions in the world. Ray and I were no longer trapped in menial jobs and running on a college student's clock.

Fall '71

Friends who weren't writers began to notice that Ray and I were drinking more. (For many writers, partying and drinking went with the territory.)

Jeanne Church, my colleague at Los Altos High School, also taught English. We let down our hair with each other regularly. Hesitantly she said to me, "I think you might think about watching your drinking a little bit. It seems as if you and Ray have really gotten into the fast lane since you moved to Santa Cruz. Just be careful, that's all. Do you realize that alcohol is a drug?"

"No," I said. "It's perfectly legal. It's not like taking prescription narcotics or shooting dope in your arm, for God's sake."

"It can be worse. Ask Jody. Her father was an alcoholic. He made her mother's life sheer hell until they got away from him."

Jody Luck was another English teacher, but I failed to see the relevance. "That has nothing to do with Ray and me," I said icily. But I thought about Jeanne's comments later. Ray and I had gotten thoroughly drunk two or three times lately—once over at our friends David and Lyn Swanger's house. They bought Scotch and vodka in economy-size half gallons because they could afford to. The conversation was good, and it had been fun to drink a little too much with them.

Only the next morning, when I had a monster hangover and dehydration, did I realize that I'd had too much. I almost never had a hangover. Ray was the same way. That night he had also pulled out all the stops at our friends' home. Come to think of it, we both never stopped drinking until we were drunk.

TEACHING

Fall '72

Next, Ray accepted an offer from the University of California at Berkeley to teach writing. He figured that the left hand didn't know what the right hand was doing—at least not in the massive California state university system. So he continued teaching at Santa Cruz as well. Ray wanted to do both jobs, although it certainly wasn't kosher.

As always, wherever he taught, Ray's students absolutely adored him. He was always openly himself, a real person, a nice man, and a very funny one. He smoked cigarettes in class or he refused to teach. He spoke softly because that's how he spoke—no booming lectures from Ray. And he read student manuscripts as carefully as John Gardner had read his own first work. Any student who really wanted to become a writer had a chance in Ray's class.

No matter what Ray said or did in class, his editorial work on student assignments and his one-on-one conferences with students were superb. He gave his students a feeling of receiving special knowledge and attention.

Maybe by the lights of academic policy he should never have worked two appointments at once, but Ray never just collected a salary. He never adopted the cynically accepted manner of "going through the motions" that is not unheard of in the realms of higher education. Every time he taught he earned his money.

WRITING

Spring '72

Ray received the Wallace E. Stegner Fellowship at Stanford University. In addition to the four-thousand-dollar cash award, he was a visiting professor, sitting in with William Abrahams, editor of the annual *O. Henry Short Story Anthology*. Ray was to serve as an example of success for the class of budding writers. He was also appointed visiting lecturer in fiction writing at the University of California at Berkeley.

By August, Ray hadn't written anything in four months, caught up in the acclaim, not to mention our move from Ben Lomond to Cupertino, and all its repercussions. I couldn't know it then, but he would be almost unable to do any writing over the next several years. Little did I sense that our grip on our personal ladder to success was weakening. Our family was beginning to slide. And because writing was at the heart of Ray's life, when his life soured, his work was not a refuge or a consolation but the weathervane of his personal storms, spinning in the wind, pointing nowhere steadily. And he needed steadiness to write.

TEACHING

Fall '73

Ray was invited to teach at the Iowa Writers' Workshop. Now what? Someone pointed out that the English Department at Berkeley was second only to Harvard's in terms of excellence and prestige. If Ray were to resign, we heard, he'd be only the second person who had ever done so. And, he was teaching there with just a bachelor's degree and some graduate course work at Iowa and Stanford!

His Berkeley appointment had been made on the perceived merit of his writing, though he hadn't had any books of stories published yet. It was a coup. On the other hand Iowa was the place where the action was for writers. Ray was sorely tempted to interact with "those of his own kind." Critically he wasn't a scholar, even if he read widely. He had simply followed his own interests. What made him a teacher the faculty wanted was his *commitment* to the art of writing. Academia—yes, stodgy old university professors, those often-maligned souls—had recognized this.

Ultimately Ray opted to go to Iowa. He resigned from Berkeley. To my enormous delight and relief, over a candlelight dinner at home, he solemnly asked me to go with him. Tears gathering in his eyes, he implied we might have a chance at a fresh start.

Ray flew back and forth during the next semester, somehow managing to cover his classes both at Iowa and at Santa Cruz. John Cheever was also teaching at Iowa that fall. Both he and Ray were put up at Iowa House, a residential housing unit for visiting writers.

In the ice and snow of an Iowa winter, Ray and John would pile into Ray's old Falcon convertible and drive to the local liquor store to buy their supplies of Scotch. They looked pretty comical, but they didn't care. They were writers everyone would have to acknowledge in the same breath when they talked about the great ones who went through Iowa.

DRINKING

Summer '72

We were looking to buy a house. Thanks to the Wallace Stegner award, it was possible we could do it. Ray and I were ready to make the commitment.

We bought and moved into a house with a garden in Cupertino at the tail end of July. "Well, let's count our many blessings. Let's get happy, and then more happy, and then happier still," I said.

"Let's," Ray said. "Would you like a drink, Maryann? I'm going to make myself one."

Yes. I would.

Later that summer Ray went to Missoula, Montana. He stayed with Bill Kittredge, a writer and assistant professor at the University of Montana.

Fittingly the two men had struck up an acquaintanceship over a table of books at an MLA-sponsored convention. (Bill became one of Ray's very best friends for the rest of his life.) They'd agreed to go out for coffee. Bill had along his second wife, Patty. She was a tall blond, good-looking, and still with a honeymoon glow.

The Montana department chairman, Earl Ganz, rode herd on the macho cowboys who comprised most of the Creative Writing Program faculty. Earl himself had been published in literary journals, a few stories styled à la Philip Roth, and was waiting to publish his masterpiece, the American Jewish novel to end all American Jewish novels.

Bill and his wife threw a party to celebrate Bill's birthday. There was some drinking involved.

At the party James Crumley, perhaps the star of the writing faculty, was determined to drink Ray under the table, as if that feat would prove he was not only a grander drinker but also, by implication, a better writer. Ray had to keep drinking and literally stay on his feet until 5:00 A.M. before Crumley, who drank along drink for drink, had to admit that Ray wasn't going to fold. The point was taken, and Ray was given the emphatic Crumley thumbs-up.

Jon and Ruth Jackson were at the party, too. Jon was a very bright student, a good ol' boy who regularly drank until he was drunk, and was perhaps the best raconteur of them all. His stories were side-splitting, and he could easily laugh at himself and his own foibles.

James Welch was there, with his scholarly wife from the English Department, Dr. Lois Welch. He was a Blackfoot, the major tribe in the area. Jim sat there drunk, with a happy, friendly smile on his face—he wasn't out to prove anything. Except that he was having a good time, which meant the more drinking the better. His novels, however, were sensitive and first-rate.

So there you had it. A group of mostly men who probably loved a good literary argument, even just for the hell of it, as much as they did debating the best way to track game or bait for fish, but who had one thing they could all agree on: Writers needed to drink. The muse wasn't going to bestow her favors on any teetotaling, namby-pamby, son-of-a-bitch excuse for a real man of talent.

WRITING

Fall '73

I said that we were starting to slide, but perhaps the more accurate image is of us being forced down the ladder one humiliating step at a time. At first there were falsely encouraging signs that our fortunes might just be in temporary eclipse. Ray was appointed visiting lecturer at the Iowa Writers' Workshop for the fall term. I didn't go with him, so he lived alone, upstairs from John Cheever. That made it easy for them to tutor each other in the art of serious drinking. It would have been a stressful routine for anyone, even a nondrinker, as Ray flew back and forth to teach his classes in Iowa and California.

The work Ray had already finished was still generating a certain momentum. His story "What Is It?" was selected for the O. Henry Awards annual volume, *Prize Stories 1973.* Five of his poems were reprinted in *New Voices in American Poetry.*

DRINKING

Fall '73

At the Iowa Writers' Workshop, Ray and John Cheever devoted much time to their other profession, drinking. They'd go out in Ray's old Falcon, the two musketeers, the Mutt and Jeff of literature, careening through the snow and ice to the liquor store. As soon as it opened, they'd buy Scotch, the fuel of choice. Neither was able to write much of anything. One day John came over to Ray's room prior to their morning run, and Ray was shocked to see that Cheever had no socks on—not a good idea when heading out into the Iowa cold.

Ray's drinking and mine became a crutch the way it never had before. I had to tend to Chris and Vance and teach school, so I was careful during the week not to overdo it. But for Ray alcohol provided a daily blackout that somewhat eased the pain of the limbo his life was heading into. He couldn't seem to go forward, and he couldn't go back.

That was the basic situation for all the years he'd spend in balls-to-thewall drinking. By now, in '73, he was drinking around the clock. He drank vodka. If he woke up in the middle of the night, he drank vodka. I swear, for a long time I think he never went more than two hours without it.

Winter '73

Ironically, as Ray's drinking progressed, fueled by his personal conflicts and his remorse, his status as a writer increased. As he became too pickled and ill to write, more and more people were reading and loving his poetry and short stories.

I WAS never physically hooked on alcohol the way Ray unquestionably was. But I was totally hooked on Ray. (The term "codependent" was not yet commonly in use, but in retrospect, that's what you'd call it.) I couldn't let go of him, and he couldn't let go of the bottle.

Even if we had wanted to get help early on, the options were limited. Treatment centers for alcoholics were rare and not widely talked about. We were, hard as it was on us, going to be among the pioneers.

Attitudes had to change. You're having a few too many? Just use your willpower and cut back. Better to be worrying if your children were getting into this marijuana stuff than if your spouse's drinking was spinning out of control. The social acceptability of heavy drinking had not yet undergone the sea change. Today alcoholism is out of the closet and holds a prominent position on the national public health agenda. But those of our generation who were afflicted had to create an awareness of alcoholism as a recognizable, genuine disease. Not a failure of character.

The people in Alcoholics Anonymous often call alcoholism a disease of loneliness. Alcoholics are people who are lonely in a crowd. They like to think they are exercising a behavioral choice, a personal decision. But they're wrong. This has to be recognized before the disease can be arrested. That's the best you can do, because it never can be cured.

This is what I was starting to learn. But like many lessons, I would retrace my steps more than once before I understood. Repetition is sometimes the road to wisdom, isn't it?

13

THAT AUGUST

Looking back on your life, some moments are unmistakable turning points. But as you lived them, the significance of the moment—of an event or action—wasn't clearly evident. Other times you likely had a premonition so strong that you knew, right then and there, that a moment was going to be pivotal and would affect the rest of your life. Further, we're all caught between what seems fated and what our free will tells us, that we are the arbiters of our choices. What we want to believe is that with the right words, the right insights, the right kiss, everything will work out.

I'm remembering moments from August 1972 . . .

The summer had started off well. In June we packed up our things at the house in Ben Lomond. The owner, a woman from Oakland, was eager to return. It was her summer home, and she only rented it out for the school year. The blue house we bought in Cupertino, with its lovely rose garden, wouldn't be ready for another three weeks, so we went traveling.

We headed north to visit Jerry and her family, as well as Ray's aunt Von and uncle Bill in Yakima, then swung over to the coast to see my half sisters and Aunt May. Seeing Jerry, I was in high spirits, as we Burk sisters laughed and joked over a bottle of gin. (Among other things, we saluted James, who had married his girlfriend, Norma.)

The situation on the Coast with my half sisters, Valla and Annette, was very basic. Although we had a good time, I felt rather detached from their views of life. Valla wanted to homestead a piece of Dad and Aunt May's land. She spoke of how she thought the future was going to be a challenge, but that with a piece of land, she could grow a garden and raise cattle and chickens to eat. She wanted a sustainable home, she said, a sustainable environment. It sounded grim.

Yeah, right, I thought sarcastically and indifferently. Such a vision of the future didn't connect with me. I saw that northwestern downtrodden spirit. By their lights our kids were spoiled. Our dog, Ginger, an Irish setter, was spoiled. Ray and I were spoiled. They worked for everything they got and had nothing extra to waste.

If we were spoiled, I took it to mean we paid attention to ourselves and didn't just passively accept our lot. And so what if Ginger was fussy about what she would eat? She was part of the Ray Carver family. At home Ginger had a big chair in the living room to sit in. We wouldn't want our dog to accept less.

My husband was going to be a professor at Berkeley that fall. He was the best writer in California and had the Joseph Henry Jackson Award to prove it (forget the person he tied with). There was Stanford a hop away from us. There was my job—I taught in the richest district in California. (Beverly Hills was a distant second.) We had just bought a big lovely house. We had a new Datsun station wagon. I had a closet of beautiful clothes for school and casual wear from Joseph Magnin in San Francisco, my favorite department store.

These were the rewards of our years of hard, hard work. We had made it. The future looked bright. I couldn't relate to pulling your family's food right out of the ground. A noble idealism, but too rugged for me. We had left farming behind, for good reasons, even if I'd always be the daughter of a farmer.

We still had some time to kill before we could occupy our new house. As Ray drove through eastern Washington, I was engrossed in Nancy Milford's *Zelda*, a biography of F. Scott Fitzgerald's wife. The kids were bored with traveling and being cooped up. Earlier in the day we'd had to separate them to curb the constant teasing and bickering. Now Chris was riding up front with her dad and Vance was in back with me.

They both started nudging me, trying to break my concentration. "Leave your mother alone," Ray said sharply. "She has a right to read her book. In peace."

He pulled the car over and had Chris switch with me. "You know, Maryann, we still have time and money, I think, to make a quick trip up to Montana. I'd like to see Bill and some other people, maybe get in a couple days' fishing. What do you think?"

I thought it was a great idea.

A sharp cry came from the backseat. Chris had been poked, hard.

"I didn't mean to," Vance protested. "It was an accident."

"Sure," Chris said sarcastically, then slugged her brother.

"We're not going to Montana," Ray said, glaring at the kids. "We're going to get back to California." He really was coldly furious as he turned the car around. Who were these guys in the backseat of his car who had once been such good kids? You couldn't even read a book around them.

So we didn't go to Missoula in July. As Ray was fond of quoting Lawrence Durrell, "Two steps to the left or right and the whole picture changes."

We swung back through Yakima and picked up Val, Jerry's son, ahead of schedule. Her husband, Gordon, was in the hospital after a serious heart attack. In our usual spirit of lending a hand to the hand that had helped us, we had offered to take Val to get him out of Jerry's hair for a week or two.

Val was a nice boy, but adding another kid to the mix was, well, trouble. Our son decided to explore the prerogatives of being the older child, for once, and, having trained under our daughter, he had a good technique. He bullied Val, and then we had to crack down on him, and the flies in Cupertino swarmed in the heat, and Chris was bored, and Ray and I were trying to set up the house. Our hands full as usual, nobody thought much of what August might bring, except that Ray was thinking of going up to Montana and fish. That's what he told me.

I got a letter from Amy. She was with Erin in Chicago, the next place she had tried to make a go of it. Her theatrical career in New York had stalled out. Now she wanted to visit us. Meaning she was on her way.

"What would Amy have done if we'd gone on to Montana?" I wondered aloud to Ray.

"I don't know. I'm beginning to feel like we're back in the car."

When I picked up Amy and Erin at the San Francisco airport, Amy was on the verge of another mental breakdown. The pupils of her eyes looked large and black, a symptom I had come to recognize. She stared mostly straight ahead—you couldn't get a laugh from her.

Slowly she improved at our house over the next few days, but even then she seemed frightened, unable to do much more than get out of bed late and drink coffee. Oh, and drop her towels on the bathroom floor after her shower.

I wanted to enjoy my new home with Ray. I wanted to be, yes, a homemaker, with flowers in vases and scrumptious food and nice music playing. I wanted to see Ray in his new study. Two years before, he had written full-time after he got his NEA grant, and by the end of the year, he had a book of stories. The book wasn't published yet, but he had 350 pages of polished fiction in his drawer, from which stories were emerging piecemeal into print.

The following year, after we moved to the Ben Lomond house, Ray taught in college for the first time. He was also a founder and editor of *Quarry*, a national literary journal. (Later *Quarry West*, the magazine was sponsored by the University of California at Santa Cruz from 1971 to 1974. Ray was cofounder and editor with D. G. Myers.) And he had kept hard at his own writing.

But not with the usual joy. He was a professional—therefore he sat down and he did it. He was writing with an eye to being published, I thought. I sensed he hoped to write us out of the rat race. However, when I had read his new stories and poems, he seemed to have pushed himself to the edge. He had used up all his reserves, and though everything he wrote that year was published and well received, it was as if Ray had extracted the new work from his raw nerve ends.

August was here. Another week and it was my birthday. Thirty-two. I missed Santa Cruz, our friends and the sense of community we had there. I missed the university. I hated to be back in a suburban bedroom town like Cupertino, where children met and played together but parents remained strangers with nothing in common except having kids.

I was half lost in thought when Ray asked me a question. I heard myself snap at him. "Oh, I'm so sorry, Ray. . . . Jesus, my nerves. All work and no play. Would you take me for a ride? I need to get out of here for a little while."

We drove up to the reservoir near our house. Parked, I sat there with Ray's arm around me. I felt depressed and anxious. I started to cry. I knew better, but I couldn't hold it back. Ninety-nine times out of a hundred, I took it on myself to cheer Ray up. This hundredth time, let him cheer me.

What he did was say: "This is supposed to be the end of the rainbow, but I don't see the pot of gold."

That stopped my crying. Okay, then, what the hell. "Since Amy is here, how about you and I take off for Monterey or Carmel for my birthday, just the two of us? That would give me something to feel good about. We could get a motel with a pool and get cool. We could talk over books. You could bring paper and pencil. Who knows? You might want to write something." My idea just spilled out as fast as it came to me.

"Sure," Ray said. "Why not? We can put three or four days on a credit card, have some seafood, walk along Cannery Row. Hit a play, some bookstores. Good idea, Maryann."

"Let's go tomorrow," I said. I didn't want to wait for my birthday.

We didn't, and we wound up having a good time in Monterey. Arm in arm, we strolled down the wharf, had drinks in the big riverboat. We should be grateful—and we said we were. We took a dip in the pool before we slipped under the covers of the motel bed.

The day after we got back to the house, Ray came into the bedroom where I was making the bed, sweating in the heat. "I've thought of a plan," he said. He did want to go to Montana and fish. Val had to go home to Washington, and no one had figured out exactly how to get him there. Put him on a plane and have Jerry meet him in Seattle?

Well, if Ray went fishing, he could drive Val to Yakima and then go to Montana. Crumley and Welch were waiting for him. They knew the good places. And I had Amy for company, didn't I? It wouldn't be as if he was abandoning me. There was no reason he could see why he shouldn't go. Why should two people have to wind up holding the bag?

"You've gone up there alone before," I said. "That's not the point. I'm not against that! I've always wanted you to have what makes you happy. You know that. Don't make it sound like I don't! Like I'm some sort of tyrant. I'm not. The one objection I do have is, right now, you're my piece of *sanity* around here."

Ray wasn't looking at me, and I couldn't quite hear what he was saying. I caught ". . . a crisis in my writing."

I knew it had been four months since he'd written anything. But this was the first time he had said anything. He looked crushed. "What I'd like to have is an illusion of freedom."

The hot sun streamed in through the bedroom window. Ray stood there in undershorts and a T-shirt. He had just taken a shower. I didn't say anything.

Ray loaded up the Datsun.

Val sat in the front seat with Ray, happy to be going home. His dad was out of the hospital and would be all right. All of us saw Ray and Val off. I kissed Ray good-bye three times through the open window on the driver's side before I'd let him go.

Cupertino Road had a stop sign at the intersection a few yards down from our driveway. Ray stopped, nothing else in sight. I ran after the car, and before Ray could pull away, I was leaning in the window to kiss him again. Finally I watched as the Datsun drove off. I rejoined the little band of Carvers and family still standing in the driveway. Vance looked at me hard. "You act like you are never going to see Dad again."

No, not true. I tousled his hair, a motherly gesture that at thirteen he routinely tried to duck. Let's go back in the house. There was nothing I could tell my son. I'd had a premonition, that's all. On this trip Ray was going to get killed. Or fall desperately in love with someone.

I busied myself with filling out paperwork for admission to a Ph.D.

program at Stanford. I had a 3.89 undergraduate GPA and 4.0 in the graduate courses I'd taken. I was sure I could get in, but at the office where I picked up forms, an older, white-haired woman whispered to me that I'd better not dawdle—age bias sets in, you know. I hadn't thought about that before. Of course there is no such bias, the woman added, rolling her eyes upward.

The next night I couldn't sleep. I lay in our new king-size bed and pulled the red satin bedspread tightly around me.

TWO DAYS BEFORE I expected him back, Ray pulled into the driveway. It was a hot, dry August afternoon. He looked terrible, worn and exhausted. There was a shattered tire in the back of the Datsun.

Later I got the details. He had been driving eighty miles an hour in the Nevada desert at night. Without warning there was the blinding crash of a meteoroid somewhere very near him, he guessed off to the side of the road. Almost simultaneously the tire exploded. He had nearly been killed.

My God, he'd been lucky.

Later that night when everyone else was asleep, we occupied the living room. Ray sat in front of the white brick fireplace. I stood near the entranceway from the kitchen. He sat there and I stood there, for a long time.

"Did you see any women on this trip?" I finally asked.

"Only one," he said.

The world shattered. But I was still myself. He was still my husband.

"I knew I'd have to tell you." He seemed relieved that it was out.

"I'll have to insist you never see her again," I said firmly.

He couldn't look at me. His eyes were focused on the moss green carpet. "She got in over her head, she told me, and I guess I did, too."

"I repeat, I want you to promise." I kept my voice steady, wanting to look in his eyes.

"I'm afraid I can't promise that." Then with a sob, he said, "I don't know if I'll make it through this alive." He began to cry, desperate sad cries I couldn't bear.

Ray came home from his trip to Montana before I
expected him to. August 1972.
PHOTO BY GARY McNAIR

I was falling apart, but Amy rallied. We had to get away from the house, I explained, and she didn't ask why, but said she'd handle all the kids. Ray and I went off to the local Howard Johnson's motel. He fortified himself at the shabby little liquor store a block from the house, buying a half gallon of vodka, bottles of orange and grapefruit juice. Enough for the duration.

In the motel room we drank as we talked, until we could sleep. When Ray was finally out, I got up and went into the bathroom and locked the door. I felt as if someone had kicked me in the stomach.

I had slipped Ray's wallet out of his hip pocket. I wanted to see if there was any evidence. Yes, there was a scrap of aqua-colored paper with her name and address, phone numbers for home and work.

I tore the paper into shreds.

There, it never existed. Gone. I cried until I threw up and could not cry anymore.

AS AUGUST RAN out its remaining days, we talked. We talked around, over, and through our "situation," as we started to refer to it. I wanted to know exactly how it happened. He had been drinking, but so was everyone else. They were celebrating Bill Kittredge's birthday, and that's when he met her. She told Ray she knew she shouldn't have come. Ray invited her to dinner the next night, some romantic Italian restaurant. They agreed to meet at six o'clock after she got home from work at the university.

We talked. And we carried on with the rest of our lives as if nothing were happening except the end of another summer and the quickening of the tempo as September loomed. The kids were getting ready for school as usual. Everything was fine. Ray and I knew how to keep up the pretenses.

I had confided in Amy. The next day she went over to the Cabana, a hotel in Palo Alto modeled on Caesar's Palace, and by evening she had a job. There was an inexpensive motel across the street she could stay in awhile. She even found a night baby-sitter for Erin. I would have been astounded if I thought I knew anymore what people were capable of. But things I thought impossible were happening, and the fact that Amy had just stepped back into the real world was no more implausible than anything else.

Before she left I told her how much I admired her courage. Amy looked at me as if I were someone she loved dearly who was a little slow on the uptake. She said that her problems had suddenly looked solvable. Compared with mine.

THE SUNDAY NIGHT before the week I would resume teaching high school, Ray and I went to a bar for more convoluted conversation about the situation. A handsome blond man was also there, and he smiled at me every now and then. Ray went wild. "Don't you get involved with anyone!" he hissed at me.

Ray had always been the jealous type, but never in a crazy way like this. It was obvious to me that he wasn't ready to dump me, but was being driven mad by the conflict. (I had no idea that his lady friend was planning to come for a visit the week I was back in the classroom.) Head games and ambiguity were new to us. Neither of us could yet orchestrate subterfuge on a personal level or read the signs of betrayal accurately.

Leaving the bar, we went to the parking lot. I opened the car door and got in the passenger seat. Ray was behind me, and I expected him to close the door. Instead, before I understood what was happening, he grabbed me, pulled me down and half out of the car.

As I hung off the front seat, he banged my head on the pavement. I begged him to stop. Please, Ray! Three or four hard blows, then he let me go. Somehow I dragged myself up inside the car, and he drove us home.

Reaching our house, I jumped out of the car and ran to a neighbor's. They let me call the police. When the cops came, I watched from the shadows as they went to the front door of my home.

Ray opened the door, Chris and Vance on either side of him. He was civilized and genteel as he invited the officers inside. Then they came out looking for me. I came out of the shadows, bleeding and crying. I asked for their help so I could get my car keys and my children. They refused.

"Lady, if you get in your car and attempt to drive, we'll arrest you."

"I'm not drunk. I deserve to have my car. But I'll call a taxi. I'm deathly afraid of him."

"Unless you can prove he's got an arsenal of guns and knives in there, and I doubt he does, we're not going to get involved. I suggest you get into your house and stay there."

"That's what I want her to do," Ray said, sounding like his old reliable self.

"After what's happened tonight, I want to leave him," I countered.

"Well, we're off," one of the cops said. "This is a domestic situation, and we never win." With that they headed back to the patrol car.

I couldn't believe the blatant sexism. It was obvious the boys' club was not about to protect me or my interests. Ray must have shown them his Berkeley instructor ID. The cops clearly treated him with respect. Courtesy was extended to everyone on my high school's faculty. Men and women were equal there, I believed; I wasn't used to discrimination. It frightened me and made me feel hopeless.

I looked at the kids. They looked like the last thing they wanted to do was to go off into the night with me. Well, how nice that they were getting some attention from their dad, something they both craved. I was just the drudge who saw to it they were fed, clothed, cared for, and loved.

I went inside, went into the bathroom, and locked the door. I was trapped for tonight, anyway. What was I to do? A fresh burst of tears spilled down my dirty, bloody face. I washed up and sat on the bathroom floor, hugging myself.

How I got to bed I don't recall. But the next morning, when I looked in the mirror, I had two black eyes. I wouldn't be starting school on Tuesday after all.

I overheard Ray calling someone from the bathroom—he'd taken the phone in with him. He said I had tried to kill myself. He had to stay home and take care of me. Right, make me sound like the mentally unstable one when I had held him together for years. I thought sadly, I have done nothing, absolutely nothing, to deserve this.

I was so drained of emotion at this point that I probably could have considered any appalling idea without reacting. Let me see. In time Ray will write about all this, "improving" the facts to create good stories. Something positive is going to come out of this, then, because it will be important for Ray's writing. I myself had said his work was the most important thing for us. I had never thought of myself as a victim who *allowed* herself to be victimized. This was all new territory to me.

It took a few days, but somehow I forgave him. I missed the first three days of school—unheard-of for me in the world I used to live in.

WHEN I THINK of that August and that house, I think of the roses. Roses and more roses. White roses, lavender and yellow roses, salmon roses, small teacup roses, large grandmother roses, the beautiful tight red roses that flowered in blooms that did not fall apart for ever so long a time.

Red roses from our rose garden, I had sung to myself.

14

MAELSTROM

What happened to us? Everything had looked so promising as the seventies started. We were living in San Jose, where I was completing my BA. Ray was commuting to his editing job at Science Research Associates. Our teenagers were growing up with no more than the usual bumps.

I circle back to the spring of 1970.

SRA had promoted Ray from editorial work to a public relations position. His good looks and tremendous charm were an obvious asset, along with the erudition he had acquired over a lifetime of reading as only a writer reads. As part of his new responsibilities, he was to represent the company at MLA conventions. The Modern Language Association is an organization for college level professors and instructors of English and other related subjects. At the national MLA meetings, department representatives from all over the country recruit new personnel, look over publishers' wares, and talk shop. In academic circles it's a big deal.

At a May 1970 local convention Ray met Bill Kittredge. Over coffee he and Bill discovered they had read some of each other's stories. The next day they decided to have drinks. The rest is history. "The Buffalo," as Bill got nicknamed, became for a long time one of Ray's best friends. He was Ray's link to a circle of Montana writers and—in a mythic sense for Ray—the wild, wild West.

When Ray got home, he was excited about having met Bill and Patty. What good people they were. Fun and friendly. I'd like them. We were going to get together again—either up there or down here. The fishing and scenery were great in Montana, and there was a whole colony of writers.

He told me that Jim Crumley had just sold his novel for more than a hundred thousand dollars. And he took everyone out on a luxury boat to celebrate. He bought his folks a truck and trailer. The things we'd like to do if we could strike it rich.

Crumley and his lucrative book, *One to Count Cadence*, were impressive. As I've mentioned, Bill introduced Ray to Jim Welch and to Earl Ganz. And in Montana Ray also met one woman in particular.

THERE WAS OTHER family news. In New York, Amy had won a part—in a Broadway production of *Borstal Boy* by Brendan Behan. She and Erin were settled in a Greenwich Village apartment, where she felt safe. (It was in a Mafia enclave.) When *Borstal Boy* won the 1970 Tony Award for best play, we were all ecstatic, pleased, and proud. We hoped that Amy's life was entering an easier and more rewarding phase.

When Ray was sent to Tarrytown, New York, to make a presentation at an IBM conference—SRA was a subsidiary—he showed his usual marvelous flair by arranging with a travel agent for me to accompany him. When my husband told me I was going, I was speechless for a good five minutes.

The Brown boys' mother, Mrs. Green, was happy to board Vance while we were gone. Chris stayed with our neighbors, a young couple who had been baby-sitting for us.

On the trip I got to see Amy in her play, twice, and to spend a marvelous few days in New York City. Poor Ray—while I was partying in the city, he was sweating through the conference until the time came for his speech. The waiting wasn't helping his frayed nerves.

He knew he was an alien in the corporate world, a total imposter. But replete with illustrations, pointer in hand, he would stand up in front of the audience at the end of the week and expound on important matters he couldn't care less about. He smuggled me into his swanky hotel room so I could stay with him until his ordeal was over and we could make a getaway.

The flight home was better than the one coming east. The New York–bound plane had run into extreme turbulence over the Rockies. The captain ordered everyone to remain seated as we were jostled sharply about. No, I had thought, this was not the right time to orphan the kids. I need this plane to keep flying. I'm about to graduate from college. It can't CRASH when I'm finally getting a chance.

This time the gods seemed to be listening.

AFTER RAY WON an NEA grant in the spring of 1970, he rented a room in Palo Alto near his job. That let him stay overnight and write, avoiding the long commute to San Jose. We also occasionally used the room for a tryst, two old married people sneaking off like teenagers to have a night together, as thick white candles burned around us.

We had long discussions about our next important moves. After my graduation, once I had a job, Ray could quit SRA and write full-time. I had wanted to start graduate work, but that could wait. I told Ray, "You're going to have the best year of writing you've ever had. You can count on it. It's a plan."

Our lives were no longer so driven by the unavoidable—pay the rent, feed the babies, work the dumb jobs. But we felt pulled in many conflicting directions. There were the needs of our teenagers. Chris turned thirteen in '70; her brother would join the ranks ten months later in '71. And the demands of our budding careers, the question of where to live permanently, the drain on our time and energy from family and friends who whirled in and out of our lives. We seemed closer to where we wanted to be but more frustrated at not being there yet.

The weeks were counting down to my graduation. I admitted to myself that I did want to see the graduates of the class of 1970 come filing into the large gymnasium in cap and gown. I would be one of them, at long last, with a newly minted BA. At long last.

• • •

WE PLANNED A special party to celebrate the publication of Ray's book of poems, *Winter Insomnia*. A guy in one of my classes was in a good band, and I made a deal for his group to play. George Oudyn, the copy editor at SRA and a friend of ours, volunteered his big gorgeous house in Portola Valley. It stood high on a hill surrounded by tall evergreen trees. The huge living room had a cathedral ceiling of wooden beams.

We set up the band at one end of the room, hung some banners overhead: WAY TO GO RAY—WINTER INSOMNIA! WAY TO GO RAY—NEA GRANT! I prepared the food with the help of my friends in student housing. We made an enormous macaroni salad to go with six turkeys, breads, and condiments. We also baked a big sheet cake and wrote on it, "Congratulations, Ray. We Love You." It looked like enough food to feed an army.

And an army of guests promptly showed up. The night of the party there was the band, the entire SRA staff, friends from student housing and my classes, friends of George Hitchcock, and writers from Santa Cruz and San Francisco. A prominent SRA editor told me I should have put out less food and more booze for a publishing party. But I figured that if the booze got low, people would go out and get more. Liquor stores were open. The food, on the other hand, was a spread that would make guests feel comfortable. None of that anxiety over whether the canapés were all there was going to be to eat!

The party was a blast. The band played and played until 4:00 A.M.— three hours for free. The musicians were laughing and cutting up with the guests and everyone was having too much fun to stop. People danced. People talked. People met people they were probably going to spend the rest of their lives with. I think anyone who was there went home eagerly awaiting the next volume from the pen of Raymond Carver, simply in anticipation of the publishing party.

AS SOON AS the news got out in the summer that I had teaching offers, Ray's boss at SRA called him aside. Dick was a friend, and he gave it to

Ray straight: Ray was very popular at work. An article about the NEA grant with his picture had appeared in *SRA Profile,* the company magazine. But Chicago headquarters had decided to eliminate his position. Dick would be happy to have Ray back in his department as an editor. On the other hand, if Ray was laid off, SRA would pay him almost a year's salary as severance. With that incentive, Ray was ready to be laid off, fired, canned, or whatever they wanted to call it, as soon as possible.

In September he said so long to SRA for good.

RAY GOT A lead on a rental house in Sunnyvale, one of the many little towns to the south and west of San Jose. It was on Wright Avenue. The property was fenced with a landscaped backyard. "We can sunbathe in the nude, Maryann, it's so private," he raved.

The family who owned the house had a last name we rolled around on our tongues, trying to imagine what they were like. Zepezauer. I had no idea.

Mr. Zepezauer turned out to be a German teacher at Homestead High, a few blocks away from the house. He had received a sabbatical leave, very rare for a high school teacher, and he and his family were going to Germany. It also meant we couldn't have the house any longer than a year.

Ray laughed when he told me the Zepezauers' main rule: We were *not* to bring their Siamese cat inside. Yet the rental agent had made Ray promise to take care of the cat if we wanted a deal!

"Then why have the damn thing?" I asked.

It seemed that Mr. Zepezauer was allergic to cat hair.

"Well," Ray said, "apparently they all love the cat. They want the cat left in its surroundings, so it will feel secure."

"Okay," I said, "Chris can take charge. She loves animals." I, on the other hand, didn't need one more creature in my house that required feeding and grooming services.

"They're also leaving some boxes of packed household goods, clearly marked, that they don't want anyone to get into."

"Of course not," I said. Then Ray and I looked at each other and laughed uproariously. "Nothing like forbidden fruit to make it interesting."

We took the house. With our next paychecks, we'd have the thirteen hundred dollars for the first payment. Ray could start writing full-time. I was in the Honors Intern Program, which would get me into a classroom and teaching by the fall.

All our plans were starting to gel, but America seemed on the verge of collapse for much of the spring. The endless Vietnam War was the root cause of unrest, but when President Nixon ordered an invasion of Cambodia, college campuses exploded in protest. Confrontations and tension escalated, until that terrible day at Kent State when the Ohio National Guard opened fire (four students were killed on May 4, 1970).

University officials at San Jose warned that students had to attend classes or risk losing course credit. This was while radical students were blocking entrances to the buildings. The standoff was fortunately defused before I had to cross a protest line. But I couldn't sacrifice the credits I needed to graduate. My sympathies were with the students, but my children needed a working mom, not an unemployable one.

WE MOVED TO Sunnyvale. That summer Chris and Vance were whisked off to Aunt Jerry's in Yakima. My sister had agreed to be the "human sacrifice" to help us out. Actually she looked forward to getting to know my kids better, and they could see their cousins.

I took an independent study class to complete the requirements for my BA. By August 1, I had to read twenty-one American novels. I was also working for my teaching credential and student teaching in the intern program. I'd get home after a long day, put on my bikini and suntan oil, and lie out on a recliner in the backyard with one of my books. Heaven.

Ray settled into his new study at the far corner of the house. He was pleased with his view of the lush yard and began to write intensely.

In August my thirtieth birthday came. Young people—or at least the media's reporting of young people—said they couldn't trust anyone over thirty. But I wasn't concerned. I told myself I was going to embark on the prettiest decade of my life. I was going to be comfortable in my skin, and with new confidence, I swung the long, silky, frosted blond hair that had become my trademark. Yes, there was no question that I was young at heart. And still looked it—I'd get carded when I ordered a drink.

Chris and Vance had a great time with Aunt Jerry and their cousins, but were glad to come home to their own rooms. They thrived in the house on Wright Avenue. In the fall they liked their schools and quickly made new friends.

When the inevitable family problems cropped up, we dealt with them. One fall day Mom and Clarence showed up on our doorstep. Basically they were at loose ends, not knowing what they should do next. They stayed awhile, my mother cooking wonderful meals. As I was teaching my own classes for the first time, I could more fully appreciate her years of dedication. She had burned out on teaching when her health went through a bad patch the previous spring. I helped her make the decision to retire from teaching at sixty-three and look for new opportunities. Shortly thereafter Mom and Clarence moved into their own digs in Los Gatos. Clarence became the caretaker of the History Club, a meeting place for several organizations, including Alcoholics Anonymous. AA surprised him by leaving the hall cleaner than any other group.

THE HIGH POINT of our social life in the Zepezauer house was a visit from Bill and Patty Kittredge.

During the spring vacation in my last semester at San Jose State, I had gone to Montana with Ray to meet the "cast of characters" at a party the Kittredges threw. I was charmed with the exuberance and energy of these people. It was an amazing assembly of writers, like the one we had experienced in Iowa. Many of the Montana writers had also studied at the Writers' Workshop so it felt like a very small world. Everyone knew one another or at least had a friend in common.

When the Kittredges came to see us, we wanted to show them a good time. We stocked up on food and booze and began to barbecue in earnest in our backyard. We did hamburgers, steaks, big salads, and all the accompaniments. There was vodka, Scotch, lots of wine and beer.

*Out on the patio: William "Bill" Kittredge, me, Tom Holland
(Amy's then-boyfriend), Patty Kittredge, and Ray. No sign of
the cats. Wright Avenue, Sunnyvale, California, 1971.*

We all sat in the kitchen one night drinking red wine, laughing and
swapping stories, until I fell happily asleep at the table. I had come off a
long day teaching high school. Ray gently took me to his study, where
we were temporarily sleeping.

We had given Bill and Patty our room, with its private bathroom.
They housed their two Siamese cats, Brownie and Emma, with them.
Brownie, especially, had a temper. That cat got angry over any change in
his routine—and the long trip from Montana was a big change. He re-
taliated by discharging rank male cat piss all over the maroon bedspread
in our room—correction, in the Zepezauers' bedroom.

After three times through the dry cleaner's, the bedspread still came
back with the odor of cat piss. We knew Mr. Zepezauer would never
forgive us. He and his family were due back in six weeks and we didn't
want to be around when his allergic nose got a whiff. As I put it back on
the bed for the last time, I said, "Now I understand what 'pissed off'
truly means."

. . .

IN THE LATE summer of 1971, cruising around in the Santa Cruz mountains, we found a rustic, dark brown wooden house in the town of Ben Lomond. It had been used as a lodge when first built. Aqua- and salmon-colored paper lanterns were strung along the open front porch. Downstairs there was a recreation room, where a Ping-Pong table was set up. We thought it would suit us well.

Ray and I didn't want to live in yet another cookie-cutter house in Silicon Valley. We managed to rent the Ben Lomond house but had to wait two weeks to move in. A trailer at the local KOA [Kampgrounds of America] was home for all of us—plus Amy, Erin, and her current boyfriend, a nice guy named Tom Holland. They had needed a place to crash. Somehow we managed to fit them in and to survive the very close quarters without becoming too uncivil.

We moved into Ben Lomond just in time. The Zepezauers had returned—we diligently avoided them. Our Ben Lomond wooden house under giant redwood trees thrilled me. Hansel and Gretel could have come around the corner at any moment and I wouldn't have been surprised. But our life in this wonderful setting was to be anything but a fairy tale.

Our kids cast a blight on the nine months in Ben Lomond. Oh, sure, we still all danced together, the four of us, plus Amy and Erin, the same as always. And had some good times—especially at Christmas, but the children weren't little anymore, as we discovered when they vocally objected to our wanderlust. What they wanted was a neighborhood where they had permanent friends. They wanted to stay put so they could be in the same school, year after year. In my heart of hearts I couldn't blame them.

Vance was an above-average athlete, and with a positive attitude, he fitted in anywhere. Chris was more like her father and struggled with her weight. She had a pretty face, but she cried in dressing rooms when she looked at herself in the mirror. From junior high on, she wore only jeans and loose tops. For her, the friends she'd had in Sunnyvale—Sue Conn, Karen Kessler, and Annabelle—were the hip crowd she wanted. Chris didn't want to make an effort to make new friends. Every weekend she insisted on taking a bus to visit her old ones.

"Chris," I said, "you're too young to be gone every weekend. There's no way we can keep track of you. It worries us sick to have you gone. Once in a great while, as a special treat, fine. But you have to make an effort to make some friends here."

Chris went into her bedroom and locked the door. She wanted to go to Sunnyvale that weekend or she didn't want to live. Later, when she unlocked the door and came out, I looked into her room and saw that she had systematically cut up $150 worth of clothes I'd charged for her at Mervyn's in Sunnyvale. I was stunned.

"Damn it all, Chris! You simply can't force our hands like this. You know I maxed out the credit card when I bought you these clothes. You were there! What the hell do you think we're going to do now!"

"I don't care!" Chris shouted back at me bitterly. "That's just the point, don't you see? I'm just like Dad. If I'm depressed, I'm depressed. And I'm *depressed*."

THE DAYS OF the Ben Lomond house were drawing to a close. We had to leave in June '72. I began checking newspaper ads and consulting realtors in the area for housing that would put Chris in Homestead High—back with her friends. It wasn't such an issue for Vance, but I was sure he'd be pleased to hook up with his old pals. Not to mention that I'd be ten minutes away from my job instead of an hour and a half.

I wasn't having any luck. One afternoon I was driving around when I spotted a vivid blue house trimmed with white shutters. It was at the end of a street and had a square sign on a stick nailed to the carport: FOR SALE BY OWNER.

It was a sprawling ranch home with a circular driveway—as I pulled in I thought this was just what we wanted. An older man with bushy eyebrows, periwinkle blue eyes, and a face with an impenetrably reserved expression came to the door when I rang.

"Are you the owner?" I asked. The man nodded. "Do you have the house for sale?" The man nodded again, not moving a muscle otherwise.

"May I see it?" I asked.

He opened the door and let me inside. I liked what I saw.

On my way home to Ben Lomond, I pressed hard on the accelerator of the yellow Datsun station wagon. We'd bought it the previous January with financing from the teacher's credit bureau. We had never had a new car before. When we got it a thin layer of plastic covered the seats, and the funny new-car smell was intoxicating.

The owner of the house in Cupertino, Mr. Hanahoe, decided that I should have the house. But how could we pull it off? We could use the four-thousand-dollar Stegner award for a down payment, but it was doled out in installments over a year. We were stymied.

I was lamenting to Claire Huddleston, a friend who was also an English teacher at the high school, when she looked at me and without hesitation said, "I can lend you four thousand dollars. You pay me when Stanford pays you."

"You'd do that for us?!"

Ray and I went to a loan company. With some explanations and negotiations, we were approved for a mortgage, using Claire's money for the down payment and closing costs. My God, we were home owners!

Our new house in Cupertino, 22272 Cupertino Road, wouldn't be ready for occupancy until midsummer. Elated, we decided to take a trip to Washington until it was ready. I hoped when we got back that the garden would be flourishing.

WE MOVED into our home, our very own house. The roses were in bloom. Then in August 1972 things fell apart, and our lives were never the same.

I TOOK A graduate course in the fall semester at Stanford, Adolescent Literature. We read Arthur C. Clarke's *Childhood's End* and John Knowles's *A Separate Peace*, among other books.

December 7 was the final exam. Pearl Harbor day. I went to the exam wearing a brown wool miniskirt and a beige long-sleeved top from Joseph Magnin in Palo Alto. I had on Italian brown leather

On a visit to Ray's Aunt Von and Uncle Bill Archer—Chris, me, Vance, and Ray.
Aunt Von took the picture. Yakima, Washington, 1972.
PHOTO BY VIOLET LAVONDA ARCHER, COURTESY OF DON ARCHER

boots that came up to my knees. My hair was long and blond. Can you dig it?

Afterward I went right home and found my husband sitting in the living room, drunk as usual.

"My, you look nice," he said, enthusiastically. "Sexy, too. Maybe we could just step into the bedroom before the kids—"

"No," I said. Then I blurted out what I'd been considering for months in the darkest recess of my mind. I almost couldn't believe I said it now: "I want a divorce. I cannot take living in this limbo. This situation is going to drive everybody over the edge." Ray started to cry. He held out his arms to me. "Please, please, Maryann, don't leave me. Please, please, just bear with me and help me get through this. You are my real lady. I love you. You are my wife!"

I was overjoyed. When the kids came home from school, I smiled and hugged them hard. I made the family a delicious dinner. We clung to the illusion of a happy family for one more evening.

A few nights later I had a very disturbing dream. People from Montana had come and filled the house. They were assertive and proprietary, as if they'd been told they could take over the place. They energetically threw clothing out of our dresser drawers. Then I saw one of them kick Vance in the stomach so hard he cried out.

I woke up with a start. Ray was already up. He was in the bathroom shaving, getting ready to go teach at Berkeley. He had a glass filled with vodka on the sink. I went into the bathroom and said, "Ray, you are going to have to leave and let us settle down and get some peace of mind." The dream was an omen and I was reacting to it.

Ray paid no attention. I was serious, and he was intentionally ignoring me. I could see the faint traces of a cocky little smile, but mainly he kept on with his business at hand—a sip of his drink, a swipe of the razor across his face.

"You have got to pack a bag today and go."

He stood there, obviously not going anywhere.

I went out to the kitchen and got a butcher knife. I had no intention of using it. I simply wanted Ray to see it and take me seriously.

I came back to the bathroom and again said I wanted him to go. He lunged at me. I threw the knife away, far out of reach so no one would get hurt. He grabbed me around the waist from behind and rammed my head into the corner. I tasted blood.

Chris, who was too young to have a driver's license, drove me to the hospital. She was embarrassed and wouldn't come in with me. The doctor who treated me warned about the risk of possible infection. My skull was cracked.

I FOUND OUT when Ray's girlfriend came down to Palo Alto to see him.

More grist for the Ray Carver mill. Now we even had a "situation room," like the military. It was our bedroom. The same room with the king-size bed, the red satin bedspread, the red-patterned Persian rug that had been magical when we bought it. The mahogany furniture came with the house. The tall mirrors on the dressers reflected our image whenever we lay in bed together.

It was amazing to be living in our own big house after having lived in rentals for years. We had a big green backyard with lemon and peach trees and an Italian rose garden. The moon was full when we moved in. It had lit up our bedroom. "Oh, God, I'm so happy," I had said the first night.

That was then. Now at dawn after another long and particularly painful night—an all-night vigil—we were both in tears. "All right," Ray said. "I'll tell you, Maryann, I love you so much I'd die for you. I would lay down my life for you."

"That's just what I'm afraid of. That's what you are going to do with all this agonizing. With all this drinking. This has gone way beyond five drinks a day. This is now a round-the-clock preoccupation. You are slowly committing suicide. I want you alive."

"I know, but I don't know if I can live." His tone turned truculent. "I don't know if you'll want me if I do."

"I'll always want you. But I want to take you alive."

We laughed wrenchingly. Then fell into each other's arms, crying, squeezing each other so hard. "Whatever you do," Ray said, his voice breaking, "don't you find someone else. Don't complicate the situation more. Please, please, just wait for me."

On Christmas Eve, Ray and I stayed awake all night again trying to deal with the crisis. Did Ray just want to have his cake and eat it too? Cliché or not, that's what he insinuated when pressed. He wasn't giving her up either. I began to realize how hopeless the situation was.

OUR CHILDREN changed. No more carefree happiness in our home. Nothing was normal now. All Ray and I could talk about, hour after hour, day after day, was the crisis. The situation. The turn of events. Heaven help the kids if they needed to interrupt us to ask a question or wanted to tell

My Stanford student ID card, fall 1972—the hardest time of my life.

us about their day at school. We made ourselves respond through clenched teeth, dutifully attending to their needs. We wanted to hurry back to the unending drinks and our endless talk.

BONNIE DAY, OUR "living poem" friend in Arcata, was no longer with Dick. Another marriage from our circle of professors and writers had bit the dust. Ray and I visited her in San Francisco over the Christmas holiday of '72. She subtly let me know that my anger at Ray was corroding my relationships with everyone else who cared about me. I knew she was right, but I had locked myself inside some sort of mental strong room with my husband. We were either coming out together or never coming out alive. Those, as my friends wanted to tell me, were actually not the only options.

I REMEMBER HARDLY anything about Christmas. The last week of '72, Ray and I went over to Berkeley to find an apartment for him. He was trying to placate me by taking me along. He took me out to a nice place for lunch, but I felt traumatized. I knew he was leaving me.

Nothing I could say to him made any difference. He planned to stay with me in Cupertino on Thursday nights into the weekend, which coincided with his teaching days at Santa Cruz, and then go back to Berkeley on Sunday. He was going to divide his time and live in both places.

We went back to our house—whose house?—and made sad love. I put on the royal blue trimmed-in-satin bathrobe that Ray had given me for Christmas a few years ago. I said something to the effect that if only he had a good wife . . . I looked down and began to cry.

He pulled me into a strong hug and lifted me off my feet. "I do have a good wife," he said. "I have the best wife in the world. There's nothing the matter with my wife. It's me. It's me."

15

"WILL YOU PLEASE BE QUIET, PLEASE?"

Three years later, 1976, began with a thousand-dollar hangover from Christmas. It wasn't that nasty queasy feeling you get from too much yuletide cheer; it was the amount we had somehow spent on food and refreshments. We had the check stubs to prove it. The holidays had brought visitors to our home to eat and drink for days on end. The family gifts we had charged to our credit cards, so that was a separate looming financial crisis.

I was desperate to raise some money. As the long, bleak month of January began, I pounded the pavement between teaching classes, trying to find a finance company that would spring for $1,000 to cover our upcoming deficit. We had to find some Peter we could borrow from to pay back the money we owed to Paul. But no dice, I couldn't get a thousand dollars to pay for that miserable Christmas. After being turned down flat by two finance companies, I gave up. I bit the bullet and somehow managed to negotiate extended payments with our creditors. Life went on.

That had basically been our situation since the end of 1972—we had just gone on. As Ray's drinking accelerated, I had tried to wait things out, hoping to hold my family together until he would come to his senses. It was a naive hope, and after four years, it was obviously unrealistic, at least to everyone else but me.

Stubbornly I assumed that Ray would come off his bender—his latest bender—and pick up his life with me. It just wasn't possible for me to write him off, not after nearly twenty years of marriage. I just couldn't do it. And I didn't want to.

BACK IN THE spring of 1973, the chairman of the Berkeley English Department had held a reception for faculty members at his home. Ray invited me. I drank a single tall Scotch and water. I chatted with various professors, enjoying being introduced as Mrs. Carver or Maryann Carver.

After the reception we had gone back to Ray's Berkeley apartment. I noted that he had a regular pillow on his bed and a smaller one taken from a couch or chair. As I stared at the little pillow, I realized it had a slight indentation. He must have had some company. At that point I could still find myself stunned by the trivial evidences of betrayal.

Ray had engineered the logistics adeptly so I'd be seen at the reception. Now I guess I was supposed to crawl in and sleep with him. The big pillow was his, obviously. It was always very important to him—to have a big perfect pillow. My other choice was to have a confrontation or a fight and then go home late at night, an hour and a half's drive.

I got into his bed and turned my face to the wall, pretending I had to sleep. I realized that Ray was teaching and juggling, barely, his personal life. That was as much as he could do. I saw that it might get a lot worse before it got better. If it got better.

As I learned soon enough, one Diane Cecily had been visiting for a week on her vacation from the University of Montana. Ray had put her on a plane that morning and then taken me to socialize with his colleagues. So it was no impromptu fling.

He had met her in Missoula at the birthday party for Bill Kittredge in August 1972. Diane was an editor at the university. Ray took her to dinner the next night and stayed with her. She was just divorced from an English professor, and they saw each other repeatedly. Ultimately our marriage went down because of this liaison, though it took several years.

In the Cupertino house I was learning to enjoy the children again. It was like when they were little and Ray was off working evenings. When he was absent the atmosphere was sorrowful but more peaceful. Most of the week it was Amy and Erin (once again living with us), Chris, Vance, and me in a fatherless house.

The undertow of despair from my situation caught up with Amy. She became increasingly manic and disassociated. One night she stripped off her clothes, jumped up on a dresser, and smashed a tall glass vase. She brandished the jagged end at the kids. I had Vance call the police.

When they came they laughed at her gibberish as they subdued her. Amy was writhing and struggling on the dining room floor. I sprang to her defense and admonished them for being unprofessional. The cops got serious and allowed me to follow them to the hospital.

At El Camino Hospital they had a civilized program with a discerning and kind staff. A doctor offered me a prescription for a mild dose of Valium. Under the circumstances I gratefully accepted it. I needed to be able to eat, sleep, teach school, and take care of all the children, including Erin. She was still a preschooler, so I had to find someone to take care of her during the day.

I would teach a class or two, then, in a free period, I'd race over to the hospital to see how Amy was doing. She'd beg me not to go when I had to get back to school. But it was already highly irregular to be leaving the school grounds repeatedly during the day. I couldn't miss any more days, either. I still didn't have tenure, and this was the last year before the school administration made its determination.

Finally, one day I rushed back to the hospital after school and was told that Amy had scaled a wall and run naked down the highway. They caught her and took her by ambulance to the county mental health facility. Now she would go through the horrible process of Thorazine sedation. It was out of my hands, as legally she was committed for a minimum of two weeks with no visits allowed.

I tried to concentrate on my teaching and block everything else out of my mind. I was on top of my student grades by the end of the quarter. The fall had been so painful and traumatic that I really had to concentrate to formulate my evaluations. It wasn't clear and automatic, the way it normally was.

. . .

ONLY WHEN RAY spent his few days a week with us did I brighten up. I had some more encouragement in the spring when Ray got word he'd been appointed a visiting lecturer at the Workshop for the fall. He wanted us all to go with him! I thought it was a breakthrough.

In June '73, Bill Kittredge came for a visit in Cupertino and Ray stuck around. They went on a two-week drunk, or as participants in these marathons liked to call it, a "pee-roller." Empty half-gallon vodka bottles overflowed the garbage cans.

I liked Bill, always had, and joked with him that he was Ray's alter ego. He was a sincere, conscientious writer and an excellent writing teacher, a walking encyclopedia of contemporary literature. No one was more stimulating for Ray. Theirs was a relationship of highs and lows— and a few moments that defied classification.

I was welcome to party with them—did I mention how "anything goes" this hip crowd was? Why not? I was the moth, Ray was the candle. Everyone else had figured that out.

When it was time for Ray's grades report to be delivered to Berkeley, we made a party out of it. I'd finished the school year myself that day, thank God, and Ray and I had gone out to lunch to celebrate, drinking margaritas and eating Mexican food until we'd definitely gone south. Now here we were careening over the bay to Berkeley.

During Bill's visit Vance graduated from junior high. Bill went with us to the ceremony, one of the family. He had lost his own family in a sad divorce a few years before in Oregon. His extramarital affair led to the breakup, and, paralyzed with shame, he couldn't bring himself to contact his son and daughter. By his lights he had a good excuse for his hard drinking.

Bill had loved and greatly respected Janet, his ex-wife, and always treated me with affection. He saw all sides of these family stories, though he tried to believe in the current slogan prevalent among the hearty, freewheeling Montana writers: "Another wife, another life." Or as Bill proclaimed dramatically, usually to much laughter: "Get your programs quick, the characters are changing."

Ever since we'd known him he'd been married to Patty, his second wife, but by '73, they were having their troubles, too. (They would separate in the fall, when Bill was a Stanford Fellow for a year. After that they still got together to party, cry, and fight from time to time.) No relationship seemed able to survive all the hard, steady drinking. That sad observation would be explored in Ray's story, "What We Talk About When We Talk About Love," which he was to write some years later.

During Bill's visit Ray created his own moments of mayhem. He went to Santa Cruz to visit Jim Houston, another writer and friend, and took along Bill and John O'Brien, a writer who'd spent several years in Alaska. Jim was working up in his study when the drunken writers arrived to roust him. (He describes the incident in *Remembering Ray.*) He tried to be quiet and pretend he wasn't there but couldn't get away with playing possum. The three interlopers soon had him in tow, drinking the afternoon away.

On the way home Bill or John threw up out the passenger window, all over the side of the Datsun. As I was scraping and hosing it down, I started to cry. I was tired and strung out. When Ray saw the condition I was in it angered him. "What are you crying about?" he demanded. I tried to explain how burned out I felt. Before I said more than a few words, he countered: "Forget Iowa. There's no point in your moving a whole household, leaving your job, uprooting the kids, just for a year there."

No amount of discussion would cause him to reissue his earlier invitation. I wrote Ray a letter trying to convey my feelings without arousing resentment and antagonism. He didn't answer me. I held off applying for a leave of absence from Los Altos High School.

I began to understand what I recently had been told, that it was impossible to debate with someone who's drinking. But to catch Ray when he wasn't drinking was now impossible, so I saw nothing to do but stumble along as best I could. I was dreading the uncertainty and loneliness of the coming fall. My instincts were right. I had to go along with Ray all the time, be a perfect "good sport"—or I'd be left behind in the dust.

. . .

TRAVELING ALONE, RAY went to Iowa in the fall of '73. Shortly he
returned to start teaching at Santa Cruz weekly, in addition to his Iowa
classes. He was assuming a mythic stature to his friends. Unlike the previous year, when his drinking made him a whipping boy for the Stanford
set, everything bizarre he did now became legendary. Ever more fla-
grant, he somehow still managed to pull things off.

Iowa didn't know he was teaching at Santa Cruz, and Santa Cruz
didn't know he was teaching at Iowa. He flew back and forth every week,
except when he called in sick or had local friends go down to Santa Cruz
and fill in. He acquired his new nicknames—"Running Dog" and
"Feather-in-the-Wind."

Ray was hired to teach again at the Workshop in 1974. But this time
he decided not to fly back and forth between Iowa and California. He resigned his position at Santa Cruz. I didn't know when I'd see him next.
After a horrible Christmas, I would be cast into a painful limbo.

On top of Ray's open-ended abandonment, Chris shocked me when
she insisted on moving out to live with Amy. Released from the mental
hospital, Amy had courageously started over once again and had an
apartment in a ghetto area. She had found a job tutoring high school students. Though I cried my eyes out, begging Chris not to leave Vance and
me, she was adamant. Amy felt that a temporary stay with her might be
good for Chris. I could see my sixteen-year-old daughter was running
away from me, too, just like my husband.

Before Ray left for Iowa, we went to see a Jungian psychologist. He'd
been drinking heavily before we went to see her. If only he weren't going
away, I thought sadly, we could meet regularly with a therapist and our
marriage might have a chance. Caught up as Ray was in his drinking,
playing the role of a wild writer, and continuing his relationship with
Diane, I couldn't imagine getting him to stay in one place long enough
to keep a series of counseling appointments. He was a man on the run.

After Ray had left California I was tortured by the realization that my
friends at school had mostly fallen by the wayside. Ray's behavior at a
couple of faculty gatherings had been so *outré* that we were virtually

pariahs in Cupertino. I had no one left. Ray had his friends—writers and their wives who drank or who could tolerate it.

Counseling was not enough to check my downward slide or my own drinking, which I did to deaden the pain. I went to my first Alcoholics Anonymous meeting in the basement of a Palo Alto church. I imagined it would be like entering the halls of hell, full of darkness and fire and hollow-eyed ghouls. I soon learned that AA wasn't a den of lost souls, but a place where people gathered to reclaim their sobriety and their lives.

I attended the Women's Professional Meeting, a group of women doctors, lawyers, teachers, and executives. When I spoke about my life, I was surprised by the feedback I got. I was trying to do it all, be a working mother, a graduate student, a busy professional, a source of bottomless support for my beleaguered husband—didn't I realize I was setting myself up? Alcoholism wasn't reserved for the losers in American society; it's often a "reward" that superachievers win.

RAY HAD BEEN writing me love letters, promising that things would be better for us, although he was, of course, still drinking. In May a student writer, Dan Domenich, who was very fond of Ray, drove him back to California.

In the summer of '74 I began to drink again. Old habits subverted fragile new ones. Ray was palling around with Bill when he could. I couldn't lick the Rays and Bills of this world, so I joined them. There is an old adage: Drunks when they're drinking can't stand sober people, and sober people can't stand drunks. Sober people find drunks inordinately boring. Drunks want to *drink* and are annoyed by anyone who won't. Before long, Bill, Ray, and I were all on the same wavelength—drunk.

That fall Ray was appointed a visiting lecturer at Santa Barbara. I took a leave of absence from my teaching position at Los Altos and entered a PhD program in literature. Renting out our house in Cupertino, off we went.

We scored a nice house in Goleta near the beach, owned by a professor who was on a year's leave. Ray went on drawing unemployment ben-

efits even after we moved to Santa Barbara and he began teaching. He insisted on driving to Cupertino every two weeks to collect the check. It was an excuse to be on the road and a chance to see all his friends in the Bay Area. I warned Ray repeatedly it was against the law, but he wouldn't listen. He was drinking, drinking, drinking, all day, every day. He ignored rules at school, so why not those of the state of California? He was a law unto himself by then.

It became a full-time job to clean Ray up and drive him to his classes. I quit the PhD program because for the first time in my life, I couldn't concentrate on esoteric issues in English Literature. Everything got worse.

At one point we landed in the Santa Barbara jail two weekends in a row. The first time Chris came and got us. Ray and I had been out together at a nightclub with a marvelous woman singer who reminded us of Eartha Kitt. We began talking to her, and she invited me to sing with her. I did. When we left Ray was driving and my Scotch-addled head was in his lap, happy to sleep until we got home. The next thing I knew Ray had been pulled over, and the cops were being unnecessarily rude. When I raised my head to protest, they took Ray to detox and me to the local jail.

The second time we were arrested, Noel Young, owner of the Capra Press, came with bail money and got us out, took us home. I'd been driving after an English Department party where it seemed everyone was enamored of us. Ray and I had held forth in witty, daring dialogue, "wild and attractive things" that we were.

The topic of Love's Towing came up, a local car-towing company. I had seen their signs in the fog coming to the party, and I said the last thing I wanted was a brush with Love's Towing! Everybody laughed. Sure enough, that was exactly who towed off our car after I was stopped by the police for slowing down excessively for a yellow cautionary light. Despite the extreme fog, I was charged with DUI. Well, truthfully, I could see absolutely nothing.

Around this time Gordon Lish called from New York. I spoke with him. Out of the blue he said to me, "You know, Ray is a great artist. If you would just let him go, if you would just free him from the exigencies of his life, there is no telling how far he could go."

I was stung in a way I hadn't felt before. "I know he is a great artist," I said coldly. "I did before anyone else." I left it there, but it was slammed into my mind that New York had officially given the writer's wife her walking papers.

Terrified, I insisted that Ray resign his teaching post. I went back to AA. Chris fled to the Bay Area to live with Ray's mother. Our son, Vance, was in a psychological shell of his own. I wanted Ray to go back to Cupertino and get well. The whole family was suffering, and the rest of the world was just waiting to see how many pieces we could shatter ourselves into.

Ray was now insatiably physically addicted to alcohol. If he stopped drinking, he faced horrific withdrawal pains. He couldn't write anything. As he said later in a filmed interview with the BBC: "I liked to drink. I liked the effect of it. I liked the taste of it. I never once associated my drinking with my being a writer."

It was in '74 that Ray also insisted that we file for bankruptcy again. I could barely handle the humiliation a second time. It wouldn't have been necessary if he'd stop pissing away his earnings. But I guess that point was out of order.

RAY'S DRINKING HAD progressed so dramatically that by Christmas, he couldn't eat but could only drink. He drank wine for the bioflavonoids, he said. When the semester ended, students came and reveled in our borrowed house in Goleta. They loved the homemade chili and all the hors d'oeuvres and Christmas cookies. They laughed and teased Ray, having no idea that the following morning we were going to pack up and leave town.

We headed north to Cupertino, with no jobs or income and Christmas just days away. Our house was filthy dirty, the residue of the uncaring tenants we had rented it to. Who cared? The only thing Ray was interested in was the booze stash. We needed something to laugh about—so we laughed at anything.

Amy and Erin were in the Bay Area, as were Ella and James and his wife. My mother could come to Cupertino, too. Jerry came down to try and help us, leaving Gordon behind to man their home front. We were going to put together some sort of Christmas, a gathering of our relatives and the kids, all our loved ones, and we'd somehow have a good holiday dinner. Maybe next year things would be better. That was the only holiday wish I could come up with.

FOR THE LEGAL proceedings in the spring of '75, we had to fly down to Santa Barbara. I finally got so driven to distraction by Ray's indifferent attitude that I hit him on the airplane. I was utterly saddened by the whole business. He, on the other, made a joke out of it. When he told the story, he'd claim that the only thing we had that the attorney for our creditors made an effort to go after was our Irish setter. Ray guessed that opposing counsel had figured out that Ginger was a purebred and might be worth a few bucks.

I COULDN'T RESUME teaching until the following year as I'd taken a leave of absence. Until the fall of '76, we had to have some income. I found a job at a restaurant called the Blue Pheasant, close to our neighborhood. It was run by two Danish men, and the food was good. So were the drinks I served. I worried about hanging on to my sobriety in these surroundings, but my family had to eat. I went to work six days a week, and we lived on my tips. Ray was the neighborhood drunk. No time for any girlfriends now.

Finally, finally—I persuaded Ray to see an alcohol counselor for three sessions at the San Jose mental health clinic. This was required before being recommended for alcoholism treatment. In a weak moment when Ray was in tears, I had gotten him to agree to give it a try.

I drove him over to San Jose and waited in the car while Ray completely snowed the sweet young counselor, hardly older than our daughter, Chris. Right out of college, she hadn't a clue about the wiliness of the man sitting in the chair beside her desk. This innocence, coupled with a hint of condescension, infuriated Ray. What was this "know-nothing little cunt" going to do for him? It was all a farce, a waste of time. Yet he was lucid enough to want out of the alcohol trap he had fallen into and knew he couldn't do it without help.

They admitted him to the San Jose treatment program. The day I went to retrieve Ray, four days after he'd gone in, I waited for him out in the parking lot. It was warm but I enjoyed just sitting there, doing nothing. I was thinking about the dinner party we were hosting that evening—it had been scheduled some time before.

THE CAST OF characters was changing, as Bill Kittredge would have said. When we were down in Santa Barbara, we'd heard the news that Chuck Kinder, after his divorce from his pretty and very intelligent wife, had gone off to Montana. Staring at the future through the windshield of the car, as he put it. Chuck was at loose ends. Or, more bluntly, he was at a dead end. Like so many writers before him, Chuck's life took a new turn in Montana as Bill's guest, for he was next in line to meet Diane Cecily. He courted and ultimately married her.

At Stanford we had become friends with yet another writer, Max Crawford. It wasn't long before Max also made his maiden trip to Montana and hung out with the good ol' boys like James Crumley. Max was from Texas, so when the Montana boys picked on him, they were picking on someone who could dish it back. He was a socialist, and his novels were concerned with social freedom and fairness for the working class.

Visiting us, he once said to Ray that it was amazing that Ray's stories championed a group of people who normally never make it into quality literary fiction. "You have no idea, man," Max said, "what you are doing for American writing. The working poor, the unemployed, the inarticulate laborer; their concerns and lives are all laid bare in your fiction."

Ray had looked at Max blankly, perplexed. He didn't analyze society like that himself. He wrote about his people and the lives they led, what he knew. Or the story just came to him. Ray never had a political ax to grind.

On another visit Max said to me, "You know, Ray drives you wild, focusing your attention on him and other women. That's all it takes to control you, to keep you so distracted there is absolutely nothing you can do about the real problem. You're too busy bouncing off the wall over some woman that doesn't mean anything to him, compared to you and his bottle."

As I was mulling over that remark again in the parking lot of the treatment center, a nurse came out. She was calling, "Mrs. Carver! Mrs. Carver!" When I responded, she said, "Come quick! Your husband has had a seizure."

The staff managed to pull him through. But he had fallen and cut his forehead so badly that it required stitches. After Ray was stable, a doctor took us both into a private office.

"Son, you can't drink," the doctor said. He was an older man, a white-haired doctor who acted paternal. "You just had what is known in the business as an alcoholic seizure. Once you've had one, it's easy to have subsequent seizures. Keep it up, son, and you can end up a 'wet brain' [clinically, the condition is known as Wernicke-Korsakoff syndrome]. You could become like those alkies who are permanently brain damaged. They have lost their ability to be thinking men."

With that pronouncement ringing in our ears, Ray's first attempt at "treatment" was over. It wouldn't be the last; and it wouldn't be the last time he wound up in a hospital. Surprise, surprise—there were levels of self-degradation left to explore. But at the moment I was more concerned with trying to think of some way to call off the party. The problem was that we had guests coming from all over, and I didn't have all their numbers. I had to face it. The show was going on tonight.

Indeed it did. The highlight was when Chuck Kinder and his new wife walked into my home. I knew they had moved to San Francisco, but never thought they'd be so brazen. They sat on the couch and never moved, not even to go to the bathroom. Ray spent the evening sucking brandy from a bottle as if it were Pepsi, his stitches concealed under a bandage, indifferent to the doctor's warning.

After that I don't think Ray and I ever spoke naturally in public. His remarks to me had a condescending edge or were icily civil. It was as if he had to demonstrate how justified he was.

RAY TOOK HIS bottle of vodka and cracked me over the head.

I don't remember what happened, but supposedly I had said to him, "Now whose bed are you going to get into?" We were at a dinner party at the Kinders' in San Francisco. It was July '75, our first stop en route to Washington State, a trip to home territory, just the two of us. Ray's mother was staying with our kids.

Personally I'd rather have been dead than go through another evening at the Kinders', though I liked Chuck, who was fun and humane. It was pure lunacy to invite us, but that was part of the titillation. Diane had once declared, "Ray, we are going to all be pushed over the edge from these fun and games."

Right.

The Kinders were at the center of the San Francisco social scene for writers. Before we went into their place Ray promised he'd be on his good behavior. That was before the explosive combination of strong personalities and lots of alcohol kicked in.

Whack. I blacked out. When I came to I was covered in blood. I saw an artery beside my ear spurting arcs of blood. Imploringly but firmly I managed to say, "Get me . . . a doctor." Someone must finally have called the ambulance—I think Diane. Going into emergency surgery at the hospital I had lost nearly 60 percent of my blood. A priest came in and performed the last rites.

THE NEXT MORNING I awoke hungry in a hospital bed. I was alive. Weak. Alert. I could be discharged, they said. But I didn't want to go home to Cupertino where Ray's mother was minding the kids. I didn't want to see anyone—except Ray. Oh yes, I was sure that when he saw exactly what he'd done, he'd be so remorseful that he'd change his ways forever.

First I got hold of Jody Luck, my high school colleague, who was friendly. She agreed to come get me, and I could recuperate some at her place.

I didn't stay long at Jody's. When I spoke with Ray, he was sorry and quiet—and set on us driving north. After I left to join him at a motel in Palo Alto, she never spoke to me again. It didn't matter how many times we passed in the school halls or inadvertently sat together at a teachers' meeting. She gave me the cold shoulder to let me know what she thought of my "reconciliation" and my unmanageable life.

What could I say?

That's where you get to. You can't explain. You can't explain it to yourself. It's your life. But the *story* of your life has stopped making sense. The small absurdities are out of control, no longer something you can smile about for a minute when you're stopped at a long traffic light, or finishing a cup of coffee, or watching a child fall asleep. What you understood to be certain, isn't. What was clear has gone cloudy. I had gone through the looking glass. The life I actually found myself in was the wrong one, not the one I'd dreamed of, or planned for, or worked so hard to achieve.

What I had to do was bring reality around, make things right, get my life with Ray back on track. That's what I believed. Because I had to. Yes, *had* to. Not a very trendy stance, is it? I guess it smacks of romantic idealism and female self-sacrifice. So be it.

Doubtless others have other explanations. And their own stories about Ray. (Chuck Kinder fictionalized his in his book *Honeymooners: A Cautionary Tale.*) But I'm the "Maryann" you find in Ray's poetry. I'm also in some of the women in his short stories. I was a source of inspiration for Ray as he imaginatively recast incidents from our lives into his poetry and fiction. I was the sounding board who knew his friends, his whole family, and the brilliance of the man long before he was anybody's notable author. You don't just toss that aside when you hit a bad patch. So there we were.

• • •

RETURNING FROM AN uneventful trip to Washington we'd almost gotten home when something went wrong again. The next thing I knew I was in another emergency room, with a dislocated shoulder. It was very painful. But I was more worried imagining walking back into school, my arm in a sling. I couldn't! With what explanation? A car accident? I knew what some teachers might think, like Jody. I could probably kiss my chances of tenure good-bye.

As we waited and waited at the hospital to get treatment, Ray promised me to stop the physical violence. He said it was the last time, absolutely, no matter what the psychological provocation or wound.

HE KEPT HIS promise. After that trip he never hit me again. But if he could keep that promise, why not others? I began to believe that I was right in spite of everything. Ray would stop drinking, would get back to his writing. We'd stay together as a family. As long as we kept talking, and as long as I didn't give up struggling to work things out, we still had a chance. I thought Ray believed it, too, despite everything.

I willed aside his edgy, defensive attitude toward me. What that attitude said was: If you had a wife like mine, or kids like ours, or a house in the wilted suburbs, wouldn't you drink? Wouldn't you be in love with Diane? Even after she married Chuck?

Maybe some would, but I don't think Ray ever entirely believed his own rationalizations and excuses. I think his family memories were too vivid and he couldn't bear to leave me and give them up. But who knows exactly why he was so conflicted. Documentaries and biographies often miss the point. There's only so much cause and effect you can untangle in anyone's life.

So much of life is of a moment. Like the faded afternoons Ray and I passed in one agreeable bar or another. Just us—no kids, no bills, no problems. Just laughter, another round of drinks, music, jokes, and the promise of later meeting together under the red satin bedspread. We took it wherever we went—to rented rooms, to rented houses, and finally to the only home we were ever able to buy. Under the soft red satin, he'd say, "Wherever you are, Maryann, is home."

"It's strange. You never start out life with the intention of becoming a bankrupt or an alcoholic or a cheat and a thief. Or a liar." Ray said that. It still cuts close to the bone. There were times I'd wonder, How can we go on? Somehow we simply did.

AT CHRISTMAS 1975, for a change, we spent the money we *didn't* have. There had been trips to San Francisco, several of them, for chic events at the Kinders'. Amy had come for Christmas with Erin. She was in graduate school in Iowa, taking another big step forward in her life. She also had in tow a writing student who was a fellow at the Workshop. Doug Unger was a charming boy—well, he was ten years her junior. (He was to be Amy's second husband. She had dumped Tom Holland for him.)

Certainly Doug didn't mind meeting Amy's brother-in-law. He proudly stated that he'd helped with the publishing of Ray's story "They're Not Your Husband" in the *Chicago Review* when he was a University of Chicago undergraduate. (The story had been circulating "underground," partially due to its racy reputation.) Doug was slight, twenty-three, his distinguishing feature a long, thin goatee that he stroked incessantly with his fingers. Amy had decided that Doug was bright, and he was—but I was bemused that she was sleeping with him after the years she'd spent with older, more experienced men.

One night after a party in San Francisco, I was half asleep in the backseat of their car when I overheard Amy and Doug discussing Ray and me. He said to Amy, "I don't know. It feels to me as if the essence has disappeared from Maryann and Ray's relationship and all that's left is the sorrow and anger that remains after the essence is gone."

Amy made a passionate rejoinder, citing all the years we had been together, the experiences that Ray and I shared indelibly. She hadn't given up hope for us, either. That cheered me immensely.

RAY RENTED A room at Joanne Dunn's house supposedly to work and to get away from the kids, especially Vance, who was getting on his father's nerves. He was otherwise back at our house. She was an English teacher and colleague at Los Altos. I trusted Joanne and was grateful she had rented the room for no more than we could afford.

Joanne lived close by, and my husband went back and forth as he saw fit. When he wanted a home-cooked dinner and to see me, he came over to Cupertino Road. When he wanted to drink or read in his room, he did that. He hoped he'd feel like writing something, but it didn't happen. What he did write in that room in Joanne's big house was a valentine he gave to me in February 1976. He had drawn a black-and-yellow bee with crayons, and written under it, "Will you 'bee' my valentine?"

I was touched when he handed it to me. He was reeking of vodka but not belligerent. This wasn't true when he sat at the dinner table and launched into another fight with his son. From a psychologist's point of view, I suppose it was a classic oedipal scene. If Vance said he was thinking of taking a class in automotive mechanics, for example, so he could learn to change the oil and make minor repairs, Ray would immediately launch into a derisive put-down. These exchanges could destroy the whole evening.

The dispute that night degenerated into a fracas that spilled from the dining room into the hallway. They had their hands at each other's throats. Vance was seventeen but looked overmatched against his lumbering, drunken father. I had to squeeze in between them and give Ray a warning look, then tell Vance to go to his room. They separated. Vance left, and I sat back down in a state of thorough, absolute desperation.

The February night of that fight, I couldn't see how I could stand any of this much longer. I left my house for an AA meeting in Menlo Park. The group recitation of the Lord's Prayer was something that eased the pain in my heart. I couldn't bear to see Ray and Vance torturing each other. Let Ray torture me instead—at least I knew why I was willing to endure it.

I was sticking with AA. Ray was sticking with the bottle. At the meeting that night I met a young-looking man of average height. His name was Ross Perkins. After the meeting we enjoyed a cup of coffee at Stickneys in Palo Alto, where the AA crowd hung out. I realized how lonely and grief-stricken I was. Ray's long association with Diane was still going on as well as an intimate friendship with Joanne Meschery, a woman he had met in Iowa. As for me, I needed something more vital and important than a lover—I needed a friend. Ross was to become that very special friend for many years.

Ross was an engineer, though he wasn't working as one when I met him. It was easy for him to reenter his profession whenever he wanted, as there was always a demand for his skills, and he had an illustrious background from his years in the space program. He had built huge satellite antenna systems all over the world—even in the Seychelles islands. He had simply gotten tired of the workaday world, and after he and his wife split up, he wanted to know himself better. The wife had gone off with a man who made good money, and Ross tried dropping out for a while. Living at that time with his teenage son, he supported them both with his remarkable ability to fix any mechanical or electronic device.

IN MARCH 1976 Ray's first book of collected stories was published by McGraw-Hill. *Will You Please Be Quiet, Please?* was a long-awaited event for us and for readers of his stories in the little magazines, *Esquire* and *Harper's Bazaar*. When he received copies of the book, Ray took me out for a late lunch at a pleasant bistro near our Cupertino house. Except that Ray wasn't interested in eating lunch or even in looking at the book. He immediately began ordering vodka on the rocks, one after another, and became weepy and sentimental.

He began talking about Joanne Meschery. She was the student from Iowa he'd been involved with, as I'd learned firsthand when I went out to Iowa in February 1974. Tom Meschery, her husband, had been a basketball star for the San Francisco Warriors and Seattle Supersonics. Ray showed me a letter from her. A love like theirs, she wrote, should have lasted years.

Joanne had a husband and three adorable children. She had settled in Truckee, California. Ray told me that financial help from the Warriors organization enabled them to buy a big house and a bookstore. Just up the road from us. Ray was supposed to visit, spend some time with Joanne and the children, while Tom was temporarily removed from the premises.

Finally Ray got around to showing me the book. The dedication read, "This book is for Maryann." There it stood in print. I was still wife number one and only.

After Christmas I had taken another job as a waitress at a shopping center to repair some of the financial damage from the holiday blowout. I quit when Ray's book was released. Excellent reviews of *Will You Please Be Quite, Please?* began to come out everywhere, though it startled me to see how Ray's characters were frequently described: waitresses, teachers, hod carriers—"people light-years away from the American Dream." But who in this country believed in that dream more fervently than these people?

A photographer from *Newsweek* came out to our blue house and took shots of Ray and some of us together. In one photo Ray is smoking a cigarette, looking intent as he stands in front of the carport. How sad and ironic that when his work was receiving all this national attention, he was too ill and drunk to write. I began to feel that the worst result of his drinking wasn't going to be the destruction of his family and loss of his friends, bad enough as these things were, but the ruination of the writer he should have been.

I didn't hold on to my first copy of the book long. Somebody stole it. It disappeared from our house during a weekend celebration with writers and friends from San Francisco. We never found out who was the thief. But Ray gave me another copy and inscribed it, "To my wife, Maryann, Love of my life, for life."

Our rocky life at home didn't change. Ray could be set off by anything. He'd launch into a tirade against me or the kids. Those closest to me were tired of the melodrama. I'd burned out Claire Huddleston, the English teacher who had lent us the down payment for the house, and Bill Hildebrand, a math teacher, who tried to counsel me and had kept me functioning at school. Bill had also driven to the airport to rescue me after a terrible scene with Ray on the airplane coming back from the bankruptcy proceedings in Santa Barbara.

Weeping in my empty house, I didn't have much hope left. I'd learned at Al-Anon, a program for spouses and relatives of alcoholics, that when drinking reaches the crisis stage, it's often the case that "Dad is drunk and Mom is crazy."

THREE AND A half lonely years had passed since Ray meet Diane. So my relationship with Ross grew closer. He knew how to be empathetic as well as fun. I was amazed by things he knew that were outside my experience, facts from the world of science, astrophysics, the workings of technology.

One night we went to his house. "If Loving You Is Wrong, I Don't Want to Be Right" played on the radio. We looked at each other intently and acknowledged the truth we heard in that song. Then we sat on his antique wooden bed with its old-fashioned headboard. Ross and I hugged each other for what seemed an eternity before we headed into what had been forbidden during all the weeks of AA friendship and support.

I got under the covers first and took my clothes off. I was shy. Ross lifted the covers and looked at my breasts for the first time. He smiled as if to say, Your body is as pretty as the rest of you. Set at ease, my heart turned on. How long had it been since I had felt this way? Loved. Without fear, anxiety, or the sorrows of drink.

EVENTUALLY RAY CAUGHT on, drunk as he was. Somehow he got Ross's number. One spring evening, with the sun spilling through the big panes of glass in our family room, Ray picked up the phone and called my friend. It touched me that he was trying to get to the bottom of the situation and reclaim his wife, even though his words were slurred on the phone. He was determined: "It has come to my attention that you are seeing my wife."

Ross was in love with me. I was still in love with Ray, or at least I told Ross that I couldn't leave him. Not when he was so far down. Under the tension of the situation, Ross and I started skipping AA meetings. He started to drink again. So did I.

The only positive development in the whole sorry mess was that Ray and I decided to take an apartment together in San Francisco for the summer. To seek more counseling. To get Ray into a hospital for treatment. To try just about anything.

That summer Jerry would be glad to have Vance in Yakima. He could find work there. He'd just completed his junior year of high school and wanted to earn money for a car. Chris was already eighteen, the age of emancipation—and did she ever know it. She had her first serious boyfriend, Shiloh, who was not every mother's dream by a very wide margin. George Oudyn agreed to try to keep an eye on her for us.

(But he laid it on me squarely only a month later: "Maryann, your kids are fucked up." What could I say—once again? They weren't living their right lives either.)

Ray and I moved into an apartment on Castro Street, just south of the gay community. It was a loft, right upstairs above the landlord's quarters. (An almost perfect description of it can be found in Ray's story "Careful.") We had to pass through the landlord's foyer to get to our place; that's where the phone was, so if we had a call, we were easily within earshot. The landlord and his wife probably wondered what sort of tenants they had but knew we were just there for the summer, so they didn't rock the boat. That left it to us.

Ray got a job in the Tides bookstore. He enjoyed the books and people—and still drank around the clock and didn't bring any money home. He spent his pay on books he had to have and on his snacks. The job didn't last anyway, and soon he was back at the apartment.

In several weeks Ray and I were going up to La Pine, Oregon, to celebrate my mother's seventieth birthday. It's a little town some 110 miles east and slightly south of Eugene. The whole family was going to come to fete Grandma Alice. But first, in that American bicentennial summer, Ray would take another stab at drying out.

He entered Garden Sullivan Hospital in San Francisco. I had stood in a phone booth, begging them to admit him. I had been rejected several times that day by several other institutions. The woman on the phone said to come in the next day and fill out some paperwork. There was one bed; there was not a bed very often. Usually a man had to wait for weeks. I said we'd be there.

The hospital treatment was a short-lived success. Ray resumed drinking in Oregon.

WE GAVE UP the San Francisco apartment and returned to our house in Cupertino before the school year started.

Vance had an exceptionally good summer in Yakima. He'd done well working in an orchard and eventually had run a crew. And he'd saved his money, as he intended. He bought a car—a red VW with a purple interior and a good sound system.

Chris, I feared, had taken a look at her father's lifestyle, and after the initial shock of the first years wore off, had concluded that if she couldn't beat him, she'd join him. Her boyfriend, Shiloh, six years older and a Vietnam vet, was only too eager to be her guide. Yet it was Chris who was holding back from marrying.

With the autumn season upon us, I resumed teaching and Ray resumed unemployment. We took up the issue of his drinking again. Two hospitalizations had not worked. Perhaps a third would be the charm. I'd heard at AA about a place up in Calistoga, north of Santa Rosa in the wine country. It was called Duffy's. But it was expensive, and we still owed a bundle for the San Francisco hospitalization. We'd have to sell the house for Ray to go into treatment again. That would also alleviate the financial pressure of living on my one salary.

Fine. We'd sell the house. That decision made, I undertook some further inquiries and made arrangements.

One Saturday morning Ray and I attended an AA gathering and then met with a father-and-son team affiliated with Duffy's. The father looked just like Andy Devine, his big stomach hanging out over his belt and his bald head sporting a broad-brimmed Western hat. The son was a good-looking version of the old man, his hair full and blond. "Before and after," Ray and I immediately dubbed them.

The old man took over. He told Ray about "hummers." These were drinks Duffy's prepared for newcomers. Consisting of a bad brand of whiskey mixed with water, the hummers got weaker and weaker until the patient was tapered off enough to avoid seizures and the worst of the dt's. The old man's aggressively authoritative manner and the descriptions of seizures and dt's—not to mention the climb down to abstinence—had Ray fidgeting in his seat. "I need to go to the bathroom," he said.

"Oh, no, you don't," the old man barked. "You're going to bolt!"

How right he was. He had Ray pegged, like that. But then Ray was an alcoholic, and all alcoholics eventually seemed to wind up with the same bag of lies and evasions. It must be pretty predictable, I thought.

Duffy's was founded straightforwardly enough by a man named Duffy, a recovering alcoholic. He knew the game. Though an ambulance could be there in a flash, the center took a nonmedical, highly personal approach. The staff consisted of ex-alcoholics, people who hadn't had a drink in years.

For the first or hundredth time, Ray had tried to quit drinking on his own the week before we had the meeting with the Duffy's men. He had sworn he'd never have another vodka.

I went out to visit Chris, who had moved into a little cabin. It was heartbreaking to see her. For company she had her little black dog, Shana, who had lost a leg in an accident. To eat she had two potatoes. Shiloh was apparently out of the picture for the moment. I gave her all the money in my purse. I begged her to come home. I'd talk to her dad. I'd beg him to lighten up.

"Fat chance of that," Chris said. "Mr. Whiskey can't help being mean. He can't help insulting everybody, never letting up until he has me or Vance in tears and total confusion. He's no better to you. He comes home from San Francisco with big, green, oozing sores around his mouth. He's got herpes, Mom. Why won't you admit these things? Why don't you face facts? By now you ought to realize love isn't enough. A person would think, like you do, that love would be enough, but it isn't."

Oh Chris, you are so right! But without love what does it matter if you have everything else? And unbelievable as it would have seemed to her right then, I knew her father loved her.

Back at the house, Ray stayed sober for less than a day. He couldn't

Chris Carver at eighteen, by the peach trees in the backyard of the blue house
at 22272 Cupertino Road. Cupertino, California, 1976.
PHOTO BY MARYANN BURK CARVER

get through a day without vodka. Not anymore. Well, it looked as if Duffy's was going to be our last, best hope.

I invited Amy and Doug to come along with us when I drove Ray there. I wanted to make it feel like a picnic, a Sunday drive in the fall through the beautiful vineyards of Santa Rosa. I got a big box of fried chicken and other snacks. Ray wasn't interested, except to drink wine. He was in a state of total fear. He squeezed my hand so tightly all the way to Duffy's, I thought it was going to be permanently numb.

Ray got settled in. (Duffy's is the setting of the story "Where I'm Calling From," which subtly conveys the notion that alcoholism is a disease, not a moral issue. John Updike later selected it for *The Best American Short Stories of the Twentieth Century*.) He couldn't abide seeing us go, so we lingered as long as we could. But eventually we had to leave. We'd see him next weekend, I promised.

In October, the morning after I listed the Cupertino house, it sold. Someone in the listing real estate agency recognized that it was a good deal and bought it. I found a house to rent nearby on Carmen Road. It was more expensive than I would have liked, but there would be money

enough for now. We had made a healthy profit on our blue house, wonder of wonders.

RELEASED FROM DUFFY'S, Ray declared he'd learned his lesson.
The place had been good for him. He realized now that he couldn't
drink the hard stuff. He'd have to stick to champagne. To my crushing
disappointment, he took two bottles of André out of a brown paper bag
and made himself comfortable in our rental home.

There is a limit to everything, isn't there? I think I had reached
mine. Ray was up all night, drinking cheap champagne and smoking
and talking nonsensically. My sleep deprivation, along with the long
hours at school under constant scrutiny and disapproval from my colleagues, pushed me over the line. I told Ray he had to leave. I meant it.

The next thing I knew, after spending a few days in a sordid little
apartment, Ray had moved in with Jean, his former secretary at SRA.
They had always been friends, teasing each other hilariously. Ray
couldn't write in his new apartment, he said, and he couldn't take being
alone. (The state of his life as he reports it in his poem, "Jean's TV," is
beyond despairing.)

RAY CAME HOME home for Christmas. At the family gathering that
Christmas Eve were Ray and I; Amy; her daughter, Erin; Doug; Doug's
father, Maurice; Doug's brother Steve, Chris (who was seeing Shiloh
again); Vance, and Ella. I was serving New York steaks for dinner, and
though I was uptight, I was determined we would be a happy family for
one night. People were drinking, but I refused to.

I was feeling crazy inside. As I was cooking Ray suddenly threw all
the fake logs into the fireplace. The resulting blaze had to be damped
down hurriedly; it could have burned the house down. Everyone scam-
pered around in our amateur imitation of a fire brigade. Ray still knew
how to grab the center of attention, didn't he? The fire under control, it
was time for dinner. I was angry. When dinner was over and I had nothing more to be responsible for, I had a drink.

I don't remember exactly how the evening ended, but everyone had a good time, I think. I kept my own dark thoughts to myself. We can't endure another year like this. Yet Raymond Carver, the writer, wasn't doing so badly. His third book of poetry, *At Night the Salmon Move,* had been published by Capra Press. McGraw-Hill's collection of his short stories, *Will You Please Be Quiet, Please?,* had been released. It won a National Book Award nomination.

On the other hand Ray Carver, the human being, was playing with fire. Not just in the fireplace. Between October and the end of the year, he had been hospitalized on three separate occasions for the effects of acute alcoholism. He'd get the new year off to a good start with yet another hospitalization, in January, his fourth.

His story, "A Serious Talk," is based on that Christmas. The moment I read it, I recognized the setting, as well as some of the incidents. They're almost identical. I am even more moved when I listen to Ray's audio recording. The inflections and tenderness in his voice for the wife of the story as she models her Christmas gift—a cashmere sweater—take me to tears. If only, I always wish.

16

TWISTED FORK IN
THE ROAD

On New Year's Eve 1976, Ray was back at Duffy's. This time he went there on his own initiative. Neither Amy, Doug Unger, nor I were involved. When he called me to say "Happy New Year" and told me "where he was calling from," my heart leaped.

I had been in and out of AA myself. I had gone initially to find a solution for Ray, because obviously I didn't have a drinking problem. Despite the fact that I had blackouts. I learned that my nervous system could no longer handle alcohol in a predictable manner. Some people get the message from liver or stomach damage—my brain was directly saying, "Enough, enough."

After yet another blackout, I couldn't remember what I had received for Christmas gifts, except for a wonderful clock from Vance. I had to reconstruct as best I could who had given me what. There were two more episodes, though I functioned well otherwise and conversed intelligently. The worst part was that I realized I could not remember I'd had blackouts while I was in the grip of one. I had four altogether, and they frightened me into ultimately quitting drinking completely.

Actually I didn't care about drinking. What I cared about was Ray, and in caring about Ray I had fallen deep into drinking. However, I never missed days of school. I didn't drink in the morning or at any time during the school week. I wasn't having seizures. I didn't drink when I lived alone. I didn't feel out of control or want to drink myself into a stupor at every opportunity.

But in the end I came to the right answer anyway: I should not drink at all.

ROSS WAS WORKING only sporadically at the time. He fixed friends' cars or toasters. He was a crack electrical engineer, so these jobs were easy for him. His friends paid him a token amount, but it was enough to keep him going, while at the same time he could "drop out." He was a self-proclaimed master of his own time, though it left him so poor I wondered if he was getting enough to eat.

A sensitive man, Ross knew that my fondest wish was for Ray and me to get back together, without the horrors of alcohol. I wanted to go back to those days when it was certain that Ray loved Maryann and Maryann loved Ray. Yet my heart went out to Ross because he was so giving to me. He focused on what would make me happy. That hadn't been a consideration for Ray in some time.

Somewhat reluctantly, when Ross had to leave his cottage in Los Altos, I asked him and his children to move in with me. It was on the level of "friend helping friend." I had never lived with anyone but Ray. Only Vance and I were still in the house on Carmen Road. He was in his last year of high school. (In my zeal to help Ross, I failed to pick up on Vance's discomfort that I was having a relationship with someone other than his father. He resented it, even if Ray treated him harshly.)

Ross arrived with his two teenage daughters, who were fourteen and fifteen—his older son, Mark, was spending time with his mother. Vance picked on Ross's kids unmercifully, especially on the fragile and vulnerable Lori. She looked like her dad and was the apple of his eye. My son was unreasonable, brutish, selfish, ill-mannered. It hurt me to see him bullying Lori, denying her food, and making her feel unwelcome. When Ross caught Vance at his game, he leaped on him and they fell on the floor fighting. I cried and begged them to stop before someone got hurt. After that I knew the situation was hopeless—we couldn't be a house of psychological healing.

• • •

RAY CAME OUT of Duffy's after his self-commitment at New Year's and resumed drinking. It was no better than when he totally swore off vodka but found himself helpless—as long as there was a liquor store open and selling, he was buying. His mind and his blood were at war, and blood was used to winning.

Restless, he left Jean's place and went to San Francisco to stay with Doug and Amy. They had a place on California Street, right next to the parish house of Saint James Episcopal Church. Amy taught Sunday school to help pay the rent. They were also sheltering Doug's brother Steve, who'd come back damaged by his experiences in Vietnam.

Ray was going to resume Duffy's hummer regimen on his own. He was embarrassed to go back a third time, and he could no longer afford it. But he knew what he wanted to do—he was always a quick study. He wanted to taper down with hummers so his body wouldn't go into shock from alcohol withdrawal. Then he could go to AA meetings and begin the long, slow process of reeducating and reinventing himself. The exact strategy aside, what Ray most wanted was to *want* to stop drinking.

From Doug and Amy's, he sent me a letter that I keep in our big family Bible to this day. It sounded like the old Ray, the man I loved more than myself.

He was subdued but not self-pitying, and sweet. He'd gone to an AA meeting at Saint James Episcopal. He wondered if I'd consider going to a meeting with him. He'd be pleased if I did.

That's what he wrote me from San Francisco in February 1977. I couldn't go.

RAY CONTACTED ME to tell me about his latest plan. He would drive up to Arcata. Dick Day, his old friend from Humboldt days, was still living and teaching there. I knew Dick would do all he could to help Ray. He was living with someone new.

The big problem was that Ray was broke. He'd spent his share of the profits on the Cupertino house. Now he needed gas money and the first month's rent. I gave it to him. Gladly.

My house was emptier than ever. Ross got a job as an engineer and moved out. The scuffle with Vance had made it impossible for him and his daughters to stay. It wasn't going to work. Yet even in the brief time we were under one roof, I realized how badly I needed someone to talk with, to care about me, to make me feel wanted. Well, I hadn't known I could break until I did, either.

WITH EVERYTHING THAT had happened recently, Ray and I still never lost touch. He wrote to me from McKinleyville, where Dick had found for him a little house with a view of the ocean. It was behind the Bella Vista restaurant. They served gourmet Italian, pricey. We had always wanted to try it when we lived in Arcata but could never afford to. The restaurant owner was a master chef, and he also owned the house. Ray impressed him; he liked the novelty of having a published author as his tenant.

Ray begged me to come up and visit him. "Come to Chef's house," he said, "and see if things might be different away from everyone and everything."

I agreed instead to meet him in wine country, in Petaluma. Ray and I walked around the square, looking in the shopwindows, but he had to find a bench and sit down frequently. Ray was sick. He was so sick and weak.

We talked all day and night. We agreed to get back together. Our eyes filled with tears of relief. Married still, after all the years! We planned to reunite in June after I finished the school year and Vance graduated from high school. I would come to McKinleyville. We were going to start over. Ray was going to get himself sober and start writing again.

BACK FROM THE weekend with Ray, I had coffee with Ross at a new restaurant in one of the chichi shopping centers a few miles from my house in Los Altos. Green plants proliferated in the dining room and hung from the ceilings in every corner of the room. Outside the sun had settled into a deep gold.

"How did the weekend go?" Ross asked tentatively. Before I could say anything, he began to berate himself. "I'm crazy. How could I have gotten into this situation? My friends say I'm crazy."

"Oh God, don't say that! You are the most eminently sane person I've ever met. And the kindest. Your kindness saved my life. I was completely devastated and hopeless. And then I met you, and I had a friend."

With that conversation, Ross understood where things stood. I had been honest. He knew that. And I was on my way back to Ray.

THE EDITOR FRED Hills of McGraw-Hill, the publisher of *Will You Please Be Quiet, Please?*, contacted Ray, having traced him to McKinleyville. Fred was coming to San Francisco and wanted to meet up. Ray was elated. In McKinleyville he experimented with leaving booze alone, but how he'd fare back in the city was anybody's guess. Ray was coming down the day before the meeting, and he invited me to come and stay with him at Doug and Amy's.

It began as a perfectly ghastly weekend. Ray drank vodka as if it were cream soda, right out of the bottle mostly, and could not have been more ornery and inconsiderate to everyone. He lashed out, ranted and raved. He seemed to be listening to voices in his head, conducting a dialogue that was a parody of what he used to write.

"Mr. Whiskey rides again," Amy commented. I started having major second thoughts about McKinleyville.

Surprisingly, though, Fred Hills's visit turned out wonderfully. He took Ray and me to a delicious seafood lunch in Sausalito. I worried about Ray drinking too much at the restaurant, and where that might lead, but Fred chose not to react. It was a quiet example of an editor doing his job excellently, trying to motivate a writer in whom he believed.

Fred talked about whether Ray would be interested in writing a novel. Yes, of course, Ray told him. In fact, he'd had an idea for a novel for a long time, but with one thing and another had been unable to get to it. This was good news to Fred because McGraw-Hill was prepared to offer Ray an advance to write one.

"I'll take it," Ray said. "And I will make you proud."

After Fred left Ray and I couldn't contain our excitement. "That's all I've ever needed," Ray said. "Just someone to tell me to write something

specific and give me a calendar to follow. To pay me. Can you beat that?"
He paused, considering something. "Take a year off, Maryann, not just
the summer. You can do that now."

I PUT IN for a year's leave of absence from Los Altos. The prospects
looked good that I'd get it. People knew my marriage was a shambles.
The department chairman and the principal hoped that time off would
help, and that I could come back to work invigorated and undistracted.

The week before I was to leave for McKinleyville I packed up the
house and helped Vance write a paper on Ernest Hemingway. He was so
conscientious and scholarly. I could see that he didn't realize—or
couldn't figure out—what exactly was going to happen to him or our
family. We'd talked about my plans, his plans, but I don't think it really
sunk in. I tried to tell myself that in the long run it would help my children if they had parents who were together and stable. But in the short
term it looked as if they would have to cope with more readjustments.

Vance had a few weeks of high school left. I found a family he could
board with and paid two months in advance. That would cover him into
the beginning of summer.

There was a nice big swimming pool, a major selling point. He could
swim a lot and sit out in the sunshine by the pool and read, or have a friend
or two over. That didn't sound so bad. He and his sister had Grandma Ella
nearby and their aunt Amy in the city. Yet even as I spoke positively about
the altered circumstances I sensed how different Vance's life was going to
be with me away, and I hoped he could handle it.

I TOOK A small plane to the Arcata airport. Ray picked me up. We
drove to Chef's house. Simple as that.

At midmorning we were sitting at the table in the kitchen, drinking
coffee after a leisurely breakfast. I wasn't expecting it when Ray looked
at me and said, "Maryann, I've fallen in love with you again."

ON JUNE 2 Ray took his last drink. He was determined he was going to
make it this time. He had been sober for four whole days when I arrived.

Vance Carver at eighteen, graduating from Homestead High School. Sunnyvale, California, June 1977.

PHOTO BY MARYANN BURK CARVER

And he held firm even on our anniversary, June 7, when we went out to dinner in Eureka.

He talked about writing again and about Fred Hills's visit. He talked of getting fishing equipment. He wanted us to fish together, not just him alone. For an anniversary present, he presented me with a silly, wonderful straw hat to wear fishing. He had an identical one for himself.

THE FATES WERE kind to Vance for a day. He had a wonderful June graduation. Jerry and three of her sons—Loren, Val, and Vawn—came down from Yakima to see the ceremony. Grandma Ella, Amy, and I were there, after a celebratory dinner. With his entire class, Vance flung his graduation cap high in the air to celebrate his freedom and the end of his days at Homestead High School.

The next day was the other side of life. Karen, his attractive blond girlfriend, had been going out with Vance for six months. She decided this was the right time to break up. She already had another boy lined up. Vance was derailed. Then his car broke down. The day before he had been smiling and jubilant. Now he was forced to consider anew what was happening to his life and where he was headed.

LET'S NOT PRETEND that a few days of sobriety meant Ray was out of the woods. He had barely chopped a few twigs. And it didn't instantly restore him to being the person he was before his brain grew addicted to alcohol.

We made some vacation plans with Bill Kittredge and Max Crawford, despite the fact that no better practitioners of the fine pleasures of drinking existed. They were joining us for a week to go fishing on Flathead Lake. A cabin had already been rented. We were going to stop in Eugene and cavort with writers there as well. We were going to go into restaurants and test the waters of alcohol-free meals. Then Ray would know if he was getting somewhere. God help us, we'd find out if there was any real hope outside the protective environment of placid McKinleyville.

I turned thirty-seven on the trip. Ray gave me a camera and film to chronicle our gang of writers. Jim Crumley came and brought his latest wife, a philosophy student with long brown wavy hair. The cabin turned out to belong to a cop. (That kept us in a sober mood.) He was blond and quite attractive and had a skinny girlfriend with long brown straight hair.

So there we were, hanging out with a bunch of writers and having a good time. And through it all, one day after another, Ray and I didn't drink.

RETURNING TO CHEF'S house, we settled down to serious endeavors. Ray applied for a Guggenheim grant. He asked friends like Jack Hicks, an English professor at the University of California at Davis,

and Gordon Lish in New York, for references. For a teaching job at the University of Texas at El Paso, Dick Day wrote Ray yet another reference—the tradition continued—as did several other friends. Ray

Bill Kittredge and I fishing on Flathead Lake. I've caught one; Bill is still trying. Near Missoula, Montana, 1977.
PHOTOGRAPH BY DIANE SMITH

had heard about that post from yet another friend, the poet Michael Ryan, who was teaching at Southern Methodist University (SMU).

As important as it was to get his professional academic life back on track, there was something else he needed to do. I held my breath a little. Ray started to write. First he did a short story he called "Viewfinder." I loved it. It's about a man who has metal arms and hands. He earns his living going door to door with a camera held in what are virtually claws, soliciting orders for a picture of the occupant's house.

In the fall Ray wrote "Why Don't You Dance?" In that story a young couple look to take advantage of an older man's household lawn sale. He has set up his bedroom furniture outside, but exactly as it was arranged in the house. The lights are actually plugged in, and the phonograph plays. It's eerie and disturbing, for there's no direct explanation of what has brought him to this collapse, although the reader is drawn to imagining the worst without a resolution.

While Ray worked I went and enrolled in some courses at Humboldt State College, one of my favorite things to do. I took Women from a Jungian Perspective, offered by the psychology department; Chinese Philosophy, using the *I Ching* and *Tao Te Ching* as texts; and Mysticism East and West. It was another step in my own realization that I was searching for God. A path that AA had started me on.

AS 1977 WAS drawing to a close, Ray and I were broke. The advance from McGraw-Hill for the novel had come and gone. I got a job as a cocktail waitress at the Red Lion, a new hotel in Eureka, and donned a maroon miniskirt and a pink blouse with ruffles tracing my cleavage. The more things change . . . but my tips enabled us to survive. Our lives were under stress again. But neither of us reached for a bottle. Not even a beer.

IN NOVEMBER RAY went to SMU to do a reading. His poet friend Michael Ryan had arranged a symposium that featured Ray, E. L. Doctorow, Philip Levine, Richard Ford, and Tess Gallagher. Ray was at once excited and apprehensive about the trip. He hadn't done a reading since he'd been sober. Could he read without having had even one drink? Then there were the parties and receptions he would be expected to attend, where the liquor would flow freely. He knew this trip was going to be an acid test of his commitment to sobriety.

"It's time to go back out there and wow 'em," I assured him enthusiastically.

Ray was thrilled to have been invited and wouldn't have missed the opportunity for the world. He and I had just read, and loved, Richard Ford's novel, *A Piece of My Heart*. Ray was eager to meet him. Also he could see Michael again, a friend since Iowa days, and have a chance to see Dallas.

The date came for his departure.

Go get 'em! Ray caught his plane and was safely on his way. I felt frightened and uncertain. I was alone, rattling around the isolated house in McKinleyville, and I sorely missed my children. It was hard to accept that all our lives were still in a precarious state.

On a trip to fetch Chris, I saw Ross briefly in the Bay Area, I sadly and sincerely told him that Ray and I were definitely back together. I then freed Ross from his promise to wait through the summer and see how everything stood. I loved him, but he couldn't go on with our relationship. So with that I lost my best friend, the person to whom I had poured out my heart for months.

CHRIS'S VISIT WAS difficult and left us both saddened.

RAY WROTE ME from Dallas. A woman had presented him with a yellow rose just before he read his new story, "Why Don't You Dance?" He electrified the huge audience. An incredible success.

The day before Ray was due home, a pink envelope arrived in the mail addressed to him. It looked like a woman's handwriting. And it certainly smelled of perfume. I held it in my hand a long time. I felt the contents. Then, throwing my normal scruples out the window, I opened it.

I read how wonderful the night they had spent together had been.

Couldn't she see him again? Yeah, that sounded like Ray. Mr. Whiskey
may have been on sabbatical, but Mr. August was back. He evidently
had not the slightest compunction about breaking my heart and scalding
my hopes again.

When Ray got home the following evening after dark, he walked in
full of authority and impatience. His step and stance were changed. In
his leather jacket and leather hat with the broad brim, he was in charge,
sure of himself. One symposium with the likes of Doctorow and Ford
and he was a literary top dog.

He was full of stories of Dallas. And he still hadn't taken a drink. I
produced the mail, including the pink envelope. I might as well have
been back on Cupertino Road five years earlier.

Ray shrugged it off. Was I going to spoil the nice rapport we'd established over a silly letter that should never have been sent? He hadn't
given her the address; she must have gotten it from Michael or some
other way. It was nothing and meant nothing, except as an experience
from a time and place that wouldn't be repeated. So let's forget it—no
unpleasantness.

What should I do? I was disappointed beyond measure. The Dallas
conference stipend was already spent. Ray saw to that. I had to go serve
drinks every day in Eureka in a garish outfit so we could keep eating.
When I told a customer that my husband was a famous writer, a really
talented man, his expression said it all—a lot of good it does you. Or
maybe he just didn't believe me.

AMY, DOUG, AND Erin spent Thanksgiving with us. They were on
their way to New York to try their luck as an actress and a writer. We
wished them well. Besides, who was I to remind people that they'd been
down a particular road in life before?

By Christmastime I'd saved enough to send Chris most of her fare
money to come home. She was in Lake Tahoe. She'd recently gone to
live and work at a ski resort with her old friends Karen Kessler and
Annabelle. From his janitor's job, Vance was able to cover his own trans-
portation. We would all be together. I clung to that vision as one stan-

dard in my life that hadn't been violated. The family came together for the holidays, through thick and thin.

My gift from Ray that year was the first copy of the hardbound edition of *Furious Seasons and Other Stories*. He'd just received it in the mail from Noel Young. Capra Press in Santa Barbara had produced a handsome volume. There was a handwritten inscription inside, on the red endpaper.

It was as touching as anything he had ever penned for me, a message tossed into the psychological sea between us, a Christmas greeting of love, "now and forever." In that holiday season of 1977 I had hope again, sent from my lost Odysseus stranded on the shores of McKinleyville, California.

After the holidays were over, Ray had a brief job at Goddard College in Vermont. This would be his teaching debut after years of drinking and being unemployed. But I realized that the journey would be more than that. I was sure he was going to do some additional traveling and looking around.

I understood, but I also felt panicky. Ray was full of energy, ready to give up Chef's house immediately and head east. What was I to do when he left me behind in California? Support myself serving cocktails while he went out to explore the world and see what presented itself? Richard Ford had mentioned that he had a farmhouse available in Vermont. And Curt Johnson, Ray's old editor friend, had a summer home in Elizabeth, Illinois, that was empty. No one used it in the dead of winter.

Vance left. He got into his red VW and headed south. Ray took Chris to the airport. Ray and I packed up the house. He simply was not going to pay rent on a place he didn't need anymore.

I rented a room in Arcata from a woman I knew. We went there. Ray and I slept together in a single bed, making cheerless love, the fog like a blanket out of Brigadoon.

ANOTHER YEAR UNFURLED its unsoiled banner. A sober Happy New Year 1978. Ray still hadn't touched a drop of liquor. That was one major sign that I felt meant he'd come back to me for good.

Ray chose to fly out of Sacramento. He could visit the Schmitzes prior to his departure. I was to drive him over the mountains and then return to Arcata, my new little rented room, and my job at the bar. No other plan was discussed.

The day of his flight we got to the Schmitzes' house without incident. They were glad to see us. I had to use the bathroom. When I came out, I overheard Ray and Dennis talking quietly in a nearby bedroom. Dennis asked Ray when he was coming back. I heard Ray say he didn't know if he'd be coming back.

Ray's true intentions were completely open to question. Only, whatever they were, I wasn't supposed to know. It took a strength from God for me to climb back in the car, full of discarded pots and pans, and set out over the mountains again. I was essentially homeless and friendless. I stopped now and then to cry and think, before I put my foot firmly back on the accelerator and drove on.

I GOT A postcard from Ray. It showed a lively view of New York City at the turn of the century. He sounded upbeat and affectionate. He was having an "illusion of freedom." That was a phrase he'd used six years ago when he'd left for Montana. I wondered if it was deliberate, or whether he simply no longer remembered which lines he used with what woman. Or maybe he thought my memories were clouded. Or maybe none of the above.

Freedom, sure, right.

The teaching at Goddard went well. Ray enjoyed socializing with Tobias Wolff, Geoffrey Wolff's brother. Geoffrey had reviewed *Will You Please Be Quiet, Please?* favorably. He went off to visit Richard Ford, his new friend whom he'd met in Dallas the previous November. But things didn't work out for a place in Vermont, so he couldn't stay long. When I heard from Ray again, he was at Curt Johnson's home in Illinois. Though the house was snowed in and isolated, he thought he could hole up and write there.

Vance came up to Arcata. He was thinking of leaving the Bay Area. I could tell from his breathing how agitated and distraught he was, how absolutely lonely and unconnected. For a night he slept in my crummy room on the floor beside my cot. I was going to go to the college and beg a dorm room for him. The winter quarter had already begun, and it was too late for Vance to register. But I was sure they'd have a spare room he could crash in.

My argument, if it went that far, was that he was going to be a student at Humboldt next quarter. That was the one good thing that had happened. Vance was going to give college a try.

Somehow I got Vance into a dorm, and he just stayed on. It wasn't an easy situation, as his status was unclear to everybody. I kept telling him he would make friends eventually, even if the situation was weird right now. I encouraged him to find a job, without making a big deal of it.

As for myself, abjectly lonely, one night I bought a bottle of wine and got drunk. I stayed in my room and cried until I couldn't cry anymore. Then I called Ray. How long was I supposed to live in this limbo? His cards and letters, his calls, had sounded comforting notes. Yet in reality our family had been flung to the four winds, all of us barely holding on emotionally or financially.

NEXT I HEARD, Ray had left Illinois and gone to Iowa City to beat his own loneliness. In Iowa City he was fine. He had been awarded a Guggenheim grant. There was a provision providing some support to the recipient's family. He could lay over until it was time to go to Texas and start his new position at the University of Texas at El Paso. He was just fine.

"I'm so sorry, Maryann," Ray said on the phone. "Please calm down. Please stop crying. I love you. I'll fly out, and we can drive back. We might as well be in Iowa City."

Please, yes.

When I told Vance about my conversation, he realized he was about to be ditched again. I would have done anything if I could have said, Come with us. Start school in Texas in the fall. But with so little money and his relationship with his father so rocky, I didn't dare. Better to encourage him to stay at Humboldt. Our friends in Arcata would rally around him.

"Please, Mom," Vance said. "Don't go until after my classes have started."

"I won't," I said. "I know exactly how you feel."

"I got a job, Mom, over at the Eureka Inn. I'll be bussing tables."

RAY FLEW BACK to California in March. Chuck and Diane Kinder were throwing a big party in San Francisco and wanted Ray to be there. She had received an inheritance from an aunt and bought Ray his ticket. I was humiliated. She had basically bought my presence, too, but I sadly realized that beggars were not likely to be multiple-option choosers.

The night before I went to the Kinders' party, I visited a few friends and had some drinks with them. It was March 10. The next day I felt weak and slightly hungover as I began the eight-hour drive to San Francisco. I wanted to see Ray; I'd see what he'd put me through at the Kinders'. Those drinks in Arcata were the last drinks I have ever had. (And so March 11, 1978, became my AA birthday.)

BY THE TIME I got to the Kinders' California Street apartment, the party was in full swing. It seemed everyone was invited. Dick Day was there. I spotted Ray; I went to him, beaming. An ailing Stanley Elkin, whose stories we'd admired forever, was holding court, one hand resting on a cane. I was introduced to Toby Wolff. I passed on through the crowd and sat down next to Clay Wilson, the cartoonist of *Zap* magazine. After several more drinks, he sketched a humorous note: D-I-V-O-R-C-E C-A-R-V-E-R. I appreciated his affection and support.

I moved on to dance with San Francisco writer Leonard Gardner. His novel *Fat City* had recently been made into a movie. The story was going around that he and his girlfriend, the writer Gina Berriault, were in Morocco when news of the movie deal reached them. Her first response was to ask if *now* Leonard would like to trade in his cardboard suitcases and invest in some leather ones. He and I danced loose and free like a couple of rag dolls.

The gossip was endless. No doubt phone wires would be burning up across the country tomorrow. Everyone would be calling friends—other

writers—to tell them about the party, and in turn they'd call more people. Everyone had to know what happened at the latest swinging West
Coast soirée. Who got drunk? Who was it that tried to drive two cars
home at once?—a sports car and the wife's Cadillac?—jumping back and
forth, hopscotching them down the street?! And what was she saying?

When we left the party we went to someone's apartment that Ray had
arranged for us to use. Hello there. Too soon it was morning.

Charming, pretty Diane had pulled off another dazzling social triumph. But one thing had been decidedly different for us. Neither Ray
nor I had a drink.

A few days later we were on the road to Iowa. We swung through
Lake Tahoe to see Chris. But no one at the resort had seen her for a couple of days. They sounded vague, as if they weren't absolutely sure we
were talking about the same girl.

We finally located her in an apartment with no furniture and no one
there but her little dog. The TV was on. My poor Chris was lying on a
thin mattress on the floor, swollen with alcohol poisoning.

We didn't have a lot of options. Beggar that I was, I called Ross.
Blessed man, he agreed to meet Chris at the airport and take care of her
if I flew her down. After much finagling to find a box that would accommodate her little dog on the flight, I got Chris on a plane. At first
she had protested that she loved the snow and the beautiful scenery
around the lake, but her brave resolve broke and she cried lonely, desperate tears.

I had sworn down in Texas I'd eventually bring both kids back into
our lives. I visualized them going to college (tuition-free, with Ray's
benefits as a professor) and having a home base again, even if that meant
dormitory rooms across town from us. For now, once Ross had Chris in
hand, her grandmother and friends would pitch in to help care for her. I
would figure out what to do next just as soon as I got to Iowa. Just as
soon as I knew what I was doing with her father. Just as soon as I knew
what to do with myself.

WE MADE IT to Iowa. Again.

17

PARTING AND APART

In Iowa City we first stayed in a rented room in the house of an Arab man and his American wife. To say it was a weird home with weird people is putting it mildly. The Arab catered to his American wife, who seemed to have some humorless, loveless power over him. Ray's poem "To Begin With" conveys the strange feeling and foreign smells that greeted us on the dark night we arrived.

The story "Kindling" also evokes the experience. Ray had been living there alone prior to my joining him. He carefully avoided using the kitchen when they were there, choosing to work around their schedules and not be seen. Once he did walk past their open bedroom door and realized that the wife slept in the bed while the husband slept on the floor beside her.

Exhausted, we crawled into Ray's bed with most of our clothes on. "You've got to be kidding," I said, trembling with anxiety and clutching the edge of a thin, sickly green blanket. He seemed to have deliberately chosen this disquieting, strange experience—more grist for the writer's mill. Never mind that his wife and children were, at the time, struggling halfway across the country with loneliness, displacement, and poverty. The irony was that Ray's Guggenheim was substantially larger than if he'd been single. He was awarded more money because he *did* have a wife and two children.

The next morning we tiptoed into the kitchen and made furtive cups of instant coffee. We drank them in the bedroom. "Let's look for somewhere else to live," I said. "Someplace by ourselves, be it ever so humble."

That's how we ended up at the Park Motel on Highway 80. It was at an intersection where several major roads converged. On a hill behind the motel a flock of trashy single-wide trailers perched. It's where Ray wrote "Poem for Karl Wallenda, Aerialist Supreme" (who died in a fall in 1978) and is the setting for "Marriage."

On Easter Sunday, Ray and I sat in the efficiency suite and watched Kitty and Levin's tragedy unfold on public TV (courtesy of a BBC production). Why couldn't Tolstoy's lovers have continued together, outlasting the vicissitudes and tumult of their lives?

Amy and Doug came by to see us. They were in Iowa en route from a disappointing, difficult experience in New York, traumatized because they, too, were on the move and currently homeless. They got into an argument in our room and almost split up. They decided that Doug would head west to Idaho and Amy would remain in Iowa City with us. Ray grudgingly gave them ten dollars to rent the unit next to ours for a night. Their next plan was to find house-sitting jobs in Iowa City for the summer.

Ray had his plan, too. First he was going to teach the summer session at Goddard in Vermont. Then we were both going to El Paso. I would fly to Vermont and we'd buy a new car and travel down the eastern seaboard. Heading west, we'd go through New Orleans and hear some jazz and eat jambalaya. In El Paso he'd take up his appointment as a distinguished writer in residence. I could go to graduate school, perhaps. Ray had it figured out.

"You'll need to write a letter of resignation to Los Altos," he said solemnly, aware of what this meant to me. I had been teaching at the high school for seven years. After some quiet thought, I agreed to write that irrevocable letter. It only took a moment to drop it in the mail.

The next day Ray began to further unfold his Texas fantasy. He was calling all the shots. No input allowed, thank you very much. We would have to stop being so friendly and accessible. We needed to be more re-served. Hold our stories back, as people would be interested in him, in gossip they'd heard. We should practice discretion in what we revealed. A noncommittal attitude would be best.

"What kind of phony nonsense is this?" I asked. Since when did we need to get that precious over a teaching job that would take hours and hours of his time—reading drivel for the most part—and attending the same faculty meetings he'd attended a hundred times before? What was the big deal? I'd done it teaching high school. Then I had a sudden chill-ing thought: I've given up my *job*. I was now dependent on this man, my husband, who suddenly was a hot dog, a snob, after being the town drunk for years.

All right, maybe it was crucial for him to prove himself for future as-signments. He was a great writer and he was sober: That was the role and posture he was assuming. This job was just the beginning. Indeed the plug was in the jug—onward to new conquests. I had better calculate my self-presentation carefully and follow his instructions if I expected to accompany the Important American Writer to Texas.

IN LATE APRIL I was called out to Washington to care for Jerry. Her health was failing. I stayed a week and watched her drink her last drink. Six weeks before I'd had my last drink; I was righteous just at the mo-ment when Jerry was ready to stop, too. She needed to try to heal her ail-ing heart.

When I got back, Ray had already moved us out of the motel to an apartment on Lucas Street that I dubbed the hippie girl's pad. In the process he somehow managed to lose my San Jose College BA diploma, the one that noted "With Great Distinction."

WITH AMY'S HELP I planned a grand party for Ray's fortieth birthday on May 25. I ordered an enormous sheet cake. We'd need it to feed all the guests I was inviting, locals and out-of-towners.

The party was held at a house that Doug and Amy were hired to house-sit. The owner was a professor of French at the university. On display in the house were books and artworks acquired over a long lifetime. Every piece of furniture, every flower in the garden, was sheer elegance and perfection.

At the party the mood was high. People were getting off just looking across the room and seeing who was there. The poet Marvin Bell came. So did Vance and Tina Bourjaily. Everybody from the Writers' Workshop was there. In a brief lull Amy and I fell into an embrace and said to each other, "Haven't we had it hard? Haven't we had it hard?" We laughed and went back to our hostess duties, offering people hors d'oeuvres and fetching drinks.

Ray loved the party. He came to think of it as the best birthday party he ever had. Everybody was there, friends and fellow writers from near and far, and he was at the center of it. For a time he stayed high on the experience and had no further misgivings about Texas and our new life together.

AT THE HIPPIE girl's pad, Ray and I slept on her mattress on the floor—it took up the entire small bedroom. I have the image in my mind still: Ray and I standing in the bedroom, teetering in the small space between the mattress and the wall, trying not to trip. I can hear him saying, "If anyone asks me what went wrong with this marriage, I'll tell them it was not large enough to accommodate your ego."

I didn't know what he was talking about. Could he mean my application to the Writers' Program at Goddard? It was his suggestion! I did apply, and he helped me edit my entrance essay, a memoir piece, which I thought was generous and kind. Soon after, Ray changed his mind. When I pressed him, he told me that he didn't think it was a good idea after all. He'd be an instructor; I'd be a student—not a comfortable situation. Having warmed to the idea so thoroughly, I was crushed.

I felt that my ego had all but disappeared, along with my diploma and a vision of my future. Sure, I did object when Ray rented another apartment a few blocks away—did we really need a his-and-hers setup? He needed it to work, he explained. Three long flights up in his "penthouse," Ray wrote the poem "The Blue Stones." It's about sexual desire.

Love has nothing to do with it, the narrator, Flaubert, keeps repeating. Then it ends, "For my wife."

I'd go over to Ray's penthouse and figure out how to create the world's most scrumptious dinner. And then talk and read. Listen to music, and read some more. And then go to bed with him in the hot humid night and make love. It was amazing to realize how much things had changed for us since 1963, while Iowa City's climate had remained the same.

In the morning he'd be impatient until he could cajole me to leave. He had work to do. He was busy. So I'd go back to the hippie girl's pad. He was isolating himself again, I realized, shutting me out. Back at my place, I wrote too. One piece was called "Apathy," and shocked Ray totally when he read it.

My frail hopes were yet intact as we celebrated our twenty-first wedding anniversary. Under rose-colored lights at a restaurant Ray and I toasted with Perrier. "Happy anniversary, Maryann," he said. "I sign up for another year." I kept the red roses he gave me in a crystal vase until they turned black.

VANCE CAME TO Iowa City after the spring quarter at Humboldt ended. Our son was so excited to be with his dad again; he idolized Ray despite everything that had happened between them. He beamed as we took pictures at the big house that Doug and Amy were house-sitting; they'd moved from one professor's place to another.

This one had a huge shaggy dog to walk and tend. There was comfortable overstuffed furniture, a piano, and a big private yard with a huge oak tree. Nightly barbecues were in order, and everyone was welcome.

My mom was in town, too. She'd come to see Amy and me, and she wanted to treat all of us at the local A&W. Root beer and fast food. Ray was not enthusiastic, nor did he at least pretend as he'd done in the past. A lot had happened to him in his first year of sobriety—the reading at Dallas, the Guggenheim grant, teaching at Goddard, the upcoming Texas appointment, and the new people and important writers he'd met and who lauded him. I had not expected that some success would affect his personality or his relationships with my mother and the rest of the family.

I've asked myself a million times since if I should simply have focused on the times when he was his old self. But I was alarmed to see his detachment and his disdain growing. Then Ray announced to me that he was leaving for Santa Cruz. He was going three weeks early to help prepare a literary festival he was involved in.

Vance had only been with us two days! He had ridden a Greyhound bus for three days to get here! How could he do this to his son?! But Ray's mind was made up. Oh, and by the way, he thought he'd prefer to go to Texas alone.

The last night before Ray left the Iowa air was so close it was difficult to breathe. In bed, I asked him, Do you love me? I waited for an answer. I waited, held my breath. After a while, I realized he had fallen asleep.

That's it, I thought. I'm going to restore dignity and meaning to my life—even if my life is of insignificant value compared with his.

I DID NOT fly to Vermont. From Iowa I left for California on July 24, 1978. I had no teaching position to return to. I didn't have much of anything. I had trashed my own life trying to keep Ray in it. Except for one thing left—a sense of my own self-worth. I tried to console myself with that slender thought.

I HAD A FEW rocky weeks in Menlo Park, south of San Francisco, until I found work as a substitute teacher. I'd also immediately set about extricating my daughter from her downward spiral. If I had not come back exactly when I did, Chris might not have made it. I never could have lived through losing her.

I withdrew my teacher's retirement and bought Chris some clothes and a car. Then I sent her and her young man, Shiloh, up to Washington to stay with my relatives. I wanted them out of the Bay Area and the drug scene. I wanted them to try a more wholesome life.

And I wrote a very long letter to Ray. I sent it to Dick Day's address in Arcata, certain that Ray would land there at some point in his travels after the Santa Cruz book festival. Better I should break the news to him when he was with his old friend.

It was like the letter that the narrator of the story "Blackbird Pie" complains about. (What a coincidence!) The narrator has a letter from his wife—but he doesn't recognize the handwriting. He insists it's not in her hand. Yet clearly it has to be. (A little psychological denial, perhaps?) The letter explains why she's leaving. And the narrator is utterly baffled why, even as he can't bring himself to look at more than snippets and passages. He won't read the letter because that way it can't become part of his reality—his history—and besides, it's not in her handwriting anyway.

Eventually I got back an anguished letter from Ray. He asked me how I could leave him *now* when, for the first time in his life, he felt he was integrating the pieces of his life. He was in El Paso finding a place to live and implied that the door still might be open for me to join him. In a wistful tone, he told me that one day he'd seen a blond driving a car with California plates and his heart had leaped up. That made me want to pack and fly to El Paso as swiftly as I could.

But almost simultaneously I learned that Chris was pregnant. If we didn't laugh . . . She and Shiloh were in Bellingham, still unmarried, but united and looking forward to having a child. I was excited to tell Ray. He was less than thrilled at the news. She was only twenty-one, unmarried. What was she thinking? He was so against her having the baby, I thought it wasn't a good sign for me to see him yet. I was torn but decided to remain in California awhile longer and see what Ray's attitude was like later in the fall. I enrolled in a graduate counseling program at Santa Clara University. The first quarter wouldn't be over until the first week in December. I'd stay in California and think about things until then.

At the end of August, I wrote him a letter. I was now ready to come to Texas but wanted assurances that we would go for counseling and get professional help. There was no reply. In El Paso Ray had run into Tess Gallagher again and taken her to a bullfight in Mexico.

FINALLY, AFTER Thanksgiving, I got a letter. Ray had asked Tess to come live with him, starting in January. He didn't know what was in store for us in this life or the next one, but he wanted me to hear the news from him.

Vance was invited by his father to El Paso for the Christmas holidays. I was grief-stricken but called Ray anyway for comfort. Sweetly and endearingly he invited me to visit him with Vance. We could fly out together.

I was so devastated that I couldn't think much, except for the *absolute* conviction that I had to go to El Paso.

At the end of December, Vance and I flew to Texas. My reunion with Ray this time was bittersweet, splendid and unsettling, joyous and miserable. When it was good, it was very, very good, and when it wasn't . . . soon he was going to be living with someone else.

We went down to Mexico for a Sunday, the three of us. We were a loving family; we were the parents of a handsome son, home from college for Christmas. We had a family dinner. We bought souvenirs. Ray held my elbow as we walked along, or took my hand.

I asked him why, oh why, he hadn't answered my letter in August. He said it was because he couldn't face counseling, not with a new job to concentrate on. Couldn't he change his mind now? Couldn't he tell his lady friend he wasn't ready yet? He wouldn't go back on his word. And I didn't ask him to, even as I cried.

We sat on the new couch in his new apartment and did a reading from the *I Ching*. He threw the coins and drew the hexagram "Sui Following" (no. 17). He had Nine in the fifth place, for which it's stated: "Sincere in the good. Good fortune."

Ray nodded, took a deep breath, and felt better. We read aloud the commentary: "Every man must have something he follows—something that serves him as a lodestar. He who follows with conviction the beautiful and the good may feel himself strengthened by this saying."

I opened the Bible, looking for some philosophical and spiritual truths to comfort and enlighten me. I found myself in Luke, staring at "One must lose one's life to gain one's life," which rocked me back onto my heels and brought forth a fresh outburst of El Paso tears. Ray and I went to an AA meeting together. Vance watched his family coming apart again, yearning for more time with his dad and wondering if he would have a place in Ray's new life in the new year.

Then it was time to go . . . home? We knew where our heart was, but we were heading back to California anyway. We said good-bye. As Vance and I boarded the plane on the tarmac I turned back to see Ray hunched over in his car, crying.

Inside, the low Muzak in the cabin switched to "Love Is a Many-Splendored Thing." Only then was I racked with silent sobs that I could barely contain.

1980s

*Toby Wolff, Ray, Jay McInerney, and Amy Burk Unger
at Pascal's restaurant. Syracuse, New York, 1984.*

PHOTO BY MERRY REYMOND

18

NOBODY KNOWS

"No one knows, do they, just absolutely no one." Ray penned that inscription in my copy of *Where I'm Calling From*. We had still been writing letters to each other. We did for another decade, as it turned out. I have kept most of them.

At the age of thirty-eight I left Ray because in my heart of hearts I believed that was what he truly wanted. He was too much of a gentleman ever to ask me to go. No matter what he said or did over the years, he stayed in our marriage. He never directly called it quits or asked for a divorce. It was up to me to go. It was probably the right thing to do, even though the emotional cost was incalculable.

Nor did Ray abandon the family that was part of his life for so long. In the eighties, he supported Vance through Syracuse University and a first year of graduate study in Europe. (Our son spent an undergraduate year abroad as well.) He put Chris through school to be a medical assistant and bought her a mobile home that we set up on my property. Later he helped her start at Western Washington University. Though Ray and I were separated, I never tried to separate him from his kids, and Chris and Vance treasured their dad's visits, his letters, his calls.

He wrote me how crazy he felt that first summer after he'd left Bellingham and us all behind. He was trotting from one writers' conference to another. At one point he was in a Wyoming motel and thought he was going to lose it completely. He felt completely ungrounded—but he didn't take a drink. Resolved to get a grip, he carried on with his plan. Attending conferences was how writers got better known, and he had to take his "show" on the road. The family business was the priority. (But, oh, how I missed my baby, and from that letter my baby missed me.)

He wrote again, a lyrical letter about seeing a doe early one day in a field. She stood still and looked at him in the morning mist, and he felt that intensity of the natural world he could so vividly convey in a few exact words.

He sent me the first manuscript of "What We Talk About When We Talk About Love." (Later the title would be used for a collection of short stories.) And an early copy of "A Small, Good Thing." Instantly I remembered when Christi had been grazed by a car. Ray had come through the nightmare of alcoholism and was back at work, more Carver stories making their way into the world. Hadn't he always said there were more stories to tell?

He wrote when *Cathedral* was published and thought for a time he might win a Pulitzer Prize. (The book was nominated for a Pulitzer and the National Book Critics Circle Award.) He told me about his feelings, for that habit of mind never changed.

He wrote how his Mercedes got sideswiped when parked. "Grief over a machine" I called it, comical and yet touching, for to own such a car was a triumph over hard times—and then the world dented it.

And he wrote to console me. Like the time he heard I'd been in an accident. I had a head-on collision with a woman in a white Volvo that left me with permanent scarring on my upper arm. But I was otherwise all right—to Ray's great relief.

Even when his time grew short, he wrote me to say that the stories in his last collection, *Where I'm Calling From*, representing twenty-five years of work, were the stories he felt he could live with. And, yes, be remembered by.

ON OCTOBER 18, 1982, we were divorced. Permanently. In the legal paperwork sense.

. . .

THE FIRST WEEK in September 1987 Ray had a pulmonary hemorrhage—like his literary hero Chekhov. He and I were talking on the phone every day at the time. Ray was staying alone in his house in Port Angeles, Washington. It was his wonderful, final dream of a place; he owned a boat and could go out and fish.

The one day we didn't talk he was at the doctor's. The next day Ray told me he'd spit up blood. The previous spring he'd been given a clean bill of health—he was "healthier than he had a right to be." That's what he wrote me then. Now the doctor had discovered some "highly suspicious" cells.

Soon there was more frightening news. Ray would be going back to Syracuse to have surgery. The surgeon would remove a lung in an all-out effort to save his life. The next eleven months couldn't have been more replete with life's yin and yang. I say that "as a student of philosophy," as I often said to Ray to preface something serious. His literary prominence rose to unprecedented levels, while his body slowly gave out.

On October 2, 1987, the surgeon in Syracuse removed most of Ray's left lung. The doctor's daughter was a Carver fan, we learned, and he went to extraordinary lengths to ensure the best possible outcome. Amy and Doug were there. After the operation the doctor spoke with them and with Tess. Amy told me he had to lean against a cabinet to keep standing, he was so completely exhausted. He had obviously tried his very best.

Ray had gone into surgery bravely telling everyone that perhaps he was on to another life. When he came out Amy said he was wild-eyed. A machine was breathing for him, and he was in distress. She invoked the AA dictum, "to let go." Ray relaxed, his eyes quieted. He was alive.

Later that night he slept.

Chris and I had kept vigil in Washington. Ray had sent me money to buy a dress and shoes, and he'd left signed checks in case we needed funds to come to his funeral.

Early in the morning we had stood in our meadow, the sun shining over Mount Baker in the distance. As the mists cleared I was startled to see a line of Canada geese in the sky—maybe fifty—and flying toward them a long row of planes. If Chris had not been there to see it, too, I would have thought it a mirage. They passed each other as we watched—the planes actually much higher—but it was a sign, a lyrical blend of nature and human technology. I knew at that moment that Ray would survive the operation.

That night Chris and I phoned the hospital. The nurse said she was glad we had called. Ray's morale seemed low. He wasn't able to talk on the phone, but he could listen to our words of love and support. He had a pad of paper. The nurse told us he wrote, "Call again." We did, and every time we phoned him, Ray would write, "Call again."

IN MARCH, RAY started having terrible headaches. His brain was affected. Novices that we all were in the ways of cancer, we did not realize that this is often the case. The lung cancer had spread, despite the surgeon's careful work and all our prayers. By April he was having daily radiation treatments at the Fred Hutchinson Cancer Center in Seattle. He had an apartment nearby and invited us to come see him.

I accompanied him to one of his treatments. When I got home, I sent him a dozen red roses. The nurses fussed over the flowers, Ray said; and he said that was a good day. He and Tess took the roses and went to a movie after his radiation treatment.

In May he had to purchase a wig, as the radiation had robbed him of his beautiful curly thick hair. He was taking a trip east. Ray wanted to look decent when he was inducted into the American Academy of Arts and Letters. John Updike officiated at the ceremony. Ray's friends James Dickey and Evan S. Connell were his fellow inductees that day, and also attending was that idol of our youth, Jacqueline Kennedy Onassis. This was reminiscent of the previous fall when, after the New York Public Library literacy-lion fest, the *New York Times* had a picture of Jackie and one of Ray in his tuxedo, talking with one of his heroes, Harold Pinter, all on the same page. If anything ever proclaimed that Ray Carver had stayed the course and achieved his dream, this did.

During the trip east, Ray accepted an honorary doctorate from the University of Hartford. "You can call me doctor now," he said with a laugh to friends. Of course he was enormously pleased, as he always had been with any recognition of his work—whether it was a poem in a little magazine or a book from a major publisher. His uncalculating enthusiasm for his work was one of his enduring charms.

In Manhattan, Ray gave a reading at a bookstore. People lined up for six blocks trying to get in. Doug, who was there, said it looked like a film opening or a rock concert crowd. Midway through the reading, hot and uncomfortable, Ray threw aside his wig. He didn't need anything but people who wanted to hear his work. Cancer-stricken Raymond Carver read in a hoarse voice to the people jammed in the bookstore, and they listened and gave him their resounding cheers.

In that astonishing month of May, Ray's last book of short stories, *Where I'm Calling From*, also came out, published by the Atlantic Monthly Press. His editor, Gary Fisketjon, had moved to Atlantic, and Ray had gone with him. The response to the book was phenomenal. His picture was prominently on the cover of the *New York Times Book Review*, under the headline "Marriage and Other Astonishing Bonds." They used a Marion Ettlinger photo of Ray wearing his leather bomber jacket. It's the picture he sent me in February for Valentine's Day.

ON JUNE 6 cancerous tumors were diagnosed in Ray's one remaining lung. On June 17, 1988, Ray and Tess went to Reno and married.

As July swelled the bounty of Washington's orchards, Ray worked hard to finish his book of poems, *A New Path to the Waterfall*. Before the month was over, I received more mail from him. This time it was three postcards, all identical, in an envelope. Nothing was written on them.

The postcards showed a picture of two hands in prayer, a Rodin sculpture. I remembered when we were in Paris. We had lost ourselves in the Rodin museum, going back repeatedly, unable to take our eyes off the magnificent works. Ray and I had seen that sculpture of two white feminine-shaped hands in prayer. Two porcelain-white praying hands.

This was how he told me he wasn't going to make it.

SEVERAL YEARS BEFORE we divorced, Ray sent me an Isaac Bashevis Singer story, "Ole and Trufa: A Story of Two Leaves." Those paired leaves are the last ones left on a tree, a metaphorical couple. As the winds and rains of November threaten, they realize that the sweet promise of spring and the serene days of summer are gone. All the other leaves have fallen, but Ole and Trufa hang on. They have each other, and that sustains them. But they begin to worry. Ole tells Trufa that he is going to fall, too, and she'll be left on the tree without him.

She can't bear to be parted and begs Ole to hang on. A leaf must stay up as long as it can. But one day a big wind comes, and Ole is shaken loose. Trufa is desolate, alone. Yet somehow she is still on the branch.

Finally Trufa falls to the ground in her sleep. But, lo, who is that on the ground beside her? It is her Ole, waiting for her! There is life after the wind and rain. There is life after falling from the tree. And in that miracle there is a higher love than what they knew when they were vibrant leaves aloft high on the tree. Their fear was of death, but in eternity was redemption.

To me the story Ray sent was more than a charming and wise folktale. Ole and Trufa were lovers. They were a couple separated by fate. They were us. And what a comfort it was—this gift from Ray. When I was lonely or desperate down to my toenails (as I would put it) or when I wished I could die (were it not for my children), I would turn to Singer's story. When I was at that level of despair, with shaking hands I'd reach for Ole and Trufa and reread their story. I'd understand anew the continuity in nature of matter; the sprouting of seeds and the growth of new leaves to maturity and the final falling of the leaves to the ground; and ultimately the spirit being born again to life everlasting. I'd reread it and take heart.

19

ALWAYS

Ray came for Christmas in 1986. Actually Christmas was over when he rented a suite at the Bellingham Holiday Inn, halfway between Seattle and Vancouver. But so what; he had come to celebrate Christmas and the date was immaterial. This was always a special time for our family. In the spirit of the season we'd be lifted out of the struggle and toil of the rest of the year. He shouldn't have to miss out just because he had a different life now.

We were all a long way from those two decades of Christmases as "the Carvers." But even after we separated we never stopped exchanging presents. Every year, every Christmas from 1955 to 1987, Ray and I gave each other gifts. It was something divorce couldn't strike from our hearts.

By 1986 Raymond Carver, author, was a man of modest means and growing reputation. He was receiving thirty-five thousand dollars a year, tax free, from the prestigious Mildred and Harold Strauss Living Grant. This windfall allowed him to write full-time for five years. The recipient was enjoined from holding other employment, so Ray happily put on hold his professorship at Syracuse University. With no other commitments and no children at home, he was free to work to his heart's content.

This Christmas Ray loaded us all up. These are the rewards, you knew he had to be saying, so enjoy. A smoked turkey from Hickory Farms arrived at my doorstep by UPS, along with cheeses of many kinds. And sausages and hams, smoked and packed in spices. And cookies from Pepperidge Farm, cakes, and other Christmas specialties.

And then Slinkies and wooden toys from the Smithsonian Institute for our two granddaughters. And black lacquered mirrors painted with golden butterflies for Chris. (God knows what he sent Vance—something luxurious, I'm sure. That year our son was living in Germany with his wife and baby.)

More boxes came. Fruitcakes soaked in rum—the only contact Ray or I ever had now with spirits. As well as a ceramic sandpiper, plump and alert. Like the man who wrote stories and sent us these gifts. And wind chimes. Ray bought me wind chimes for my porch. From a company called White Swan in Oregon. They ring to this day. To my ears, when the wind is just right, they chime, "Hello, hello," the way Ray used to say on the phone.

RAY PHONED ME after he got into town. "Hello, hello." He was calling from the Holiday Inn.

His mother was with him. Ella was in her seventies, but her Southern belle manner had endured. Chris and her two little girls, Windy and Chloe, were coming over to visit him. This had become the ritual several times a year. The girls looked forward to swimming in the hotel pool and eating meals in the coffee shop where Grandpa Ray just signed his name to the bill.

"He didn't even have to get money from his wallet!" Windy told me.

Ray was calling to tell me he'd call me tomorrow. He wanted to get together for Christmas. Which technically was over, but I knew what he meant.

"You think about it," he said, "about when you could get away, where you'd like to meet. I'll call you tomorrow at noon—at high noon—and you tell me."

We hung up.

RAY WAS IN town. We'd get together briefly, I supposed, to exchange gifts. Nothing more. But my heart skipped. It was always like this when he called. Or sent me flowers for Mother's Day or my birthday, or a big package of books, or a manila envelope crammed with book reviews and poems.

High noon on the dot Ray called again. My gorgeous ex could meet commitments. If he said he'd call at noon, he called at noon. To have his life in order had become a good thing—his wild romantic period followed by a calm classical one, his second life.

"Let's go to that Mexican restaurant in Fairhaven," I suggested. "Dos Padres. I'll meet you upstairs. It's a separate space called Rose's Cantina."

"Sounds good to me," Ray said.

TWO DAYS AFTER Christmas Day, Ray and I met in Rose's Cantina. He was still breathtakingly handsome. He took off his sports coat and sat down; his mildly faded purple shirt suited him well. He looked fit, with the same strong presence that never ceased to attract me, and he seemed on top of the world. He was forty-eight, my favorite age for a man.

When my handsome father was forty-eight he had taken me with him to the liquor store in Lynden, Washington, seven miles from our home. It was primarily a drugstore but they kept some liquor in stock. The druggist behind the counter asked my dad for identification. State law required anyone purchasing alcohol to show ID, no matter their age.

"Forty-eight?" the druggist exclaimed. "Are you really forty-eight? You look more like twenty-eight."

My dad had laughed. He repeated the remark all the way home: "Forty-eight? Forty-eight? More like twenty-eight." And he'd laugh again. That sealed it for me. Forty-eight was the best age. The age of my dad, so many years gone now, when I watched him buy a bottle of whiskey to share with his friends. Full of life and "mature handsome," I called it. Like Ray was today.

But he was also *the* Raymond Carver. His stories that I had first read in draft and that we used to discuss and edit together had a following all over the world. Many thousands of people loved his work.

The room was pleasant, dimly lit, and music was playing. We both ordered Perriers with lime. Our drinks came in large elegant wine-glasses. I thought, We can play any record we want on the jukebox. Song after song, we could play them all if we wanted to—no lack of quarters.

We were four years divorced.

Maybe the jukebox had "Groovin, on a Sunday Afternoon" . . . the song we played over and over when we lived in Sacramento—those sunny days together—when we were younger and danced together. Now in '86 Ray was living with Tess Gallagher, though they each had their own house. He called her his "companion." What was left to Ray and me was the letter in the mailbox, the phone call, the trip to visit grand-children, and the occasional, odd sighting, those unplanned moments when once-married couples spot each other across a street or in a restaurant.

As the afternoon drifted on, the dim red lights and the music en-veloped us and made winter's cold seem far away. It was like the old days, to sit across a small table from Ray and relax, stretch my long legs out, slip off my shoes. We didn't touch. Then he reached under the table and I lifted my feet into his hands. My peasant feet, always happier bare than shod.

A HOT, BLACK night the first summer we went out together, before he touched my breasts, Ray had held my feet. We were in Jerry's rented house in Union Gap, talking with her in the kitchen. It was a Saturday night. I was wearing white shorts and a salmon-colored halter, scanty clothes for '55. But I wasn't self-conscious. I knew the exposed parts of my body more than passed inspection. (Yes, teenage hauteur.)

I was sitting with my legs stretched out. Ray looked at them a long while, or so it seemed to me, and then he lifted my feet into his lap and affectionately rested his hands on them. He would squeeze and pat my feet from time to time—my big, too-wide feet! I was utterly astonished he liked them, and so self-conscious and embarrassed by this scan-dalously intimate attention that I could barely sit still.

"Your feet," Ray had said, with another squeeze. "I just love your feet." Then he went on talking with Jerry. Surprisingly she seemed to be enjoying herself. This wasn't a typical local boy—Ray was witty and interesting. I realized my sister had never enjoyed a conversation with me this much, our twelve-year age difference too wide a gap. But Ray was different, even though he was young, too.

Another round of Perriers came.

Ray released my feet. We talked about Chris and Vance, our grandchildren, what was happening in their lives. Reluctantly I left our table to go to the restroom. Ray went to the men's.

I was thinking of too many things. "Love of my life, for life," he had written ten years ago in my copy of his first major press book, *Will You Please Be Quiet, Please?* That was a time when he was so ill from chronic drinking. Did anyone but me notice that he was on the verge of killing himself? Nobody talked about it. Until he stopped.

Back at the table, another song came on. We sipped Perrier, talked about his recent publications, what he was working on now. Besides our children, that was the important thing. His work had been our business, the family business. Even with all the emotional scars, his work justified so much of what we'd put ourselves through. That's what I believed.

I started to explain about the firewood business I had launched. It was out in Deming. I had a partner, the best selective logger around. It was really the only thing I could harvest from the family farm I lived on.

For no reason, or because I'd been speaking about the farm, I could see an image of my dog Bogey, bright and clear. He was smiling at me, looking at me unwaveringly. Come here, it meant. Around Bogey's head was a white light, an enormous circle of bright white light. At moments like this your brain races, searching for a connection, some meaning. Ivan Ilyich—that's what came to me.

He's the main character in a Tolstoy novella, *The Death of Ivan Ilyich*. Ivan has bruised a hip or leg—nothing serious, he assumes—but his condition steadily worsens. As he lies in bed, alienated from his family and friends, he keeps wondering how such a trivial injury could have brought him to the threshold of death. At the end he sees a bright white light. It's the love, pure love, that is the heart and soul of the universe, the presence of God.

Ray was looking at me. "I've got to go now," I told him quietly. "Sorry. It's Bogey. Bogey, my dog. He needs me. He's at the vet's." Bogey was named for Humphrey Bogart. He was an Australian shepherd dog, black and white and very furry, with long curly hair and the brightest, sweetest eyes. He had such an incredible soul.

"Okay," Ray said, slightly hesitant in that appealing way some men have. "Okay. I'll see you later. For sure I'll see you later."

Early one morning in December, Bogey had crawled to my bedroom door, his breathing raspy. He had never fully recovered from a bite to the throat by another dog, a black dog, Sinner, who belonged to a neighbor. My mom took Bogey to the vet's five days before Christmas. She thought it would be better for us all, and for the dog. And he still might get better.

By the time I got to the vet's after my hasty exit from Rose's, Bogey was nearly gone. I was not too late. But it was the end. When it was all over, my friend Don came and carried Bogey home. We buried him under my big fir tree. I didn't go back to town, I didn't go anywhere. But the whole day was luminous in my mind.

BEFORE RAY AND I had gone into Rose's, I had watched from my car as he parked his. He got out and, carrying presents, walked over to mine and got in. He hugged me; for five minutes he hugged me. When he finally let me go, Ray took a deep breath, slowly exhaled. The air from his lungs sounded how I imagined the valves of a dirigible release. I could feel his tension.

"Relax, Ray," I said. "I'd like to see you relax."

I knew how busy he was and how much he was on display. Even now, I can be a little startled when I glance over somebody's coffee table and unexpectedly see Ray's picture on one of his books or on a book about him. This man I knew better than myself, inanimate in a photo, so unlike him being held down in one place.

Ray nodded. We made some small talk sitting together in the car as he toyed with the loosely tied belt of my dress. Casually, he slipped it off and put it in his coat pocket. I didn't say anything. He wasn't being aggressive or flirtatious. No, I think, he was calming himself, the way he used to with that first cigarette. The dress would be pretty unpresentable without the red silk belt, and I didn't think I had another one that went with it. But I let him have it.

I gave Ray his Christmas present. It was a statue of a woman with long hair and a gorgeous body, her legs in stride, in motion, her breasts erect. It was carved out of oak. I had found it at a Montreal art gallery, or it found me. The gallery owner simply gave it to me after he saw me staring and staring at it, so much longing in my eyes.

Ray took his gift. We got out of my car and went up to Rose's.

HE FINISHED THE last book of poems and died at his home in Port Angeles on August 2, 1988. In the Arkansas country tradition his body was viewed at home. The mourners quietly filed by the four-poster bed where he was laid out, too bloated, hairless, and still really to be Ray. But it was.

I saw the statue I'd given him on the bedside table. Somebody had polished it exquisitely. It gleamed like gold and smelled like lemon. Beyond grief, I thought of the man I had cherished. Of that Saturday night long ago in my sister's kitchen when seventeen-year-old Ray Carver had lovingly held my big feet.

Shortly before he died I had been sitting in a lawn chair when a UPS truck lumbered up my driveway. I took delivery of a box. Inside was a signed copy of the Franklin Library edition of *Where I'm Calling From,* a beautiful volume bound in maroon leather with gilt-edged pages. The maroon ribbon bookmark had been placed in the story "Distance." I opened to the marked page and read the brief exchange between the boy and the girl, his answer to her when she playfully asks if they will always love each other. Always, the boy says. Always.

Chronology
Raymond Carver, 1938–88

1938   Raymond Carver born in Clatskanie, Oregon, May 25.

1941   The Carver family moves to Yakima, Washington.

1943   Ray's brother, James, born in Yakima, Washington, August 18.

1955   Ray, seventeen, completes junior year at Yakima High School. He has a summer job in Union Gap and meets Maryann Burk.

1956   Ray graduates from Yakima High School. He immediately moves to Chester, California, to work in a sawmill with his father and uncle.

In November, Ray returns to Yakima.

1957   June 7, Ray marries Maryann Burk in Saint Michael's Episcopal Church, Yakima. He works as a pharmacy deliveryman and attends some classes at Yakima Community College.

A daughter, Christine LaRae, born December 2.

1958   Ray and Maryann move to Paradise, California. Ray enrolls in Chico State College.

A son, Vance Lindsay, born October 19.

1959   Fall semester, Ray takes Creative Writing 101 at Chico State, taught by John Gardner.

1960   Spring semester, Ray founds and coedits *Selection*, a literary magazine funded through Chico State.

In June the Carvers move to Eureka, California. Ray works in a sawmill.

In the fall he transfers to Humboldt State College in nearby Arcata.

1961   "The Furious Seasons," Ray's first published short story, appears in *Selection 2* (Winter 1960–61).

In June the Carvers move to the farm of Maryann's father, north of Bellingham, Washington.

In mid-August the Carvers return to Arcata.

1962   Ray edits and writes for *Toyon*, Humboldt's literary magazine. Spring semester, Ray's first play, *Carnations*, performed at Humboldt. He has small-magazine acceptances: *Western Humanities Review* in Utah takes "Pastoral" (later named "The Cabin") and *Target*, a poetry magazine in Arizona, takes the poem "The Brass Ring."

1963   In January, Humboldt awards Ray an AB degree. He takes a job at a library at the University of California at Berkeley. Maryann stays on for the spring semester, then joins Ray for the summer. In August the Carvers move to Iowa City, Iowa. With a thousand-dollar stipend, Ray begins studies at the Iowa Writers' Workshop.

1964   January 21, Maryann's father, Val Burk, dies. She travels to Washington for the funeral without Ray.

In May the Carvers return to California and live in Sacramento. Ray takes a custodian job at Mercy Hospital.

1965   Ray works nights at Mercy Hospital, writes short stories and poetry at home during the day. He takes a poetry-writing class at Sacramento State, meets teacher and poet Dennis Schmitz. Maryann takes sales job with the Parents' Cultural Institute.

1966   Ray receives news that "Will You Please Be Quiet, Please?" will be included in *The Best American Short Stories 1967*.

1967   Carvers file for bankruptcy in the spring.

Deciding to become a librarian, Ray enrolls in the University of Iowa to obtain an MLS degree. June 17 Ray's father dies; Ray leaves Iowa and does not return. The Carvers move to Palo Alto, California. Ray hired as textbook editor at Science Research Associates (SRA) in July.

1968 Maryann awarded one-year scholarship to study at Tel Aviv University. SRA gives Ray unpaid leave of absence.

In June the Carvers move to Israel but return abruptly to California in October. Ray's association with the editor Gordon Lish begins.

1969 In February, Ray is rehired by SRA as an advertising director. This brief foray into the world of commercial publishing gave him valuable insights he was able to use later to market his own writing.

1970 Ray promoted to a PR position. He travels to New York to give SRA presentation. Maryann accompanies him, visits her sister Amy, performing in Brendan Behan's play *Borstal Boy*. Ray receives National Endowment for the Arts (NEA) Discovery Award for poetry. "Sixty Acres" selected for *Best Little Magazine Fiction 1970*. Book of poetry, *Winter Insomnia*, published by Kayak Books.

In June the Carvers move to Sunnyvale, California.

In August, Maryann begins teaching English at Los Altos High School.

In September, Ray's position at SRA is eliminated. Maryann's salary, his severance pay, and NEA grant enable Ray to write full-time without taking another job.

1971 In June, Gordon Lish has Ray's story "Neighbors" published in *Esquire* magazine. Ray appointed visiting lecturer in creative writing at University of California at Santa Cruz.

In August the Carvers move to Ben Lomond, California. Short story "Fat" appears in September issue of *Harper's Bazaar*.

1972 Ray awarded Wallace E. Stegner Fellowship at Stanford University, also appointed visiting lecturer in fiction writing at University of California at Berkeley.

In July the Carvers buy their first house in Cupertino, California.

In August, Ray goes fishing in Missoula, Montana. He meets many hard-drinking writers and academics, including editor at the university Diane Cecily, and begins an affair with her.

1973 Ray is appointed visiting lecturer at the Iowa Writers' Workshop

for the fall term; continues to teach at UC Santa Cruz, flying
back and forth.

"What Is It?" appears in *Prize Stories 1973*, the O. Henry
Awards annual; five poems reprinted in *New Voices in American Poetry*.

1974   Spring term, Ray lives alone in visitors' housing (Iowa House), upstairs from John Cheever. Ray appointed visiting lecturer at University of California at Santa Barbara.

In the fall, with a one-year leave of absence, Maryann enters Ph.D.
program in English at UC Santa Barbara.

For the second time Carvers file for bankruptcy.

Acute alcoholism compels Ray to resign his academic positions in
December; the family returns to Cupertino. Maryann takes
cocktail-waitress job to support the family until her teaching job
resumes the following fall.

1975   Unemployed, ill from chronic alcoholism, Ray writes very little.
Enters treatment center in San Jose, has seizure from alcohol
withdrawal. After release continues to drink. His marriage suf-
fers increasing antagonism and infidelity.

1976   Ray's third book of poetry, *At Night the Salmon Move,* published
by Capra Press, Santa Barbara, California.

In March *Will You Please Be Quiet, Please?*, a collection of short
stories, published by McGraw-Hill. It's his first major press
book. From summer to January 1977, Ray hospitalized three
more times for treatment of acute alcoholism.

At Thanksgiving, Maryann and Ray separate so Ray will have to
confront his alcoholism and take responsibility to get well.
Carvers' house in Cupertino sold to pay for his treatment expenses.

1977   *Will You Please Be Quiet, Please?* nominated for National Book
Award. Ray moves alone to McKinleyville, California, to try to
stop drinking.

In April, Ray and Maryann agree to reconcile.

June 2 Ray stops drinking. His "second life," as he calls it, begins.

Vance graduates from high school; afterward Maryann reunites with Ray in McKinleyville.

In November, *Furious Seasons and Other Stories* published by Capra Press. At writers' conference in Dallas, Texas, Ray meets poet Tess Gallagher and Richard Ford, who becomes a lifelong friend.

1978   Ray receives Guggenheim Fellowship. From March to June, Maryann and Ray live in Iowa City again.

July 24 Maryann returns alone to Bay Area.

In August, Ray takes up appointment as distinguished writer in residence at the University of Texas, El Paso. He begins relationship with Tess Gallagher. Ray writes book reviews for the *Chicago Tribune, Texas Monthly,* and the *San Francisco Review of Books.*

1979   January 1 Ray and Tess Gallagher begin living together in El Paso. He defers Syracuse University appointment as professor of English; his Guggenheim Fellowship provides support during this period.

1980   Receives National Endowment for the Arts Fellowship for fiction.

1981   In March *What We Talk About When We Talk About Love,* published by Knopf, edited by Gordon Lish.

1982   October 18 Ray and Maryann divorce.

1983   Ray and Cynthia Ozick selected as first Mildred and Harold Strauss Living Grant award recipients. The award provides $35,000 a year, tax free, for a five-year period.

In September *Cathedral,* published by Knopf, is finalist for National Book Critics Circle Award and Pulitzer Prize.

1984   *Fires: Essays, Poems, Stories* published by Vintage Books, New York. Between 1984 and 1987 Ray and Tess Gallagher travel to South America and Europe.

1986   In November, Ray's poetry collection, *Ultramarine,* published by Random House. At Christmastime, Ray visits Maryann, his daughter, Chris, and granddaughters, Windy and Chloe, in Washington State.

1987   Ray represents United States at the International Pen Conference,

Zurich. In June, *The New Yorker* publishes "Errand," his last short story.

In September Ray has pulmonary hemorrhage; he's diagnosed with lung cancer.

October 2 most of one lung is removed.

1988   In March cancer has spread to his brain; he starts radiation treatment.

In April, Maryann, Chris, and two granddaugthers visit Ray in Seattle. It is the last time his family sees Ray alive.

In May collection of short stories, *Where I'm Calling From*, published by Atlantic Monthly Press, edited by Gary Fisketjon. Ray inducted into American Academy of Arts and Letters. He receives honorary doctorate from the University of Hartford.

June 6 cancer detected in his remaining lung.

June 17 in Reno, Ray finally marries Tess Gallagher.

August 2 succumbs to cancer, shortly after finishing his last book of poems, *A New Path to the Waterfall*. The *London Times* headlines: THE AMERICAN CHEKHOV, RAYMOND CARVER, DEAD AT FIFTY over a full-page obituary.

Selected Works
of Raymond Carver

Winter Insomnia. Santa Cruz, Calif.: Kayak Books, 1970.

Put Yourself in My Shoes. Santa Barbara, Calif.: Capra, 1974.

Will You Please Be Quiet, Please? New York: McGraw-Hill, 1976.

At Night the Salmon Move. Santa Barbara, Calif.: Capra, 1976.

Furious Seasons and Other Stories. Santa Barbara, Calif.: Capra, 1977.

What We Talk About When We Talk About Love. New York: Knopf, 1981.

Fires: Essays, Poems, Stories. Santa Barbara, Calif.: Capra, 1983; New York: Vintage, 1984; New York: Vintage Contemporaries, 1989.

Cathedral. New York: Knopf, 1983.

Where Water Comes Together with Other Water. New York: Random House, 1985.

Ultramarine. New York: Random House, 1986.

Where I'm Calling From: New and Selected Stories. New York: Atlantic Monthly Press, 1988.

A New Path to the Waterfall. New York: Atlantic Monthly Press, 1989.

No Heroics, Please: Uncollected Writings. London: Collins Harvill, 1991; New York: Vintage Contemporaries, 1992.

All of Us: The Collected Poems. New York: Random House, 2000.

Index

MB is Maryann Burk; RC is Raymond Carver; *m.* means "married."